THE WAR VETERAN IN FILM

THE WAR VETERAN IN FILM

Emmett Early

McFarland & Company, Inc., Publishers
Jefferson, North Carolina, and London

LIBRARY OF CONGRESS CATALOGUING-IN-PUBLICATION DATA

Early, Emmett, 1939–
  The war veteran in film / Emmett Early.
    p.   cm.
  Includes bibliographical references and index.

  ISBN 0-7864-1471-5 (softcover : 50# alkaline paper)

  1. Veterans in motion pictures. I. Title.
  PN1995.9.V44E27   2003
  791.43'652355 — dc21   2003001403

British Library cataloguing data are available

On the cover: Nicolas Cage and Mathew Modine in *Birdy* (1984).

Manufactured in the United States of America

McFarland & Company, Inc., Publishers
  Box 611, Jefferson, North Carolina 28640
  www.mcfarlandpub.com

Acknowledgments

I would like to acknowledge the contributions made by my wife, Ann Early, and my son, Liam Early. I would also like to thank the following for their support: my old friends Harold Vreeland and Don Skiles, Tom Schumacher of the Washington Department of Veterans Affairs, Tom (Doom) Wear, Bruce Harmon, Ricardo Swain, Hispanic ex-marine, Frank Kokorowski of the King County (Washington) Veterans Program, and thanks also to Jesse Wing, for his sage advice, and to Stephanie Ogle of Cinema Books.

Contents

Chapter 3: Returning in Disguise

Sam said to Lonnie [her boyfriend], 'My mom said not to worry about what happened to Emmett back then, because the war had nothing to do with me. But the way I look at it, it had *everything* to do with me. My daddy went over there to fight for Mom's sake, and Emmett went over there for Mom's sake and my sake, to get revenge. If you went off to war, I bet you'd say it was for me. But if you're planning on joining the Army, you might ask my opinion first. The ones who don't get killed come back with their lives messed up, and then they make everybody miserable.'

— Bobbie Ann Mason, *In Country*, p. 71.

There was once a young fellow who enlisted as a soldier, conducted himself bravely, and was always the foremost when it rained bullets. So long as the war lasted, all went well, but when peace was made, he received his dismissal, and the captain said he might go where he liked. His parents were dead, and he had no longer a home, so he went to his brothers and begged them to take him in, and keep him until war broke out again. The brothers, however, were hard-hearted and said: 'What can we do with you? You are of no use to us; go and make a living for yourself.' The soldier had nothing left but his gun; so he took that on his shoulder, and went forth into the world.

— The Brothers Grimm, "Bearskin," p. 467.

Athena, greeting Odysseus, on the shores of his homeland, regarding the trials he must still endure:

Endure them all. You must. You have no choice.
And to no one — no man, no woman, not a soul —
reveal that *you* are the wanderer home at last.
No, in silence you must bear a world of pain,
subject yourself to the cruel abuse of men.

— Homer, *The Odyssey*, Robert Fagles trans.,
Book 13, lines 349–353.

Introduction

On Veterans Day, the parade forms with the local military and high school marching bands, the drum majorettes, and the Kiwanis Club clowns. Then come the ragged clusters of war veterans marching. They wear remnants of uniforms. Some are wearing medals on their jackets. Some wear service organization hats with badges. They are middle-aged or elderly men, depending on the war in which they fought. There is a flatbed truck or two from which the disabled can wave from their wheelchairs. The crowd lining the streets wave and some shout words of gratitude. Flags are everywhere.

What is going on here? This is not the recruiting parade full of anticipation or even a victory parade with energy and glamour. Rather it is a faint echo of the fervid hoopla. Men and women participate in these parades because they are attached to the memory of their military service. Duty and obligation continue to pull their war veteran identity out into public. The wars the veterans represent are long past and rapidly fading memories for the civilians in the crowd, although, for the veterans, the war's memory is a living, even vivid part of his everyday life. Thanks extended to war veterans, which the parades tend to elicit, are honest expressions, but they are often extended by politicians and civic-minded civilians who have their own motives, and by members of the veterans' families, who know how meaningful military service in wartime can be. But the message is there, the flaming memory of war has cooled to a weak ember, glowing weaker as each post-war year passes. The fate of the war veteran is to carry in his mind something that remains undiminished, vivid, and poorly comprehended by the citizens who surround him: a never-ending need to thank and be thanked.

But there are only a small fraction of war veterans marching on Veterans Day. The rest are hidden in the population. Your neighbor who tends his garden. The carpenter on the roof. The war veterans believe they rec-

1

ognize one another. Who are they and what do they do with their memories?

The War Veteran's Homecoming

Wars create stories. Like a disturbance in still water, war veterans reenter their cultures, becoming sources of stories. Wars get sensational attention in cinema where drama has historical meaning and popular appeal, not to mention vista shots with pyrotechnics, which supplement the acting. War veterans, although they are connected to the wars that created them, are often less commanding as movie subjects when the war fades from prominence in the collective memory. As war memory fades, war veterans merge in the collective consciousness, so that veterans of one war can be compared to another and certain common characteristics prevail among the veterans of all the wars. Films about war veterans present an archive of how the veterans faired and how they were regarded. To my knowledge, war veteran movies have not been collected and examined together as a genre separate from war films. Nor have their collective narratives been examined that describe how the veteran reentered his culture and the effect that he had on the culture, and the effect that the culture had on him. Those movies should be examined together, for there is much information in the narratives about the wars with which they are associated, the cultures of the war veterans, and, most importantly, about the veterans themselves.

War veterans, regardless of the wars, seem to have a great deal in common. Looked at together as a group, war veterans take on a motif that has an archetypal commonality, as implied by the three disparate opening quotations. The Vietnam War created a remarkable disturbance in U.S. culture, generating fiction and movies in the latter half of the twentieth century. Several authors (Walker, 1991; Lanning, 1994; Devine, 1995; Turner, 1996; Lembcke, 1998) have discussed Vietnam War veteran films. Walker discussed Vietnam War veteran movies as a film scholar relying on genre categories. He used the regrettably truncated term "Vietvet" (a term of quickspeak that only Anthony Burgess could love), in his otherwise worthy review. Lanning, in his book, also contributed a scholarly collection of war veteran film offerings, many of them, unfortunately, already no longer in circulation. Doherty (1993a&b) commented on the war veterans in films before and after the imposition of U.S. mid-century cinema censorship, and Selby (1984) on the '40s *film noir*. Vietnam War veteran movies are represented in large numbers, compared to movies about veterans of other wars, and certainly represent a contemporary rip-ple in U.S. culture that has somewhat obscured the broader war veteran perspective. No one, to my knowledge, has examined the collective nar-rative of the war veteran in film from a broad multi-war perspective.

Several authors, most notably Dean (1997) and Lembcke (1998), have used films about Vietnam War veterans to show that the veterans' image has been manipulated by the political right and left, and by press and other information media, including the film industry known as Hollywood. A broader look, with a perspective to include veterans of all wars who are the subjects of films, seems warranted to see if Vietnam War veterans are a truly unique lot in the history of war veterans, or, perhaps more accu-rately, another example of the cultural impact of war on society.

But while there is no genre of war veteran movies, they virtually span the history of film and populate the movies of nearly all the film genres, including comedy, mystery, adventure, romance, horror, *noir*, and partic-ularly action. No musicals, so far.

The War Veteran in Literature

Prior to the twentieth century introduction of the moving picture, war veterans were depicted in literature since the beginning of what we think of as literature of the Western world. The first two works of written literature are about war and the war veteran. As Homer's *Iliad* is to war, his *Odyssey* is to the warrior's homecoming. *Nostos* is a Greek word, used frequently in Homer's *Odyssey*, which best sums the meaning of the war veteran's homecoming. Schein (1996, p. 21) observed that *nostos* referred to "returning to light and life." Schein noted that Odysseus' "distinctive heroic achievement" was "surviving death and returning home" (p. 22). Odysseus spent ten years engaged in the siege of Troy, after being reluc-tantly drafted, and ten more years finding his way home, losing all he had, his war spoils, his crews, his ships, before finally reaching his homeland. He approached his home disguised ignominiously as a tramp, before reclaiming his wife and property by strength of combat. The difficulty Odysseus had returning home is the first example found in the Western world of the war veteran's story, and, as such, is an archetypal template for all war veteran stories to follow.

As scholars remark, much of Odysseus' trip and most of his trials take place in a mythical world, for which we have little reference today beyond symbolism (Pucci, 1987; Schein, 1996). Characters such as the Cyclops, Calypso, Hermes, Circe, and the Sirens are not of the real (conscious) world, although they were evidently common motifs in ancient Greek oral lore that fed the writing of the *Odyssey*. Some say Homer was not a single person at all, but rather the name of a group of scribes organized by the tyrant Peisistratos, who collected written works at the time of the introduction of the alphabet, as a wealthy person might collect art today (Nagy, 1996). The modern Peisistratos might wish to take control of the Internet. In any case, Homer was, in a real sense, the first literary recorder of popular culture, if culture is defined as the sharing of knowledge, beliefs, and values.

Great contributions to war veteran literature continued from Homer's time. Stanford (1963) examines various authors through literary history, from Ovid to Nikos Kazantzakis and James Joyce, who have taken up the challenge of describing Odysseus' trials. Virgil in the *Aenead* picked up the Trojan survivors after the war and followed their own odyssey through adventures that led finally to the founding of Rome. Sir Walter Scott recorded an epic of fiction in his novel *Ivanhoe*, looking at the returning crusaders and the influence of the Middle East battlegrounds on the warriors. The brothers Grimm recorded two rather similar fairy tales about war veterans, "Bearskin," and "Brother Lustig." Both have the war veterans bargaining with the devil for a way out of their isolation and poverty. William Faulkner's novel *Sartoris* chronicles the post–Civil War life of a Confederate army officer. Céline, in his novel *Journey to the End of the Night*, recorded the wanderings of a World War One veteran of the French army. Erich Maria Remarque wrote perhaps the most anticipated war veteran novel, his sequel to *All Quiet on the Western Front*, *The Road Back*. The recent best seller *Cold Mountain*, by Charles Frazier, depicts the epic journey of a Confederate Civil War veteran making his way home after deserting from a field hospital. The consistent theme that prevails in these stories is the war veteran living in restless isolation. (A collection of war veteran novels that have been made into film are listed in the References section at the end of this book.)

The War Veteran as Symbol in Film

Historian Brent Toplin observed that film picks up where oral tradition and later written literature left off.

> However we think of it, we must admit that film gives us a new sort of history, what we might call history as vision. Its earliest predecessor, oral history, tended to create a poetic relationship to the world. Then, over a

2000-year period, written history created an increasingly linear, scientific relationship. Film changes the rules of the game and creates its own sort of truth, creates a multilevel past that has so little to do with language that it is difficult to describe adequately in words [Toplin, 2000, p. 38].

Today we can safely say that film productions, particularly movies, and the popular mutation, television video, are collective creative efforts, commonly subsumed under the sophisticated rubric of cinema, that have been our uniquely twentieth century popular culture. Indeed, movies, as a collaborative art, have provided us with a record of the returning veteran from various wars, as he is viewed within his own culture, as well as the culture in which the film is produced. Whether or not the war veteran is central to the movie plot, how the war veteran character is portrayed in the context of his return gives us a sampling of how society viewed him. Jeremy Devine wrote in *Vietnam at 24 Frames a Second*, "Movies are integral in creating a mass cultural psyche surrounding combat and the people we ask to risk their lives in it" (1995, p. 11). Movies actually create a significant portion of the popular historic archive of knowledge regarding who the war veteran was and how he fared.

(I refer to the war veteran in the masculine, although I acknowledge that women have served in combat and continue to fight in several cultures. War veterans are also nurses and women in related combat support professions. I use the masculine only in the sense that the vast majority of combat veterans are males, as a writer of sexual trauma would use the feminine, to similarly reflect the regrettable dominance of females in that category.)

What I have listed in Appendix 2 are all the films, to my knowledge, that concern war veterans. No doubt there are many more that exist and hopefully I'll eventually add them to my list. I've printed in bold those that are commented upon as representative of one thing or another. I will mostly focus on films made in the United States, not out of preference so much as limited exposure and access to war veteran films from other countries. I doubt that there is a nation in the world that has not been affected by a recent war. Not all of the films listed are on video and a significant number are no longer in print. I am grateful to Seattle's Scarecrow Video for access to their extensive video archive.

By *war veteran* I mean someone who has served in combat while in military service. Such a person may still be in the military at the time of the story, or he may be, as is more usually the case, a civilian. I draw a distinction between the war veteran who remains in uniform and fighting the same war, as in *Apocalypse Now* or *Uncommon Valor,* and the war veteran who moves on to another battle in another war. An example of the war veteran still serving in the military, who moves to another fight, is found in David Lean's lush film *Ryan's Daughter*, where the British army war veteran is sent from the front lines in France to light duty in Ireland's County Mayo. Other examples of career military men who remain in the service after combat are found in Francis Coppola's *Gardens of Stone*, Peter Hyam's *The Presidio*, and John Ford's *Fort Apache* and *She Wore a Yellow Ribbon*.

In some cultures the distinction between war veteran and others becomes blurred with long-term conflict. The original meaning of the word "veteran" comes from the Latin *veteranus*, meaning a person of long experience. When it comes to combat, however, any experience can be a long one. The term "wily veteran" is commonly used today to depict the experienced ballplayer or long term employee who has learned many economical ways of expending energy to accomplish his or her tasks. That knowledge, in the right circles, is considered wisdom.

The use of the war veteran image cuts a swath through cinema quality from the very pinnacle of high quality (e.g., *The Seventh Seal, Taxi Driver*), to the low down exploitation B-movie (e.g., *Satan's Sadists, Deathdream*) — just as the war veterans themselves cannot be generalized as a cultural group beyond their common experience in war. However the quality of the film, the statements made about war veterans give us a feeling for their culture. It is therefore difficult to depict war veteran movies collectively, because war veterans are featured in so many different ways. Veteran Hollywood director John Ford used U.S. Civil War veterans frequently as symbols and protagonists for his dramas: *Fort Apache, The Sun Shines Bright, She Wore a Yellow Ribbon, The Searchers*. War veterans are protagonists in dramas, heroes and anti-heroes, as well as characters in supporting roles who deliver a message, and sometimes, by virtue of their war veteran status, become a cultural symbol and a statement about the war's impact on the culture. These are veterans of wars who non-veterans approach or avoid with guilt, distaste, curiosity, fear, derision, and sometimes respect. There are war veterans who were wounded in the war, some physically, some mentally, while many carry both types of wounds as burdens of encumbrance. Just after their return and discharge from the military, war veterans are given the task of adjusting to a world that has gone on without them. They act as noble heroes and ignominious antiheroes. (Those who would romanticize war veterans should remember that Hitler was a war veteran.) Their unique experiences in combat, what they have learned in battle, their training and sacrifice, become credentials to motivate action, mayhem, fantasy, romance, and mystery.

To comment on war veteran films is to inevitably comment on the cultures that produce and sustain them. The soldiers carried their culture with them to Vietnam, Palestine, Korea, or the Somme, and recreated their culture again in the trenches and bunkers of the combat zone. As they return home, the war veterans and those around them realize how they have been influenced by the war experience and the culture they fought in. It is only after they return home that alienation results from the friction that is created by the changed war veteran and his culture. Sean Penn's *Indian Runner* catches that friction in the Vietnam War veteran's return, while *Ivanhoe* reflects the changes in the behavior of the knights involved in Richard-the-Lionhearted's crusade. The U.S. *noir* films of the post–World War Two era depict the friction of a cynical, dark culture for the veteran on his return. The friction always strikes a cultural note. Whether the note is one of prejudice, resentment, bitterness, sadness, romance, adventure, or nostalgia, is what I propose to discuss.

Film, like theater, is a popular collective art and therefore comes close to the spirit of Homer. It is an inherent feature of the modern movie that its creation is a group effort. Although one person, a director or producer, may have control of the production, and may even write the scenario and manipulate the camera, he or she still relies on others for the finished product and is perforce influenced by them. One could compare a movie production crew to the group of writers who are said by some to constitute Homer. The first class war veteran film *The Stunt Man* gives us a spirited example of the movie production crew with its tradition, its star-jadedness, and its newspaper city-room atmosphere of sensation fatigue.

Movies are so expensive to make that, as a collective effort, none can be made without some expectation of at least monetary success or the support of a zealous institution. The fact that such an expensive project can be launched and completed, and survives on video, is a statement of its cultural appeal. Whether studio-made or independent, the distribution and success of a film indicates that a note has been struck in a significant portion of the movie-going public.

Many of the films listed in Appendix 2 are explicitly about war veterans as protagonists (e.g., *Best Years of Our Lives, Crossfire, Manchurian Candidate, Desert Bloom, Jacknife, Jacob's Ladder*). An example of a film with a war veteran implicitly stated is *Taxi Driver*, in which Travis Bickel's military veteran's status is stated, while his combat experience is only implied by the esoteric Marine Force Recon patch on his jacket. However, his combat status is essential to the plot. Other films deal with war veterans only incidentally in supporting or character roles (e.g., *The Big Lebowski, Gosford Park, Rushmore, Spitfire Grill*), but, again, their combat experience is pertinent. Often we see war veterans exploited as action figures in heroic movies (e.g., *The Blue Dahlia, First Blood, Lethal Weapon, Devil in a Blue Dress*). A variation of this theme is the drama that uses a war veteran as a driving force in the plot (e.g., *Cornered, Bad Day at Black Rock, Cutter's Way, Dead Presidents, Absolute Power, Gardens of Stone*). And then there is the war veteran movie made *during* the war, depicting the fear generated in anticipation of the warrior's return (*Motor Psycho, The Visitors*).

There is a group of films that take on the archetypal form of the war veteran returning home in disguise or dramatically changed (e.g., *Ulysses, Ivanhoe, The Sun Also Rises, Birdy, Born on the Forth of July, Deer Hunter*). A significant variant of this theme is the fake war veteran's return, as seen in *The Return of Martin Guerre*, and its U.S. Civil War imitation *Sommersby*. Although the term "fake war veteran" is not really correct, as is often the case, the "war veteran" is authentic, but the "fake" is that he impersonates someone else, as Odysseus did when he finally made his way back home.

Another important group of war veteran films, certainly an ancient theme of its own, is the veteran struggling with the impact of the war on his personal philosophy (e.g., *Seventh Seal, Key Largo, Some Came Running, The Man in the Gray Flannel Suit, Ulee's Gold*), and the impact of prolonged captivity, as P.O.W. (e.g., *Rolling Thunder, Some Kind of Hero*).

When war veterans are portrayed as bad guys, they generally are considered emotionally disturbed, as in *Black Sunday, To Kill a Clown*, and *Wild at Heart*, or as a reluctant antihero, such as Ed Harris' complex character portrayal of Shang in Louis Malle's *Alamo Bay*, or culturally driven anti-heroes, as in *Dead Presidents*. Elia Kazan's *The Visitors* presents war veterans in a generally negative light in which even the positive is tainted with compromise.

In many cultures, the war veteran becomes a haunting symbol, such as Septimus Warren Smith's suicidal veteran in *Mrs. Dalloway*, and the brain injured Indochina War veteran, Pierre, in *Sundays and Cybele*. And occasionally the war veteran movie itself is portrayed as a critique of society, as in the aforementioned *The Stunt Man* and the study of the war veteran film director James Whale, *Gods and Monsters*. Lembcke (1998, p 162) gives an extensive critique of the Jane Fonda project *Coming Home*, designed as a critique of the Vietnam War era.

The most comprehensive of the film portrayals of the war veteran are what I have come to call triptych films, featuring the boy before the war, the warrior in the field, and the war veteran after he returns home. Films such as *The Deer Hunter, Forrest Gump, Dead Presidents, Born on the Fourth of July*, and *Birdy*, satisfy the criteria. Ironically, to be consistent with the triptych tradition in art, the picture in the center is considered the most important. For the war veteran, the relatively brief period of war takes on such salience in the course of his lifetime, that the period actually seems bigger on the inside than it does on the outside, a tribute to the resilient power of memory.

CHAPTER 1

The Wounded War Veteran Returns

War, combat, is a hard act to follow. Everything after combat in wartime is anticlimax. The war veteran's wounds are both physical and emotional. He is seasoned by hard experience and wary of new experience. The war veteran's fighting spirit, however, is not necessarily diminished, although his determination to survive might be compromised and society may receive him rudely upon his return.

Being physically wounded does not necessarily imply that the veteran was emotionally traumatized and has acquired posttraumatic stress disorder (PTSD). On the contrary, some of the latest research has shown that anesthetic, such as morphine, administered immediately after being wounded, and in some cases for months thereafter, may actually interrupt or inhibit the re-experiencing rumination that seems to be involved in creating hyperarousal and avoidance symptoms that characterize PTSD (Pitman, 2000). Many war veterans, who are physically wounded, however, carry PTSD from prior traumatic experiences before being wounded. One of the hardest experiences to endure for some combatants was to have to return to combat after a stay in a hospital, moving from sedentary life that allows for reflection and worry into an all-too-familiar danger.

PTSD is a disorder that will receive frequent mention in this review, because the symptoms of the disorder are common among war veterans, even though most of them do not qualify for a diagnosis of PTSD, according to the psychiatric diagnostic nomenclature (American Psychiatric Association, 2000). Research has recently shown that persons qualifying for Criterion A (the trauma) and meeting some but not all the other criteria, have remarkable vulnerability to other disorders, such as depression, substance abuse, or other anxiety disorders (Marshall, et al., 2001).

Symptoms of PTSD that are common in war veterans relate to a sense of having no future, experiencing heightened startle response (e.g., jumping or cringing involuntarily at loud, unexpected noises, and its sister symptoms of hearing loss and a shallow tolerance for noise), night terrors, nightmares, other forms of sleep disturbance, intrusive recollections and dissociative flashbacks to wartime experiences. Other common symptoms include grief, dysphoria (e.g., feelings of emptiness or hopelessness), and guilt about surviving when friends and comrades have died, or guilt about participating in the ravages of combat. Hyperarousal, irritability, fear of repetition of hostilities, and a feeling of being fated to die, are also among symptoms of the disorder not uncommon among many veterans who are never diagnosed with PTSD.

The war wound carries the memory of the war and embodies in the veteran and those around him the meaning of the sacrifice. Aged World War I veteran poet Robert Graves, a man with a rich and varied cultural life, commented at the end of his lifetime that he was never able to look in the mirror without recalling his war experience (Reid, 1995).

It is the emotional and spiritual wound, however, as Dean (1997, p. 23) points out, that tends to get the press, when the war veteran comes to symbolize a cultural trend. He writes using regrettable hyperbole, "Finally, in the past ten years, the image of the Vietnam [War] veteran as a troubled individual has resisted modification because the Vietnam vet has become the quintessential 'stressed-out' American and a reference point whenever the subject of PTSD is considered in any context." The victim of U.S. culture comes to symbolize its stressors, but perhaps no differently than the World War I wounded Tommy symbolized the scars of Great Britain (e.g., *Mrs. Dalloway* and *Fairytale: A True Story*). In the period of the Great Depression, the scene of unemployed war veterans rousted from shantytowns was also a ready symbol of government injustice (*Heroes for Sale*).

Heroes for Sale, 1933

William Wellman directed *Heroes for Sale*, released in 1933, which was from a screenplay by Robert Lord and Wilson Mizner. Richard Barthelmess plays Tom Holmes, a U.S. soldier who is wounded carrying out a heroic mission to capture a German soldier. Gordon Westcott plays Roger Winston, who was on the same mission across no man's land, but quailed at the last and stayed in a shell hole. When Tom returns to the shell hole with the prisoner, he is hit by enemy fire and Roger returns with the prisoner, believing Tom is dead. Roger is praised by the general, promoted and decorated for heroism. Tom, meantime, is picked up by German corpsmen. He is treated as a POW and released on armistice. His sympathetic German doctor explains that he must take morphine to cope with the intractable pain of steel fragments that remain lodged near his spine. Tom and Roger meet on a troop ship sailing home. Roger is a major with a Distinguished Service Cross, while Tom walks stiffly with a cane. In private, Roger confesses and whines, while Tom is magnanimous: "Nothing we can do about it. I've been in the shadow of death so long, nothing in life seems very important anymore."

Tom's troubles continue after his homecoming. While Roger receives a hero's welcome and takes an executive job at his father's bank, Tom conceals from his mother that he is morphine addicted. He takes a job as a clerk at Roger's bank, but in the throes of opiate withdrawal cannot concentrate and is finally fired. (Interestingly, the pusher on the street wears a suit and fedora, and sells an ounce of the opiate for $200.) The bank president, Roger's father, scoffs at his son's defense of Tom being a wounded war veteran: "You fellas forget the war is over. It's time to quit beating the drum and waving the flag."

Tom is turned into the police and is sent to a treatment farm, where he is subsequently discharged as "cured." With his mother and father both dead, Tom moves to Chicago and takes up lodging at a soup kitchen/rooming house. There he meets the good-hearted Mary, played by Aline MacMahon, daughter of the proprietor, and Ruth, played by Loretta Young, a comely resident across the hall. Tom and Ruth are smitten and Tom is inspired. Tom meets another resident who plays a rather comical foreign-born Communist proselytizer, Max (Robert Barrat). Tom takes a job where Ruth works as a laundry route truck driver. Quickly he is recognized through his inventiveness in increasing his route, and the boss rewards him with promotion. Tom's fortunes improve rapidly and he and Ruth are married and have a son, Bill.

Tom's fortunes turn again, however, when Max, the Communist, turns out also to be an inventor who creates a laborsaving laundry machine, which Tom helps him promote to the boss, with the promise that it will not lead to the laying off of any workers. However, the company changes hands and the machine indeed causes employees to be laid off. The workers are disgruntled and finally riot. Tom tries to dissuade them, but instead gets swept up in the human tide and is arrested in the riot. His wife, Ruth, is killed by a police baton trying to find him. Tom is convicted of leading the mob and sent to jail for five years. Max, the hypocritical Communist inventor, however, grows rich selling the laborsaving laundry machines and converts to capitalism, saving Tom's share for him. When Tom is finally released from jail, he is hounded by Red Squad investigators as if he were a pedophile and simultaneously made wealthy by the money from the invention that Max has saved for him. Behaving like a guilty war veteran with his disability check, he gives all his money to the food kitchen where his friend Mary works. Mary has been caring for his son, Bill. They have been giving food away to the hungry. Tom funds their kitchen in perpetuity and goes off on a tramp with other Depression-driven jobless men. Under a bridge, on a rainy night, where tramps are stopping, he meets Roger, his wartime buddy, whose bank has collapsed. Roger is hapless, but Tom, remaining optimistic, quotes FDR just as they are rousted. The tramps are identified as ex-servicemen and put in boxcars by cops and hauled across the state line.

This 1930s product of so-called "pre-code" U.S. cinema presents a war veteran whose sacrifices have been brushed aside and who has been victimized by wartime injuries and leftover sequelae in the form of intractable pain. The film conveniently drops the pain issue after Tom is cured at the State Narcotics Farm. His ignominy, however, continues when he finds himself trying repeatedly to do the right thing, only to be mistreated and misunderstood. The film ends on a paradoxically ominous note. Tom's young son, Bill, arm in arm with Mary, stare at a plaque commemorating the Tom Holmes Memorial which feeds the hungry. Little Bill says, "When I grow up I want to be just like my dad!"

William Wellman was himself a war veteran (Thompson, 1983, p. 21). He was a volunteer with the Lafayette Escadrille in 1917 after joining the French Foreign Legion. He flew with the Chats Noir (Black Cats) and was awarded the Croix de Guerre, with palm, for his combat actions. He was shot down and wounded. After treatment he was discharged from the French flying corps and was honored when he returned home. He grew restless, however, and enlisted in the U.S. flying corps before the end of the war. He crashed again during a demonstration as a flying instructor. This time he survived with more serious injuries, including a back injury that caused him pain the rest of his life. He gave much attention in his career to the story of the warrior in various forms. Wellman lost a close friend and fellow American while flying with the Chats Noir, and in a symbol of his survivor's guilt, he used his own picture as a downed World War I flyer, who was reported killed, in his 1942 movie *Thunder Birds*.

The Best Years of Our Lives, 1946

The returning of veterans from World War II was a part of the dramatic upheaval caused by the course of the war effort. During the Vietnam War there was much talk about returning veterans, notably ethnic and racial minority veterans, who would take up arms against their domestic oppressors. The subtler kinds of damage were not anticipated, such as the loss of wages and family disruptions caused by PTSD and the common accompanying disorders of depression and addiction. It was the World War II generation, however, that dealt with the greatest numbers of the populace trying to settle down at the end of a war.

How do you tell the story of the returning Second World War veterans? One approach is to tell a small part of the story and hope its representative of some larger truth for returning veterans. William Wyler attempted this when he directed *The Best Years of Our Lives*, which was released in 1946. He picked a fictional Midwest town, Boon City, and described the lives of three returning veterans, who hitch a ride on a B-17 heading for the bone yard of discarded aircraft. The veterans are Homer Parrish (played by Academy Award-winning double amputee Harold Russell), a navy veteran who burned his hands off on a red-hot hatch door of a sinking tin can. Dana Andrews plays Fred, an air force bombardier captain, who was a soda jerk before the war and must return to his old job. Fredric March plays Al, an infantry platoon sergeant, who returns to his bank job to be placed in charge of GI Loans.

The screenplay is by Robert E. Sherwood from a novel by Mackinlay Kantor. All three returning men become veterans "nervous out of the service" in their own fashion. The Harold Russell character, Homer, must adjust to his disability and accept the love of his girl-next-door sweetheart, Wilma, played by Cathy O'Donnel — "a swell girl."

Frederick March's character, Al, drinks too much, struggles with sleep disturbance and anger. Dana Andrews' Fred has to come down from the responsibility and nightmare-generating memories of terror, to cope with an acquisitive wife and no prospects for a decent job. After guiding bombers to their targets amidst bursting flack, Fred must go back to work as the jerk in the drug store that's been bought by a chain.

The movie cuts between the three, periodically bringing them together, with the bulk of the acting on the shoulders of yeomen like Andrews and March.

A nice plot twist has Fred falling in love with Al's adult daughter, Peggy, played with mesmerized decorum by Teresa Wright.

The three vets meet at Butch's, a tavern ("the best joint in town") owned and operated by a piano player (as opposed to pianist) named Butch (Hoagy Carmichael). Butch even teaches Homer to play the piano, and though it is not a key plot point, it shows Homer victorious.

Harold Russell lost his hands in an army training accident. He was active in veterans volunteer service, particularly AMVETS, until he died in 2002 at the age of 86. He had a small part in *Inside Moves* (1980), which his obit describes as dealing with a suffering Vietnam War veteran (Page, 2002). *Inside Moves*, however, depicts John Savage as a young man suffering

Three vets, "nervous from the service," meet with others at Butch's Tavern in
The Best Years of Our Lives (RKO, 1947). From left to right are Dana Andrews
as Fred, Myrna Loy as Milly, Al's wife, Fredric March as Al, Hoagy Carmichael
as Butch, and Harold Russell as Homer Parrish.

crippling injuries after a suicide attempt. The film does not mention his
veteran status, which is perhaps an example of the symptom syndrome
acquiring a stereotype.

There are two odd discontinuities in *The Best Years of Our Lives*, which
was a major studio release in 1946 and swept the Academy awards that
year. Al has a teenaged son who expresses distaste for the samurai sword
that his father presents to him; instead he asks his dad about Hiroshima.
We never see the boy again, even though Al's family drama is central, with
his tolerant wife, Milly, played by Myrna Loy, and daughter Peggy's yearning for Fred, the bombardier. It is as though the film symbolically cuts out
the boy's questioning, keeping him out of the picture.

The other discontinuity occurs at the wedding when Peggy and Fred
kiss, with Peggy having no knowledge of the resolution of their major
stumbling block, his marriage to Maria. We know Maria has initiated a
divorce, but Peggy doesn't share our knowledge.

Some of the 1946 lines seem as quaint as the automobiles of the era.

Fred shows his affection for Peggy by saying, "I think they ought to put you in mass production." Al decries returning to his job: "Last year it was kill Japs, this year it's make money." Al is offered a bank VP job, an ostensible promotion, at $12,000 a year.

When naïve Fred finally connects with his nightclubing wife, Marie, played by impatient, blonde, Virginia Mayo, says, "Now we can have a real honeymoon, without a care in the world, just as if nothing had ever happened." We see the impact of her words on Fred's face, who knows how much he has changed. Fred argues with Marie. She asks angrily, "Are you all right in your mind? You talk in your sleep. Can't you get those things out of your system? Snap out of it!"

Perhaps the most touching scene involves Homer's test of Wilma. He invites her to help him prepare for bed and demonstrates how helpless he is without his hooks, when much of his movie performance was spent showing off his cleverness and bionic adaptability. Wilma, the angel of tenderness, tucks in Homer and kisses his forehead.

The final scene seems rushed to editing despite the leisurely 172-minute length of the film. The scene is a prolonged wedding ceremony between Homer and Wilma, a wishful symbolism to hope that the citizens of the United States of America would accept its war wounded and maimed. Tacked on, and anxiously cut, Fred has the last line when, after he kisses Peggy, he invites her to spend her years with him with "no money, no decent place to live, working, getting kicked around...." (Compare this to the marriage scene in *The Men*.)

The last lines, which seem almost compulsively tacked on, utter the reality for many war veterans, particularly the veterans with unpleasant disabilities. Their long-term reception is more often represented by the needy, wanton Virginia Mayo's Marie, as the whining, impatient, uncaring society, who cries, "Snap out of it!"

The Men, 1950

The Men was released in 1950 and is dedicated with following perspective: "In all wars, since the beginning of history, there have been men who fought twice. The first time they battled with club, sword, or machine gun. The second time they had none of these weapons. Yet this, by far, was the greatest battle. It was fought with abiding faith and raw courage, and in the end, victory was achieved. This is the story of such a group of men. To them this film is dedicated."

Directed by Fred Zinnemann, the film is about World War II paralyzed veterans on a hospital rehab ward. It stars Marlon Brando as the patient Ken, known as Bud to his wife, Ellen, who is played with charm by Teresa Wright. Everett Sloan is Doctor Brock. Jack Webb as another patient, the sarcastic Norm, and Arthur Jurado is Angel, whose family visits for a day. Story and screenplay by Carl Foreman.

Brando's face is puffy. He becomes a spokesman of sorts for all the rehabilitating veterans. But initially he is negative and refuses to join the other vets on the ward. "Don't disturb him," says Nick, "he's readjusting." Bud is transformed by the surprise visit of his wife. At first he rejects her and tells her to get out. "I'm like a baby. Normal is normal and crippled is crippled, and never the twain shall meet."

In spite of his initial resistance, he starts working on his recovery and even develops a hysterical idea that the use of his legs is returning. The doctor has to turn his therapy around to inhibit his patient's false hope. "Before you change the world you have to accept it the way it is."

An unhappy note is struck when the popular and the most advanced patient, Angel, dies suddenly. Bud, in grief over losing Angel, cries out to Ellen, about the risk of marrying a paraplegic. She retorts with her best Teresa Wright pluck: "I'm not marrying a wheel chair, I'm marrying a man." The marriage theme is similar to that of the double amputee, Homer, and his swell girl-next-door in *Best Years of Our Lives*. Bud tries to stand unassisted for the ceremony and starts to slump as they join hands.

The movie ends on a positive, but realistic note. The problem of impotence is briefly discussed. Unfortunately, nothing is said in the movie that would have woven a more complex thread involving the emotional impact of combat with veterans' physical and emotional readjustment challenges.

Bad Day at Black Rock, 1955

Directed by John Sturges and released in 1955, *Bad Day at Black Rock* features Spencer Tracy as John J. Macreedy, a war veteran returned from World War II, where he fought with the Japanese-American company in Italy. He comes to the town of Black Rock in the Arizona desert like a samurai, looking for the father of the man who died saving his life. The film begins with a scene designed for the then new wide screen technology with a modern diesel passenger train arriving at a small town, looming across the flat desert plain.

Tracy's Macreedy wields iron strength of character, while the townspeople weasel around him trying to cover up the fact that the man he seeks was the "Jap farmer" murdered during a spate of anti–Japanese jingoism at the start of the war. Macreedy, with his useless arm, satisfies the criteria for playing the wounded vet, but he manages with his one good arm to out-fight the town bully, Coley Trimble, played by the menacing Ernest Borgnine.

Tracy's stalwart character has the acerbic wit and self deprecation that resembles the real-life war hero with one working arm, Senator Bob Dole, who has become a popular comic figure in advertising with puckish humor, as the man with indomitable spirit. (He advertises both Viagra and Pepsi.)

If the wounded war veteran is a metaphor for many kinds of troublesome post-war traits, the town with something to hide describes a societal and cultural shadow that generates war. The town's murderous racism is a buried secret that locks the townspeople together like a pathological family. Tracy's Macreedy observes all this with distaste and states that he is ready to resign from the human race, as soon as he completes his last duty. As long as the citizens of Black Rock hid and denied their crime, they behaved like the family riddled with abuse, doing further harm to avoid acknowledging their collective shadow. It seems that Tracy's Macreedy is as much at odds with the citizens of Black Rock as many of the war veterans come to feel in their own home environment.

Bad Day at Black Rock has a screenplay by Millard Kaufman, from a story by Howard Breslin. Anne Francis plays the helpful Liz Wirth, Dean Jagger plays Sheriff Tim Horn, and Walter Brennan is the town doctor. Lee Marvin plays a tough guy, Hector, who fights Macreedy. And Robert Ryan is Reno Smith, the guy who rules the town.

Spencer Tracy portrays his tough Irish character, but he's really not an action character, and he doesn't quite pull off the one-handed war veteran. What he does manage to convey is the man who isn't afraid to die. Something of the "one-percenter" motorcycle outlaw underneath his respectable suit and tie.

A Hatful of Rain, 1957

A Hatful of Rain was released in 1957 and concerns a Korean War veteran who is the victim of wartime traumas and deprivation, surviving for 13 days wounded in a cave. He becomes a morphine addict from the treatment of his wounds. This iatrogenic malady becomes a social struggle when morphine becomes heroin. Fred Zinnemann directed the movie as a stark drama that deals head on with the personal and family malaise of heroin addiction, but neglected to exploit the much bigger issue of causation and meaning of the pain being relieved. Don Murray plays the vet, Johnny, who has to come to terms with his adoring father (Lloyd Nolan) and his pregnant wife, Celia (Eva Marie Saint), who believes her husband is seeing another woman. (No man married to Eva Marie Saint would be seeing another woman.) Anthony Franciosa plays Johnny's brother, Polo, who is neglected by his father in favor of Johnny, and who is hopelessly in love with Johnny's beautiful wife.

Johnny's plight grips the whole family and finally brings them all together, pitching in to help Johnny after he finally confesses. Celia calls the cops as an act of mercy: "I want to report a drug addict. He's my husband."

Henry Silva plays the heartless heroin pusher, Mother. He has the image of an ambiguous ethnic other with high cheekbones and a dark-eyed, cutthroat stare. (Silva reappears as the sinister Korean servant in *The Manchurian Candidate*.)

Several films depict the plight of the alcoholic vet (*Jacknife, Cutter's Way*) and some play the whole addiction problem for laughs (as in *Rushmore, Fort Apache*, and *Up in Smoke*). Only *Desert Bloom* and *A Hatful of Rain* directly tackle the addiction problems of the war veteran. I don't find any film, however, that is willing to make the direct connection between emotional pain and addiction, although the bloody *Rolling Thunder* gives us a rationale for violence in the pain-seeking former POW.

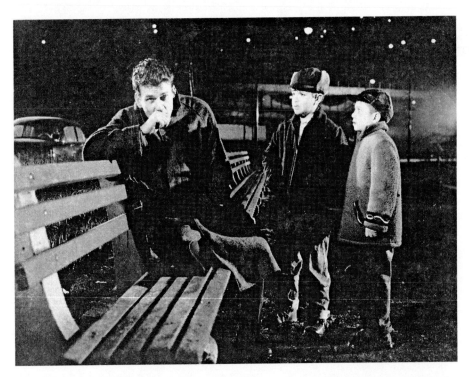

Don Murray plays Korean War veteran Johnny in Fred Zinneman's *A Hatful of Rain* (20th Century–Fox, 1957). Johnny is abject and sick, sitting on a park bench, addicted to heroin but without a supply. Two kids look on. One asks, "Are you gonna die, mister?"

The plot of *A Hatful of Rain* was adapted from a play by Michael Vincent Gazzo. It presented some depth of pain on the parts of Johnny and Polo, who were abandoned by their father after their mother died, surrendering them to an orphanage. Johnny went off to the army and the Korean War. ("Two years in the army and another lousy year in the hospital.") The film also gives us no solace in the ghastly high-rise project apartments with institutional tile in the halls where Johnny, Polo, and Eva live.

Lloyd Nolan, as the brash, opinionated, domineering father, narrowly channels his love through admiration toward Johnny. He brags about Johnny in the bar as someone with courage. In contrast, Johnny does a lot of cringing in seizures of pain, staggering about dark, wet streets. At one point he is sitting on a bench and a child walks up and watches him convulse; bending over, he asks, "Are you gonna die, mister?"

The stark, merciless, black-and-white photography makes us feel that they are all living in a cave in that 1957 cement tenement house. The film itself has the cold chiaroscuro chill of the Korean War. The one spark of warmth, carried first only by Celia and Polo, is the family solidarity, which finally coalesces and starts to glow when Johnny finally confesses his painful addiction, and Pop shows he really cares.

Johnny's father, at an inappropriate time, of course, related a story about when Johnny was a boy. He was told he would grow rich if he worked, and he took a shovel and dug and dug, but no money appeared in his pockets. He finally gave up when it started to rain, and when he put on his hat it was full of water. "Poor Johnny, he worked and he worked, and all he got was a hat full of rain."

The Sun Also Rises, 1957

A more subtle wound, known only to the veteran who attempts to be intimate, is sexual impotence, portrayed in the film version of Ernest Hemingway's *The Sun Also Rises*. Released in 1957, the film was directed by Henry King, starred Tyrone Power and Ava Gardner, and featured a lively Errol Flynn. It failed to survive and make the conversion to video. Power's Jake Barnes is ironically cast as a stiff war veteran, working as a successful reporter, who is ambiguously injured in the book version, which becomes in the movie a wound, caused by a piece of shrapnel in the back, that is candidly and succinctly described as leading to impotence. When Jake receives the bad news from the doctor, he pauses, lights a cigarette, and asks, "I can still smoke, can't I?"

Ava Gardner plays the gadfly Lady Brett, who herself is the wife of a war veteran. Symbolically, Jake cannot consummate a relationship, and his dilemma is played off beautifully against the young, naïve, and proud bullfighter, who is positively brimming with machismo. The bullfighter attracts Lady Brett and Jake accommodates her by introducing the two and then courteously stepping away.

The Sun Also Rises is a wicked, bitter twist of a title, referring to the problem of impotence in the war veteran. This theme is taken up in other films as well, most directly in *The Big Chill* and *The Men*. The topic comes up also in the issue of social isolation and maladaptive behavior (*Sundays and Cybèle, Distant Thunder*), and particularly when it is secondary to substance abuse (*Desert Bloom, Rushmore, Cutters Way*) and paranoia (*Taxi Driver*). Impotence in the war veteran means that he is ineffective, spent, dogged by death, the reaper who cuts a swath before him preventing intimacy, forcing the veteran to seek isolation as salve, insulation, and prophylaxis to avoid the anxiety of intimacy. Happiness not allowed — Emmett's plight in *In Country*. Success systematically avoided. The World War I veteran, Septimus, in *Mrs. Dalloway*, best exemplifies the extreme of this sad fate.

The Sun Also Rises, for some reason, was never released as a video. If remade today as a film, like the *Razor's Edge*, another Tyrone Power war veteran film, it might fare better.

Ryan's Daughter, 1970

The war veteran in David Lean's film *Ryan's Daughter* does not technically "return home," but is rather reassigned from the hospital, where he was recovering from wounds received fighting with British forces at Passchendaele, to a remote garrison on Ireland's west coast. Major Randolph Droyan is let off on the road and is seen standing beside an ancient stone signpost with a carved cross. Director Lean has the major posing his slim, angular figure frequently against the beauty of the land and seascapes of County Mayo's coastline to emphasize his posttraumatic isolation.

The major was wounded and drags his left leg. He is posed with the local fool staring at him. The major is played by Christopher Jones. He has a scar running down from one eye that suggests his sadness and the traumas he has endured. Michael, the gamboling fool, is played by John Mills, whose performance is remarkable. His gross, stiff-legged limp is played in contrast to the major's. Michael's face, on the other hand, is unconcealed agony, whereas the major is masked in English middle class stoicism.

The film's title refers to Rosy Ryan, played by Sarah Miles, the adult daughter of the local publican. Rosy's father, Tom, played by Leo McKern, happens also to be the local informer, posing as an IRA sympathizer while informing the British garrison of rebel activities. Rosy is seen in the beginning of the film flirting with the local schoolteacher, Charles Shaughnessy, played by Robert Mitchum. They marry, but Rosy discovers with convincing disappointment that her husband cannot satisfy her. When she meets the major, however, she is smitten. The sudden passion in the meeting between Rosy and the major has an arduous intensity that takes them both aback. Their mutual fervor has the feeling of *Last Tango in Paris*, as their embrace sends them bouncing against the Guinness sign on the wall of the pub.

The major has been sent to command the English garrison as a cushy R and R assignment and will eventually have to return to France. The driver who picks him up confesses that he too was at the front, but the Second Battle of the Marne was too much for him. He also was sent to relax in the rugged peace of western Ireland.

The major is taciturn and remote. He is besieged by flashbacks to combat, usually stimulated by sounds, such as the start of a noisy garrison steam generator, or by the stressful circumstances that occupy the plot.

When Rosy and the major begin to tryst, there is a compulsive fatalism in both of them. The plot tension develops as the town becomes aware of their affair through the mimicry of the fool. When the IRA cadre attempts to land German weaponry on the stormy coast, it is Rosy's father who informs the British, but the town rabble blame Rosy, "the British soldier's whore," as the informant, beat her, cut her hair, and force both her and her sad, loyal husband from the town.

David Lean's spectacular epics *The Bridge on the River Kwai, Dr. Zhivago,* and *Lawrence of Arabia* had preceded the 1970 release of *Ryan's Daughter,* and his tradition of exquisite photography on an epic scale was continued. The spectacular use of the natural conditions on the Irish coast, the creeping fog on the battered rocks, the gale winds and spraying surf, the primitive stone structures in the Irish town, serve to mute some of the posturing and melodrama of the epic.

There is a poignant scene after the IRA smugglers have been apprehended, after the love affair has been exposed to the public scorn and retribution, in which the major and Michael, the fool, meet on the beach.

The fool shows the major where more ammunition has been hidden and opens boxes of dynamite and blasting caps as if he were a sideshow magician. Each box has a mirror on the underside of the lid, giving it a glittery light. The major a moment earlier indicated something final was approaching when he gave the fool his last cigarette, and then the silver case. Rosy and her husband hear the suicide blast from the beach as they are preparing to leave town.

In the aftermath of an attempted landing of German ammunitions for the IRA, the Major, played by Christopher Jones (right), confronts the Fool, Michael, played by John Mills (left), who is salvaging the remains. The Major holds a box of blasting caps in his hand, in this scene from David Lean's *Ryan's Daughter* (MGM, 1970).

The sad husband and his wife have to march through town, while the mean denizens watch from their windows. Only the fool and the priest accompany them. Trevor Howard plays the Catholic priest as a strong character who tries to single-handedly keep the town on its moral course.

A very poignant scene occurs early in the film when the ranking officer, a captain, played by Gerald Sim, greets the major at the garrison. The captain is about to depart for leave, prior to being transferred to the Front in France. He asks the major to tell him what it is like at the front and the major responds with booming silence. The captain confesses, "I'm a coward, you see—can't master it." He says that he most fears shaking "like an epileptic baby." "You've done your bit," he tells the major as he departs, as if he were lucky the worst is over. Just as the door closes, the garrison steam generator begins its rhythmic thumping bang and the major starts to shake at the noise.

The British in Ireland of that period during the Great War were regarded as an occupying enemy force. A villager remarks with scornful sarcasm when she sees the major's war ribbon: "A crippled, bloody hero." The Irish patriots find themselves allied with the Germans, not out of favor for Germany, but because they are also fighting the British. The Catholic priest, Father Collins, finds himself acting as the force for charitable humanity in spite of his nationalist loyalties and his own religious moral code, while all about him the old world values seem to be crumbling like the eroded stone towers of the past.

Johnny Got His Gun, 1971

Johnny Got His Gun is a creation of director Dalton Trumbo, who adapted the film from his own novel. Released in 1971, the film is now on video but out of print. Its topic is a U.S. veteran of World War I who wakes up in a hospital dismembered and without a face. His form is draped in a sheet that is built up to be tent-like, almost as an object of worship. Only his head of curly hair is visible. The chief doctor, who is himself on crutches, wants to keep the veteran alive as a specimen, claiming that he cannot feel a thing and his study will benefit others. However, the veteran's voice-over contradicts the doctor. It begins with a flat (if you will), disembodied voice, "What happened. Where am I." And in a poignant note for anyone who has ever awoken on a gurney in the ER, he cannot feel his limbs.

Fortunately there are a series of flashbacks as we see the veteran, Joe (played by Timothy Bottoms) as an adolescent boy with his father (Jason Robards) and mother (Marsha Hunt) and his girl friend, Kareen, played by Kathy Fields. We see Joe as he is about to enlist, spending the night with Kareen in her bedroom. She undresses under a sheet on the bed in a manner that mimics Joe's post-war circumstances.

The sequences of Joe and his father are particularly sweet. Father takes Joe and his friend fishing and Joe manages to lose his father's favorite fishing pole: the one he'd said "set him apart from other men." He tells his dad at night in their tent as they are lying side by side. Joe cries out in voice-over from his hospital bed, "I'm sorry father. Sorry I lost your fishing pole. I loved you." In another sequence, when he discovers that his face is gone, he cries out, "I can't live like this. Help me, mother, I'm having a nightmare and I can't wake up."

Director Trumbo mixes a variety of film media. In the grainy opening credits a series of newsreel clips portray world leaders meeting and reviewing troops. The hospital scenes are filmed in black and white, scenes also with a grainy film quality that seem to have been shot at the time.

The flashbacks are in color and move from realistic to abstract and surreal. Donald Sutherland appears in the role of sardonic, sad Jesus. "You're a very unlucky man and sometimes it wears off."

Finally, as a result of his father's suggestion in a dream sequence, Joe manages to communicate, first with a loving, devoted nurse, and then to the doctors, by tapping out Morse code with his head. He asks them to let him go out to public places where people can see him. When he is denied this, he begs them to kill him. This he is also denied. The chaplain calls the general stupid and the nurse prays for forgiveness. The final sequence in sepia black and white has a melodramatic old movie quality as the hospital people leave his room and turn out the light.

The last that is heard is the flat voice of Joe repeating, "SOS, Help Me." Followed by a drumbeat and fade. Then comes the statistics in red letters on a black background: "War dead since 1914 80,000,000." "Missing or mutilated 150,000,000." "*Dulce et decorum est pro patria mori.*"

Dalton Trumbo was blacklisted as a Hollywood writer during the era of the McCarthy anti-communist hearings. *Johnny Got His Gun* was first published as a novel in 1939. This was the only film he made as a director and he was said to have gone about the country trying to promote it. (Trumbo was responsible for writing many notable films, including *Spartacus* and *Papillon*.) The film is bitter and unyielding in its confrontation about the suffering that war brings to human beings, as contrasted with the pomp and arrogance of the leaders. It makes bitter statements about the motives of old men as one sings like a carnival barker, "So many young girls these days falling into old men's arms. Where have all the young men gone?"

To Kill a Clown, 1972

Released in 1972, *To Kill a Clown* was directed by George Bloomfield. The movie reflects the antiwar side of the Vietnam War as it was still in progress. Alan Alda, in a rare anti-hero role, plays Ritchie, a mad former army major, a Vietnam War veteran, with his knees shot off. He walks with two canes and is assisted by two canines, Dobermans of ferocious demeanor. The film concerns two innocents: the immature artist, Timothy Fischer, is played by Heath Lamber; his wife, Lilly, is played by Blyth Danner. They are residents in a summer retreat that is owned by Ritchie on Chokeberry Bay. When Ritchie arrives, Lily is at first attracted to him as a more mature man. However, he soon turns nasty when he decides to discipline the silly, impulsive Timothy, using his vicious dogs as guards.

Ritchie tells Lily about his days in Vietnam. He says that he brought souvenirs from Vietnam, although he didn't appreciate their significance until he, himself, was left for dead, his knees shot off, and awoke with his .45 pistol gone. "Some bastard gook has it on *his* wall." Walker (1991, p. 87) refers to Alda's portrayal of Ritchie as "Hawkeye gone berserk." Walker's interpretation of Ritchie's madness is flawed. "Apparently, he got the impression from his upbringing that only those who fight can gain manhood, and the idea that the fight in Vietnam deprived him of his drives him insane" (p. 87). Ideas do not drive one mad. It is a more likely and parsimonious explanation that being severely wounded and left for dead was sufficient to destabilize his mind.

The movie has an interesting but weak screenplay with an ambiguous ending by director Bloomfield and I.C. Rapoport. It is based on a novel, *Master of the Hounds,* by Algis Budrys.

Coming Home, 1978

The contrast between the physical and emotional wounding in war is highlighted in the controversial film *Coming Home.* Released in 1978, directed by Hal Ashby, it is a story about a wife of an army officer, played by Jane Fonda. While her husband (Bruce Dern) is away at war, she works in a VA hospital and falls in love with a paraplegic veteran from Vietnam (Jon Voight). When her husband returns, he seems to be emotionally more wounded than the paraplegic veteran. This otherwise excellent drama was tarnished by Fonda's offensive political activism during the war. She went too far, in the eyes of many war veterans, in going to the enemy in 1971 and giving them succor and support, posing on an anti-aircraft gun, as if she were taking sides. "Hanoi Jane" became the Vietnam War's Tokyo Rose. Lembcke (1998), as mentioned earlier, appears to be knowledgeable about the details of the writing and production of *Coming Home.* Fonda, he reports, commissioned Nancy Dowd to write the script after her (Fonda's) return from Vietnam. While controversial, the film does, however, play up the contrast between psychological and physical trauma and acknowledges the tragedy caused by both wounds.

Walker (1991, pp. 120–121) suggests that Fonda set up a scenario in which her character, Sally, "cures" the disaffected Vietnam War veteran of his impotence, while the experience brings her to sexual satisfaction as well. It seems that for Ms Fonda, being a symbol can work many ways.

Cutter's Way, 1981

Cutter's Way was originally *Cutter and Bone,* after a novel of that name by Newton Thornburg. Directed by Ivan Passer and released in 1981, *Cutter's Way* has a murder mystery plot featuring two men who were friends before the war. One went to war and the other dodged the draft. The war veteran, Alex Cutter, is played to the hilt by John Heard. Cutter drives the movie plot after Richard Bone, the prettyboy gigolo, played by Jeff Bridges, witnesses a man dump a woman's body in an alley and drive off.

Cutter has been severely wounded on the entire left side of his body. He wears an eye patch and has a stiff prosthetic leg and missing arm. He is also psychologically traumatized. He boozes, he rages, he neglects and drives his wife, Mo (played with compassionate sadness by Lisa Eichorn), to distress, and he presses his friend, Bone, to persist in proving the arrogant rich man is the killer. Cutter taunts the passive Bone into taking action, as he pursues the killer with reckless disregard for his own well-being. Heard is perfect conveying the man for whom life after Vietnam is an anticlimax. He speaks for everyone who went to serve in combat to every Clintonesque pretty boy who dodged and deftly avoided the challenge of the battlefield. His energy, however, is compulsive, adrenaline-driven, and cannot last. But while it lasts, he has the power of one who knows no fear. His sarcastic humor cuts to the bone of personal fear.

Cutter has lost an arm, a leg, and an eye but not his adrenal glands. He is driven, although he is not necessarily suicidal. Suicide, he says, takes too much commitment. But he has decidedly given up *trying* to live. At times he is not even sure he *is* alive. "When I wake up in the night alone and I can't sleep, I have to get up and look in the mirror to see if I'm still here." He taunts his companions at the table in a bar, which is crowded with African-American men shooting pool. Cutter shouts "*nigger*" loud enough to be heard by all, and then refers to the men, who loom over their table menacingly holding pool cues, as spades. Bone weakly explains his friend's crazy behavior: "It's the war." Cutter retorts with mind-bending mock indignation, "What war? I wasn't in no war."

Cutter grows impatient with Bone's passivity. In a comic scene, Bone is standing on a California pier plunking at targets with an amusement booth rifle. Exasperated, Cutter jerks out his .45 semi-automatic pistol and blasts away at the target to the startled horror of the vendor.

The truly great war veteran scene is when the drunken Cutter drives home and encounters his neighbor's car blocking his driveway. He backs up and charges, repeatedly crashing and pushing the car into his neighbors' yard. Then before the cops arrive, he drinks mouthwash and dons his Vietnam fatigue jacket, and audaciously points out to the cop that he knows the meaning of duty. It is not hypocrisy, but the flagrant exploitation of his disability, charged by the old existential one-percenter philosophy of not caring whether he lives or dies.

The rich man, who they think did the crime, is spotted in an Old California parade, arrogantly riding a posse horse, his face smug as Mussolini

John Heard (center, pointing gun) is Cutter in *Cutter's Way* (United Artists, 1980), a Vietnam War veteran who takes aim with his pistol at the amusement park booth out of impatience with his friend, Richard Bone, played by Jeff Bridges (second from right), as their mutual friend and co-conspirator, Valerie (Ann Dusenberry), looks on aghast.

behind mirror sunglasses. He is J.J. McCord, played with sculpted jaw by Stephen Elliott, and he becomes the object of Cutter's Vietnam revenge.

The music of *Cutter's Way* is enchanting, with Eric Harry on glass harmonica and Walter Repple on zither.

Birdy, 1984

Birdy, directed by Alan Parker, was released in 1984. It is what I have referred to as a war veteran's triptych film, with most of the action seen in flashback from the post–Vietnam War perspective. The movie centers around two boys from the slums of "Philly," the confident, well-adapted Al, played by Nicolas Cage, and the socially maladapted Birdy, played by Mathew Modine. Birdy has a fascination for birds. First he trains homing pigeons with Al's help. Then, when his mother destroys his cages after an accident, he breeds canaries and gradually grows more and more fascinated with the bird identity. The accident that caused his mother's not-uncalled-for reaction occurred when Birdy jumped off a high structure trying to fly.

The film cuts alternately between the post–Vietnam days and the boyhood before the Vietnam War. Both boys go into the army and both are severely wounded. The doctor at the army mental hospital, who is treating Birdy, sends for Al, who arrives in uniform with Combat Infantryman Badge, his face wrapped in bandages, obviously not yet thoroughly healed of his wounds. The compassionately limited doctor is an army major, played by John Hawkins. The doctor explains that Birdy was missing in action for a month. We see Birdy in a flashback, later in the film, already wounded, sitting in a med-evac helicopter. The helicopter is hit by enemy gunfire and crashes. Birdy is thrown clear from the crash and watches the mangled corpses in the burning wreckage, then sees flocks of tropical birds overhead in the distance that seem to be incinerated by a napalm air strike.

Al comments sarcastically to the Doc that "the army takes care of its own, they certainly took care of me." He points out the irony, saying that he has a steel jaw that is more fragile than a glass jaw. Al's job, the Doc explains, is to try to get through to his old friend, the catatonic Birdy.

Birdy, in the hospital, does not communicate. He sits in contorted squatting positions and seems to mimic bird postures. He will not eat unless he is fed. The phrase, he eats like a bird, fortunately was not used.

Technically these men are not yet out of the army, but they are veterans of the war. We see Al in the hospital gym lifting weights, watching an amputee in a wheelchair shooting hoops, and another amputee climbing a rope. The ironic sign behind him reads: "Welcome home, soldier, the USA is proud of you."

The hospital is remarkable for its stark tile and prison-like steel caged staircases. The shoddy suburb of Philadelphia neighborhood seems to exist on the decrepit periphery of a city dump. There is no sentimentality here about the good life. Al says to Birdy, surrendering to his seeming failure to get through to his friend, "They got the best of us, Birdy. We're all screwed up." He talks about the sweet smell of his own burned flesh. "I don't know what I look like, Birdy." He cries, holding his inert friend in a close embrace. "We should hide out and not talk to anybody." At this point Birdy expresses his first post–Vietnam words. "You know, sometimes you're full of crap, Al."

The final scene has a refreshing surprise, a camera trick that follows a chase scene to a resounding drumbeat. There is good music by Peter Gabriel, with several refreshing choruses of "La Bamba." The screenplay was based on a novel by William Wharton, which had the story taking place after World War II, letting the boys come of age during the war and then

Nicolas Cage, as Al, sits in the hospital room holding Birdy (Mathew Modine) in his arms, two wounded Vietnam War veterans who knew each other in childhood, in Alan Parker's *Birdy* (TriStar, 1984).

fighting at the end. The novel is a must for anyone who has ever had a love affair with a canary.

The catatonia that Birdy displays is caused by trauma, and the post-traumatic symptom is what used to be called hysteria. Birdy, we know, was already deep into his imaginary world before he ever went into combat. It is not improbable that one could emerge from such a disorder with the dramatic quickness that we see in *Birdy*.

Born on the Fourth of July, 1989

If anyone can transform the adrenaline charge into a visual image montage it is Oliver Stone. As a Vietnam combat veteran who became a successful mainstream film director and popular international celebrity, Stone commands a special mention in this discussion of war veteran films. (Other war veteran filmmakers are James Whale, who served as a British officer in the trenches of World War I, William Wellman, a volunteer flyer with Lafayette Escadrille, John Ford, who won a Purple Heart as a navy officer filming the Battle of Midway, Samuel Fuller, who was highly decorated with the First Infantry Division, and former B-24 pilot Robert Altman, who flew combat missions in the Pacific Theater.) Stone, himself, has developed a cult following and popular appeal. He has become controversial in the making of fictional movies based on historical events and characters, such as *JFK* and *Nixon*. He captured the war veterans' attention with his trilogy of films about the Vietnam era: *Platoon, Born on the Fourth of July*, and *Heaven and Earth*. To a certain extent he fosters his own popular myth by his biography, dropping out of Yale, teaching at a school in South Vietnam (1965–66), and then volunteering for the army and serving as an enlisted infantryman in the 25th Division from 1967 to 1968.

Born on the Fourth of July was released in 1989 and is another example of the triptych concept of spanning the Vietnam War era. The film is based on the autobiography of Ron Kovic, (screenplay by Kovic and Stone), and follows Ron from his youth, watching a Fourth of July parade in Massapequa, Long Island, and playing war games (Bryan Larkin plays Ron as a lad), to the high school kid wrestling and contemplating his future with his friends. The mature Ron is played by Tom Cruise. There is a sudden segue from his senior prom to Vietnam, skipping Marine Corps boot camp. Ron appears as a battle-seasoned rifleman near the Cua Viet River in Vietnam. Civilians are gunned down in their hooches in a scene emphasizing the disorienting state of high tension and dangerous ambiguity. After the civilian casualties are discovered, a real firefight develops with the NVA counterattacking. Ron is firing into the sun's glare and realizes he has shot another Marine. He tries to confess to his CO afterward, but is ordered to carry on. A few months later Ron is himself shot and brought down, the bullet severing his spinal chord.

Director Stone keeps the viewer riveted with continuous scenes of med-evac and field hospital, followed by sudden segues to the infamous Bronx VA hospital scenes of rats and burbling body fluids, and Ron's futile attempts to walk with braces.

Stone knows no subtlety. When Ron returns home, he finds his family and neighbors awkward and embarrassed. He tries to be upbeat, but is finally drawn into alcohol and drug use by another vet friend, Timmy, played with empathy by Frank Whaley, who seems to be the only one comfortable with Ron's paralysis.

Ron gets into a drunken screaming match with his mother, played by Caroline Kava. She seems to be a rigid woman who fostered his teenage athletic competitiveness and encouraged him to join the Marines, convinced that he was doing the right thing. She is most alarmed by anything sexual and offended when he is drunk and swears at her, waving his catheter. She shouts, "Don't say *penis* in this house!"

Ron's father is played by Raymond J. Barry as a quiet, passive man who remains loyal to Ron and wants everybody to live in quiet harmony. When he seems to lack enthusiasm for his son joining the Marines, Ron counters, arguing, "you served, uncle Bob served." He is loyal to his son, helping him with his adjustment, but finally has to ask him to leave when he clashes with his mother.

The film segues next to a Mexican resort colony of Vietnam War veterans. Hard drinking and drug use occurs amid an apparently accepting and exploiting Mexican hostelry. Chief among the excessive debauchers is Charlie, a paralyzed veteran, played with spitting fire by Willem Dafoe. Charlie goes berserk after prolonged debauchery and fights with everyone, as Ron joins him in departing in a taxi. Charlie then fights with the taxi driver, who finally dumps them out on the desert and drives away, leaving them stranded. Charlie then picks a fight with Ron, taunting him, calling him a fake veteran and then a baby killer. They grapple in their wheelchairs, falling out and wrestling in the sand until they are exhausted.

In another segue back to the States, Ron seeks out the family of the Marine he thinks he killed in Vietnam. This sequence picks up the theme that had been stated earlier with the marching bands of veterans of previous wars, encouraging concepts like valor in battle and the passing of the combat status to successive generations. Ron confesses to the family in a painful scene in which it seems that he ends up being emotionally abusive to them by confronting his own guilt. This scene was factually not part

Paralyzed Vietnam War veteran Ron Kovic is played by Tom Cruise in Oliver Stone's *Born on the Fourth of July* (Universal City Studios, 1989). Ron is being wheeled into a war protest demonstration by an undercover vet played by Peter Crombie.

of Kovic's real experience (Toplin, 2000, p. 13) and is given as an example of Stone's exercising artistic license in the manipulation of historic fact to create "broader truths." The film's finale has Ron demonstrating and rioting at the 1972 Republican convention in Miami (which the real Kovic never did) and then speaking to a cheering crowd in the 1976 Democratic convention. Stone seems to lose Ron's character in the sweep of collective events at the end of the film.

Born on the Fourth of July is a problem film, but not because it is based on an autobiography and is in a sense a heroic story of survival. As that, it captures a certain zest of men who expect to die and live on with absolute abandon as an anti-climax. It is a problem because there are certain clichés that evolve from war veteran stories, and Stone shamelessly exploits most of the clichés and draws them out so broadly he borders on parody. Kael (1991, p. 251) refers to Stone's "visual rant." For example, the prolongation of the Fourth of July parade scenes, showing he odd quirks of aging veterans. It seems that in his quest to depict reality, for he knew the situation well, his combat veteran's cynicism got the better of him. He could not believe that his audience would understand and so he over-expressed his symbols and ran the pointed scenes implying the injustice too long. His style reminds me of a war veteran I once knew who described lobbying his state legislator at a reception by backing him up against the wall and splashing him with red wine to symbolize blood.

Ron as a boy has an unreachable girlfriend, Donna (played as a child by Jessica Prunell and as an adult by Kyra Sedgwick). He never manages to really hook up with her. After he is paralyzed, he tries again to meet with her, but she is caught up in sixties counterculture sentiment. "War is *so* wrong."

Pauline Kael (1991) criticizes Stone for overplaying Ron's innocence before enlisting, although the story as it is portrayed seems not far from what many veterans remember.

Snow Falling on Cedars, 1999

Released in 1999 and directed by Scott Hicks, *Snow Falling on Cedars* conveys the damage of war in a more subtle turn, although the staid drama would have become stultified had it not been for the impressive Northwest Puget Sound coastal atmosphere. Credit is given to the Washington State Parks, though the town in the film was credited as Greenwood, BC. Based on a popular novel by David Gutterson, *Snow Falling on Cedars* is another triptych film, devoting a respectable amount of time to the prewar boys and their loves, before brief scenes from World War II, in both theaters. The combat scenes are done in quick cuts, juxtaposed with the trial of one war veteran for killing another. The heart of the movie is the court room drama mystery devoted to the post–World War II trial of the Japanese-American war veteran of the Italian campaign for killing another war veteran of the Pacific War, his former childhood friend. The trial is covered by a reporter for the local paper, who was himself a veteran who had lost his arm in combat.

The background of *Snow Falling on Cedars* is the contest of drives, prejudices, and conflicting loyalties. The war disturbed this fictional Northwest island culture, depriving the Japanese-Americans of their farmlands, which the post-war settlements did not erase.

The war veteran twist in *Snow Falling on Cedars* is mainly in the characters of the reporter, Ishmael, played by Ethan Hawke, and the Japanese-American fisherman Kazuo Myamodo, played by Rick Yune. The veterans each have their remoteness and an inability to communicate feelings. Ishmael, who had his arm amputated as the result of a war wound, is moody with emotional isolation. When subtly critiqued by his mother for his remoteness, the loss of the arm seems like the lesser wound.

Ishmael is seen in flashback as a boy, falling in love with a daughter of a strawberry farmer, Hatsue, played as a girl by Anne Suzuki, and as an adult by Youki Kudoh. Their love relationship is kept secret, meeting in the rain forest, trysting in an old growth cedar tree's roots. When Pearl Harbor is bombed, the anti–Japanese fervor causes the Japanese-Americans to be rounded up and shipped to internment camps. Ishmael's father is the publisher of the San Pedro Island newspaper and stands up for the Japanese-American families, placing his principles before his financial interests. Ishmael, throughout the movie, has his character compared to his father's. In Gutterson's novel, Ishmael's father is a veteran of World War I.

Under pressure from her traditional mother, Hatsue is coerced into rejecting Ishmael, writing to him from the internment camp a dear Ishmael letter just before he is wounded in a Pacific Island assault.

The man who is thought to have been murdered is a fisherman, who was also a war veteran, whose mother bought Hatsue's family's farm. The man who married Hatsue, Kazuo, just before he goes off to fight in the U.S. army in Italy, tries after the war to buy the land back from Carl Heina just before Carl dies mysteriously on his boat. It is weakly established in the movie, but more strongly in Gutterson's novel, that Carl and Kazuo were boyhood friends. During the trial, Ishmael discovers evidence that will exonerate Kazuo, and Ishmael's struggle is overcoming his jealousy and prejudice to turn over the evidence to the trial judge. Ironically, one the longest flashbacks to the war takes place when Kazuo recalls killing a young wounded German solder by bashing him on the head, in a manner similar to that which he is accused of doing at the trial.

Almost stealing the show is Max Von Sydow, who plays the aged defense lawyer, Nels. What really steals the show is the wonderful photography of Robert Richardson, featuring the foggy grays and snowy forests of the Pacific Northwest coastal islands. The moody atmosphere is accented

After choosing between honor and love, Ishmael Chambers (Ethan Hawke) hugs his beloved Hatsue Miyamoto (Youki Kudoh) in *Snow Falling on Cedars* (Universal Pictures, 2000). Darkness hides his left arm wartime amputation. His sleeve is tucked in his overcoat pocket. He has just acted to free her husband from custody and thereby to perpetuate his loneliness. (Photograph by Doane Gregory.)

by the mournful music of James Newton Howard, featuring the solo cellist Ron Leonard, and Mozart's *Laudate Dominum*.

Screenplay adapted from the novel is by director Hicks and Ron Bass. One has a strong sense of before the war and after, and the great disruption that the fighting caused in the lives of a generation of the island community. Although as hard to come by as meaning from tragedy, the film leaves us with a sense that some justice has been served in this remote corner of the world.

Comparing Wounds

The lovers' discomfort with the wounds of the veterans recalls the folktale from the Brothers Grimm *Bearskin*, about the destitute war veteran who is offered a pact with the devil. If he will neglect himself for seven years, never washing, cutting his hair, etc., and wear a filthy bearskin, he can at the same time have bottomless wealth. Bearskin befriends a traveler who offers him one of his daughters in marriage. Bearskin is rejected by two of the older daughters, but accepted by the dutiful youngest daughter. Bearskin gives her half a ring and goes off, outwits the devil, and returns a wealthy, handsome man.

Most of our wounded veteran tales depict the awkwardness of dealing with the reckless, moody veteran and his wounds. Recall Tom, the pain-ridden veteran in *Heroes for Sale*, and Homer, the sailor with his hooks for hands in *Best Years of Our Lives*, and Ken, the paralyzed veteran in his wheelchair (*The Men*), and the moody, addicted Jack in *Desert Bloom*. In a deft turn, the film *Coming Home* features the physically wounded and paralyzed veteran against the emotionally wounded but physically whole counterpart, finding the former noble and the latter disturbing.

A film such as *Born on the Fourth of July* could not have been made during World War II. The so-called Hays Commission refused to allow such images of drunken men or modern "soldiers in unsavory situations" on the grounds that such scenes gave aid to the enemy (Doherty, 1993a, p. 38). Such scenes were only allowed in historical dramas. Modern war films were rendered virtually bloodless and gruesomeness was unacceptable. Ironically, the very core of the naivete that Stone decries in his film was the innocence maintained by the censorship code.

When examining the role of the war veteran, independent of the war, we can glean some commonalties of war veterans and the cultural influences that make each war's veterans unique.

Heroes for Sale, released in 1933 and *A Hatful of Rain* (1957) deal with the not uncommon problem of iatrogenic opiate addictions. Both men, World War I veteran Tom, and Korean War veteran Johnny, were wounded in their respective wars and both acquired addictions to morphine as a result of prolonged treatment for painful conditions. The scope of the Depression Era *Heroes for Sale* is more sweeping, following Tom after an unrealistically quick cure of his addiction *and*, it is assumed, his intractable pain, through a series of ups and downs, treating him like a populist saint. Tom's character was unquestioned, especially after his cure. A *Hatful of Rain* similarly shows the circumstances of the environment oppressing the veteran. He lives in a neighborhood of hideous, bare cement apartments that are part of a massive housing project. The circumstances of the drug addiction are elaborated by *Hatful* director Fred Zinneman. The pusher, Mother, and his henchmen are '50s wayward hipsters, and Mother (Henry Silva) is a menacing psychopath with ambiguous Asian/Hispanic features. The drug dealer in *Heroes for Sale* wears a suit and tie and looks like a tough Caucasian without remarkable ethnicity.

The crucial cultural difference between the two films is seen in the role of the veteran. Tom, in *Heroes for Sale*, is a victim of injustice. His combat heroics went unrecognized. When he was finally treated, he was quickly cured and went on to perform noble deeds that were sometimes crushed by circumstances outside his control. Johnny, in *Hatful*, is regarded as a hero by his dad who extols his suffering, but Johnny regards his military experience with contempt, "two years in the army–another lousy year in a hospital bed." His wartime traumas are recalled in nightmare fashion. The ultimate upbeat in the Korean War veteran's story is the fact that his family becomes unified in his support.

Tom Holmes, the World War I veteran, walks away from family and, Christ-like, hits the road with the poor. His child idolizes him from afar. His wife has been martyred in the worker unrest that followed from Tom's attempt to help. His role predates Luis Buñuel's *Nazarin*, that gave the saintly character who does harm a satiric ring. *Heroes for Sale* contains the 1930s romanticism, giving credence to the nobility of humankind, while *Hatful of Rain* reflects the stark realism of the post–World War II era.

A somewhat different comparison is raised when two films on the subject of war-related paralysis are examined. Fred Zinnemann also directed *The Men*, which was released in 1950, portraying the rehabilitation problems of paralyzed veterans of World War II, and Oliver Stone directed *Born on the Fourth of July*, about a veteran's rehabilitation from paralysis during the Vietnam War. *The Men* seldom refers to the war directly. Bud, Lt. Wilcheck, was a platoon leader who was awarded a Silver Star, which is a major combat award. The drama is centered on his struggle to develop a will to live and then to engage in a relationship with his understanding wife. The culture of this film is confined to interior scenes where the veterans pull for each other, while the medical treatment is dignified and reasonable. The structure of recovery is solid behind a traditional society. Stone's film is far more expansive. It excoriates the Veterans Hospital treatment of Ron Kovic, which he presents as a rat-infested nightmare. Ron's family is awkwardly ambivalent toward his disability. Ron fights and rages, abusing drugs and alcohol for a while in a period of social and cultural alienation — south of the border. When he returns to a sense of direction and purpose, he becomes a political activist actively opposing the war and the government's actions.

Both films give us close-up looks at the paraplegic veterans in despair. *The Men*, however, zeroes in on the inner struggle resulting from Bud's decision to marry and strive for a normal life "capable of retraining." *Born on the Fourth of July* reflects the action orientation of the 1970s during the time of the Vietnam War veterans' return. (The film was released in 1989.) Despair is dramatized as self-destructive rage. (See the similar fury displayed in Lt. Dan's behavior as a double amputee in *Forrest Gump*, released in 1994.)

The Return of the POW

Odysseus when he lands in Ithaca, first conceals, dissimulates about his having been a prisoner of war. England's King Richard I, captured while returning from his campaign in the Middle East, was held for ransom by a German nobleman, but was not technically a POW. Movie director James Whale began his theatrical career directing plays while a POW in Germany, putting on entertainment for his fellow prisoners. Generally, however, POWs do not fair well when they are able to return home. There was a very high rate of PTSD among surviving POWs in the Pacific Theater during the Second World War and the conditions appear to worsen for many as they age (Port, et al., 2001). The sequelae of starvation, torture, and beatings can be profound. Kurosawa's "The Tunnel," a segment of his film collection *Dreams*, illustrates the anguish when captivity follows defeat and the loss that marks the return of the POW.

One of the complications that arise for the returning POW and his family is the discovery that the personality traits, which are necessary for surviving his incarceration, such as unyielding determination, idealism, the compulsive fostering of fantasy and mind exercises, are not the ones needed for adapting to family life at home. Films like *Some Kind of Hero* and *Rolling Thunder* illustrate in fiction the real dilemma of men who return after a long period of captivity to discover that their families have adapted to their losses and moved on. Philpott (2001) described this in his biography of real life Vietnam War POW Jim Thompson, the prisoner held more than ten years and who returned to find that his wife and four children had adapted to his death and were living with another man.

Other films that deal with war veterans who were briefly held as POWs (e.g., *First Blood, Cornered, The Fallen Sparrow, Ruckus,* and *The Deer Hunter*) are discussed in other chapters. *The Fallen Sparrow* deals specifically with the aftermath of torture. The returning POW can be seen as a metaphor for the plight of many who dedicate themselves to ideals or goals, only to find that their families have adapted to life and moved on.

The Manchurian Candidate, 1962

The Manchurian Candidate was a big Hollywood movie when it was released in 1962. Directed by John Frankenheimer, it had an advertising icon of the Queen of Hearts. With Frank Sinatra as Major Bennet Marco of the U.S. Army, and Laurence Harvey as the troubled Korean War Medal of Honor winner Raymond Shaw. Janet Leigh has a very clever, lighthearted role that saves the movie from becoming overbearing. She plays Rosie, Major Marco's love interest. Angela Lansbury is the Queen of Diamonds, the wicked mother of the war veteran, Shaw, and wife of blowhard Senator Iselin, played as a clownish satire of Senator Joe McCarthy. The story by Richard Condon, adapted by George Axelrod, addressed a number of issues related to the Cold War fear of Communism, while it exploited a dramatic assassination plot, based upon mind-bending hypnotic dissociation, induced through evil "Oriental" brain-washing, perpetrated by the Soviet Pavlov Institute.

The movie begins before credits showing a patrol, led by Marco, being ambushed and captured. Then we cut after the credits to the Medal of Honor winner, Shaw, stepping off an airplane to be greeted by a crowd of press and his scene-stealing mother. In a manner later copied by *Jacob's Ladder,* we learn that Marco and other survivors are having nightmares, which Marco, being an intelligence officer, takes literally. The dreams are cleverly enacted, showing an initially confusing scene of a ladies' lecture incongruously attended by the lethargic combat squad, the scenes then changing to show the ladies as Soviet and Chinese officials. The lecturer becomes a smiling, bantering Asian man, Yen Lo, played by Khigh Dhiegh, exuding both confidence and malice, who jokes about Americana: "tastes good like a cigarette should, ha ha." He is demonstrating that Sergeant Shaw has been thoroughly trained to kill when in a trance, once he turns

Frank Sinatra (left) plays Korean War veteran Major Marco in John Franken-heimer's *The Manchurian Candidate* (MGM/UA, 1962). He watches Laurence Harvey, as Christopher Shaw, play the deadliest game of solitaire.

over a queen of diamonds, when ordered to play solitaire. The evil doctor demonstrates his accomplishment by having Shaw kill two of the Americans, strangling one and shooting the other, emotionlessly, while the other entranced soldiers watch without reacting.

Sinatra's Marco is assigned to investigate Shaw and in a nice drinking scene, the inebriated Shaw tells Marco about his hatred for his mother, who was instrumental in destroying the only loving relationship he'd ever had. Before entering the army he had fallen in love with the daughter of a senator labeled as a Communist by the demagogic Senator Iselin.

In the development of the story, the hapless Shaw is directed by his mother, who, it turns out, has been a Soviet agent all along, to kill the senator who has sworn to block her husband's nomination for vice president. He also kills the senator's daughter, his own fiancée, without breaking out of his trance. When he is finally confronted by Marco, who has identified the queen of diamonds hypnotic cue, Marco deftly uses the trance technique to uncover the plot.

When Harvey's Shaw realizes that he's killed his lover and her father, Marco, now in charge as the hypnotist, tells him to "forget about it." (Great technique!) Finally at the convention center, Marco intervenes, but only after Shaw has killed his mother and stepfather, the ridiculous Senator Iselin, with a sniper rifle.

The Manchurian Candidate is probably the first movie to give us the sense of the war veteran as a walking time bomb, who will go off if someone says the wrong thing. (The jittery, aggressive Buzz, played by William Bendix in *The Blue Dahlia*, was a victim of brain injury.) Shaw was portrayed in 1962 as a victim of Communist brainwashing. It was the Communists who would be so heartless as to conspire to assassinate a national leader to further political ends. Unfortunately, I have, since seeing *The Manchurian Candidate*, been unable to see Angela Lansbury without thinking of the queen of diamonds.

Black Sunday, 1977

Black Sunday, despite its title, is not a dark comedy or *film noir*. It is better classified as an action drama of a James Bond sort, in which an Israeli terrorist expert is pitted against a former Vietnam War POW pilot who has been brainwashed by terrorists to fly a Goodyear blimp carrying a huge bomb over the Super Bowl football stadium. The film's thesis is reminiscent of the classic *Manchurian Candidate*, but has substituted melodramatic special effects for the sinister mind control of the latter. The crazed former POW is played by Anthony Perkins surrogate Bruce Dern, who managed to deliver his mix of whiny temper, edged with emotional instability, which here worked to give an otherwise predictable action plot a kind of Vincent Price sinister twist. The movie was directed for action by John Frankenheimer and had Robert Shaw as the anti-terrorist agent. The thesis awakens the collective angst that there is something not to be trusted about combat veterans and men whose wills have been made to crack. Seeing and believing this film, and its aforementioned Korean War brother, one would not vote for John McCain to govern anything. The film ironically also illustrates the fear that many war veterans have with or without PTSD: don't bunch up, stay away from crowds.

Rolling Thunder, 1977

A B-movie about revenge was made in 1977 and called *Rolling Thunder*, perhaps for the American bombing operation of the same name. William Devine plays Major Charles Rane, a former POW, who arrives home to San Antonio by plane with another Texas former POW, army master sergeant Johnny Vohden (Tommy Lee Jones). The major, Charlie, finds out that his wife has been having an affair with a policeman, Cliff, played by Lawrason Driscoll. Charlie is quite stoic about this and we learn that his philosophy is a rather Buddhist sense of "all things will pass." He illustrates this when his rival, Cliff, makes a noble gesture at meeting with him. Charlie drinks with his rival and merely requests that Cliff not call his son a moron. Cliff says he admires Charlie for his courage, and says so ironically, "Them gooks had no mercy. You're lucky they didn't ruin your life." Charlie reveals that he has developed a fetish by demonstrating how he was tortured and urging Cliff to inflict pain upon him.

The plot turns when some robbers come after a box of silver dollars given to Charlie by a local company at his airport homecoming celebration. They torture Charlie, but he refuses to tell them where the coins are hidden. They finally force Charlie's right hand into the garbage disposal. About then Charlie's wife and son come home and the son leads them to the money. The robbers then shoot his wife and son but leave Charlie passed out and bleeding.

Rolling Thunder then becomes a story of revenge, as Charlie sharpens up the hook prosthesis on his arm, practices with his guns, and enlists a barmaid and his friend, Johnny. Armed with shotguns and dressed in their Class A uniforms, the men trace down the robbers and shoot them up in a brothel south of the border.

The film was written by Paul Schrader, adapting the screenplay from his own story with the help of Heywood Gould. The story comes impressively close to the biography of Jim Thompson, the longest held U.S. prisoner of the Vietnam War (Philpott, 2001), who returned home to find his wife and children living with another man. Thompson, however, maintained his dignity until he succumbed to alcoholism.

Rolling Thunder was directed by John Flynn. Linda Haynes plays the barmaid with measured abandon. She says at one point, after Charlie has involved her in a violent scene, "Why do I get stuck with crazy men."

Charlie replies, "That's the only kind that's left." He describes himself as already dead when she tries to make love to him. Like Charlie, the movie fails to take advantage of her talents. Charlie demonstrates mind over matter to the point where nothing matters, nothing is attached.

Some Kind of Hero, 1982

Some Kind of Hero is a film, released in 1982, which doesn't quite know if it is a comedy or a drama. Directed by Michael Pressman, it stars Richard Pryor as Eddie Keller, a hapless returning POW who was captured on his first operation in Vietnam with the 101st Airborne and spends the next four years as a POW. When he is finally released, he is met at the airport by his manager, an army PR colonel, played by Ronny Cox. Eddie is awed by the media attention. He discovers in a kind of sad, anxious series of setbacks, reminiscent of Buster Keaton or that sad clown act of Red Skelton, that his wife is in love with another man, his daughter may not be his, his business is bankrupt, and his mother is in a nursing home after a stroke and about to be booted out because of lack of funds. Not only that, but his back pay is held up, apparently because he signed a confession while a POW in order that his dying buddy could get to a hospital. Margot Kidder plays Toni, a call girl who befriends him. Eddie finally tries to rob a bank, after happening upon an old army buddy in the middle of a bank heist. In a series of misadventures he ends up with gangsters' money, which he uses to pay off everybody in a hurried finale that attempts to make it all seem OK.

Some Kind of Hero unfortunately doesn't work as either comedy or drama. The right idea, that of showing the culture shock of a returning POW held for four years, is portrayed in a thin and muddled drama that tries to take on too much. Wasting a golden opportunity, what it fails to do—a fault common to many returning war veteran films—is show the effects of psychological trauma in the ordinary, mundane everyday ways that it manifests.

Akira Kurosawa's Dreams, 1990

Akira Kurosawa's Dreams was released in 1990 and represents an end mark of Kurosawa's magnificent collection of directorial works. The film consists of a group of richly photographed vignettes written by the director. The fourth segment, "The Tunnel," features a World War II army officer (Yoshitaka Zushi) walking on a deserted mountain highway. He is carrying his possessions in pack and bags. As he approaches a tunnel, a fierce dog comes barking and howling out of the darkness. The dog, a German shepherd, is strapped with some sort of military gear. The dog's snarling growls, as he menaces the man, fuse into the sound of gunfire. The veteran proceeds undaunted into the dark tunnel, walking through a ghostly-lit passage until he emerges into the light again at the other side, and hears another's steps following. A figure of a stiff soldier in World War II battle garb emerges from the vacant, echoic tunnel, his firm steps resounding. As he emerges his figure is revealed with a ghastly white face. He marches out and snaps to attention. "Private Noguchi!" shouts the veteran. "Yes, Commander!" shouts the soldier. "Commander, is it true? Was I really killed in action? I can't believe I'm really dead. My parents don't believe I'm dead." The veteran replies. "I'm so sorry, but you died in my arms." Private Noguchi snaps to, does an about face, and walks off into the tunnel.

There follows an even more clamorous sound of troops marching to echoes of commands. Out of the tunnel come four columns of soldiers, all in white face, who stop on command. The leader announces with martial zeal that Third Platoon has returned with no casualties. In brief, passionate statements, the veteran mournfully announces that Third Platoon was annihilated. "You were all killed in action. I wasn't killed. I survived. I can hardly look you in the face. I sent you out to die. I was to blame. I can't deny my thoughtlessness and misconduct." He tells his troops that he wished he had died with them instead of being taken prisoner. "I know your bitterness. They called you heroes, but you died like dogs." He tells them to go back and rest in peace. They, however, remain immobile until he gives the proper orders. As the sounds of the marching platoon recede, the menacing dog returns, his snarls again fusing with the sound of gunfire.

Kurosawa follows this grim scene with a vignette of beautiful images of Vincent Van Gogh's paintings, seen by an aspiring artist at a museum. The artist merges with the paintings and actually talks to Van Gogh at work in a hay field. Martin Scorsese plays Van Gogh with an impressive likeness, except for his New York City clipped accent. The delightful, colorful dalliance gives needed relief from the war veteran's plight, and a nice statement about the director's ideas of art in cinema. It is significant that Kurosawa himself was an aspiring art student until he began training in 1936 as an assistant director. His first feature film, Sanshiro Sugata, was released in 1943 (Richie, 1996, p. 220). Kurosawa was never in the army. Yet, this film is a collection of his personal dreams. The director himself wrote the script. Which leaves one to conclude that this is about Kurosawa's guilt and perhaps an image of the collective guilt of his contemporaries.

CHAPTER 2

Symptoms of Survival

Guilt and Revenge as Motivating Forces

In the opening and closing of Steven Spielberg's impressive 1998 World War II film *Saving Private Ryan*, the aged war veteran is seen in the graveyard of the D-Day casualties of the Normandy landing. The veteran walks to the site and falls to his knees. His sentiment reverberates through the minds of many war veterans who are living with the dead: Have I been worthy?

Accentuated sense of duty, guilt, loyalty, need for revenge, a sense of having no future, are the symptoms of survival. Not necessarily the symptoms of posttraumatic stress disorder (PTSD), but rather simply the symptoms of surviving prolonged circumstance of combat and readiness.

Duty and loyalty are important values to war veterans, values that often stand in sharp contrast to the values of the society in which they return. Motorcycle clubs became attractive to some combat veterans who valued the brotherhood bond, to be duty-bound to cover the back of any brother in need. Lavigne (1993, p. 140) describes the Hell's Angels Motorcycle Club forming from crews of World War II bombers. (One can hear the echoic roar of many B-17 reciprocating engines starting up after a motorcycle club meeting.) Urban police, fire and emergency services departments took their share of returning war veterans, as well, for similar reasons.

Revenge drove war veterans to return to combat and settle the score for the loss of comrades, as seen in *China Gate*. Revenge tends not to ever be resolved, even for war veterans who survived repeated tours of combat, no matter how many are killed. Trauma-born revenge continued as racial and ethnic hatred, becoming an unremitting source of obsession.

Guilt was also a contaminant carried home. Guilt served as the ineffable stopper that held the veteran back from success and the ability to truly savor his life. *Gardens of Stone* presents guilt of those professional soldiers who are unable to train soldiers on their way to war. *The Presidio* features the war veteran with guilt by association to the war and the deeds of others. The combination of these symptoms and values made more powerful by their association to war traumas, made for lives devoted to helping or hating others.

Many statements about guilt, such as *Akira Kurosawa's Dreams*, are taken as anti-war. But the term "anti-war" is a political declaration, whereas looking back on a war with grief and guilt is a natural expression of the reality of war. Guilt can also be exploited, cultivated and perpetuated until it becomes psychopathology.

The Searchers, 1956

In John Ford's *The Searchers*, released in 1956, John Wayne plays Ethan, a Civil War veteran. He returns to his brother's home in Texas three years after the end of the war with his recent past questionable. It is implied that he may have been involved in a robbery. When asked to join a posse and take an oath to the Texas Rangers, Ethan refuses, stating that he already swore an oath to the Confederate States of America. Ethan proves himself to be a hard, lonely, bitter, and bigoted man. When Martin, a young man who was adopted into the family and is part Cherokee (and part Welsh), appears in the house to greet him, Ethan clearly expresses dislike for his Martin's Native heritage. Martin is played by Jeffrey Hunter with cosmetically darkened skin. Ethan makes a distinction between blood kin and Martin. He calls Martin "blanket head" on several occasions, always with the abrupt contempt of a muleskinner. After Comanches (played by Navaho) raid the family home while most of the men are away in the posse, Ethan and Martin find the family murdered and the women taken prisoner. We are made aware of a secret love between Ethan and his brother's wife, Betty. Ethan and Martin set out after the raiding party across the vast landscape of the Texas plains, following them into New Mexico. Ford filmed on location in Monument Valley, with the winter scenes shot in Canada.

There is no great emphasis placed on Ethan's war experiences and influence, although it could also be argued that the whole plot involves the influence of Ethan's war experiences. In his biography of Ford, Andrew Sinclair refers to John Wayne's portrayal of the lonely, vengeful Ethan as "a western Odysseus" (p. 213).

John Ford's direction gives the film a heroic, but extremely hard edge with its westward ho imperialism and sense of Manifest Destiny. The Comanche warriors charge across expanse of river or plain in frontal assaults on horseback, getting themselves picked off by cowboys firing pistols and rifles while exchanging quips. There is a comical scene in which a plump Comanche "squaw," Wild Goose Flying in the Night Sky (played by Beulah Archuletta), is unknowingly married to Martin, who thought he had been trading for a blanket. The Comanche men are referred to as "bucks." The white girls are no good after living with "bucks," and the only merciful thing to do is kill them. "They ain't white, they're Comanche." When Ethan finally talks face to face to Chief Cicatrice (aka, Scar, played by Henry Brandon), he says, "You speak pretty good American, for a Comanche."

The screenplay was by Frank S. Nugent from a novel by Alan LeMay. The script abounds in racist remarks, not uncharacteristic of the day. Scalping is what we now refer to as abusive violence, as is Ethan's shooting the eyes out of a dead warrior's corpse. Ethan himself has no room for religion, only for revenge. When the "reverend" is praying over the graves of his brother and family, Ethan walks away impatiently, "Put an amen to it." When Ethan and Martin come upon a herd of buffalo, Ethan shoots one, then compulsively, angrily continues to shoot at them, arguing that he's depriving the Comanche of meat.

The Searchers has its humorous moments, with the character Mose, played by Hank Worden as a stoned or brain-injured fool. When Martin's true love, Laurie, played by Vera Miles, is about to marry a foolish guitar-playing cowboy with a pronounced comic twang, Martin engages the man in a comical fight, a good old Western brawl in which they fight nearly fair, and no one is really hurt — no brain hematomas, retinal tears, or spinal cord injuries result.

Veteran Ford favorite Ward Bond plays the local reverend who has a second professional role as captain in the Texas Rangers. He, in which capacity it is unclear, refers to Comanches as "childish savages."

Debbie, the little girl who is kidnapped, is played by Lana Wood. Her sister, Natalie Wood, plays the grown-up captive girl, who is finally rescued and carried home in Ethan's arms. The drama ends with Ethan turning away from entering the house, and walking back toward his horse alone. That picture of Ethan framed in the doorway, solitary, unable to enter the warmth of the house, is another icon of war veteran loneliness.

The concept of revenge is usually allied with the theme of unfinished business left over from psychological trauma, particularly that which involves human violence. Revenge also carries with it a sense of fate, and Ethan is resigned to his. He appears to be wanted for a crime that is so vague, it seems almost to be surviving the war on the losing side. John Wayne is often criticized for his limited acting range; however his big man's rage is believable, as he seems fairly to explode with intensity at times. He plays a man who is fated by his attachment to the past, whose actions require that he be forever alone.

Director John Ford volunteered at age 47 to serve in World War II, and was commissioned in the navy despite bad eyesight. He had already been commissioned as a lieutenant commander in the naval reserve at the time the war was declared. He was made chief of the Field Photograph Branch of the Office of Strategic Services. He was on site filming during the Battle of Midway and legend has it that he was shooting film on top of a power station as the Japanese airplanes attacked, shouting and cursing at them for not turning at the time for optimum camera effects. He was knocked unconscious by one explosion, recovered and continued filming. He was wounded by shrapnel by a second explosion and received a Purple Heart. His film was finally released as *The Battle of Midway* (McBride, 2001, p. 336). Ford was active throughout the war. He made a parachute jump into Burma and landed with the troops on D-Day at Normandy directing his cameramen.

Anatomy of a Murder, 1959

Anatomy of a Murder, directed by Otto Preminger and released in 1959, has James Stewart playing a leisure-loving lawyer, Paul Beeker, defending a two-war veteran, Lieutenant Manion, (Manny, played as an insouciant con man by Ben Gazzara), against the charge of murdering the man who raped his wife. His attorney uses a kind of pre–PTSD defense of "irresistible impulse" caused by a dissociative reaction, "not uncommon in soldiers in combat."

The defense rested on the issue of loyalty and the "irresistible impulse." To counterattack, George C. Scott, in his first movie role, played the dapper prosecuting attorney shouting rapid questions at the defendant: "Have you ever had neuroses, psychoses? How many men have you killed?"

Adapted from a popular novel by jurist Robert Traver, the movie retains the delightful doubt cast at the end as to whether Manny and his tart wife (played saucily by Lee Remick) didn't pull the wool over everybody's eyes. We are never sure about Manny. As a veteran of two wars, he is tough. His true feelings are unknown, perhaps even by himself, hidden behind a series of opercula, like the moving cups hiding one pearl.

Defendant and two-war veteran Lt. Manion (Ben Gazzara, far right) looks on as his attorney, Paul Beeker, played by Jimmy Stewart (middle, head turned away), confers with his investigator Parnell Emmett McCarthy (Arthur O'Connell), as Manny's wife (Lee Remick, left) smiles at the news, in Otto Preminger's courtroom drama *Anatomy of a Murder* (Columbia, 1959).

Sundays and Cybèle, 1962

In the 1962 French art film *Sundays and Cybèle*, the war veteran, Pierre, played by Hardy Kruger, is a survivor of the French Indochina War. We see him in the black and white abstract credits in his fighter plane attacking a village and crashing, and we see the terrorized expression of a Vietnamese girl. In a sudden transition to Pierre waiting as a train passes, we see him in flashes, as if part of the film.

The story begins ten years after he crashes his plane. He seems to be brain-injured; he has a flat expression and is unresponsive to his girlfriend, Madeline (played lovingly by Nicole Courcel).

While hanging around the train station after he sees his girlfriend off to work, he meets a little girl leaving the train with her father. The father asks him directions to a school. He follows them as the father hurries the girl away toward a walled school. Cybèle is played by Patricia Gozzi. She

Hardy Kruger plays Pierre, a French-Indochina War veteran in *Sundays and Cybèle* (Davis-Royal Films, 1962). His girlfriend, played by Nicole Courcel, has difficulty reaching him emotionally. He seems indifferent to her.

is doe-eyed pretty, sharp, and given to imagination. After the father turns Cybèle over to a nun, he hurries off, promising to be back on Sunday, and in his rush, leaves behind the girl's satchel at the gate. Pierre picks up the satchel and reads a letter the father has written, explaining that he will not return. On Sunday Pierre returns to the school, is mistaken for the girl's father, and takes Cybèle to the park. The winter scenes display the approach of Christmas. The theme of their first day together establishes their relationship rules. Cybèle drops a rock into a pond and says "Pierre, regard." She points to the rings on the pond water. They will enter a magical space through the center of the rippling rings. Cybèle says that the nun did not have her right name, but refuses to tell him what it is until he brings her the cock on the church tower.

The relationship between the numb, depressed war veteran and the little girl is moving, romantic, and sad. We feel they are doomed. The romance is in the girl's imagination and in the eyes of the quiet Pierre. The frequently repeated phrase in the film is Cybèle saying, *"Pierre, regard."*

Pierre has episodes in which his primitive fervor is let loose. He is reluctant to go along with his girlfriend to a wedding on a Sunday, a day that he has been dedicating to taking Cybèle to the park. Pierre, his girlfriend, Madeline, and two couples from the wedding walk into a fair. Pierre protests about the noise. They all mount bumper cars, Pierre and Madeline in one. Pierre becomes dizzy. Somebody crashes into them and he climbs out of his car and hits the man. A huge fight ensues. As his girlfriend and her friends drag Pierre away from the melee, he is delirious, saying, "Is she dead? Did I kill her?" Later, when they pass a fortune-telling booth, a gypsy lady takes him into her private space and asks him if he is interested in the future. He replies, "I'm more interested in the past." One of the wedding party men explains to the other that Pierre "was found half dead after a plane crash in some jungle village."

Christmas brings the dénouement. Pierre steals a Christmas tree and carries it fully decorated into the park. Then he takes down the cock from the church tower and presents it to her as a gift. Cybèle gives him a matchbox containing a piece of paper, on which is written her name. In the meantime police have been called. Cybèle is missing from school; one of the wedding party men calls the police about Pierre. Madeline followed them on one of their Sundays in the park, but she concluded that Pierre was but a child himself and their relationship was pure. The police, however, kill Pierre, and when the policeman picks up Cybèle, who has run off into the woods and fallen in the snow, and asks her her name, she cries, "I have no name. I'm no one now."

Sundays and Cybèle is adapted from a novel by Bernard Eschasserioux, *Les Demanches de Ville D'Avray*. The story speaks to the war survivor's sense of social alienation, which is not to be mistaken for malice. It is an existential expression of painful sensitivity. For Pierre, the child Cybèle was his connection to a trauma-truncated memory of the apparent killing of a girl in a jungle village. The profound connection between the war veteran and the girl is the romance of unconscious projection on his part, and on hers as well. He is her knight in shining armor and she places him in their magical circle. When Pierre steals the gypsy's knife they stab it in a tree and listen to the tree's wisdom, and what they hear is what they imagine. Pierre, *regard*.

Rio Lobo, 1970

Rio Lobo stands for a number of Western movies based in the post–Civil War featuring war veterans in gunfights, hard riding, and two-fisted drinking. Released in 1970, *Rio Lobo* was directed by Howard Hawks in his own tradition. It starred perhaps the greatest action figure of U.S. cin-

ema, John Wayne, as Chord McNally, who is a Union army cavalry colonel at the end of the Civil War. He is in charge of a detail to guard a train
with a gold shipment. Rebel soldiers ambush the train and ride off with
the money. Colonel McNally's friend is killed when his neck is broken
leaping from the train. The rebels are finally captured and imprisoned, and
when the war ends, McNally is waiting for two of the rebel soldiers, a Captain Pierre Cardona, played by Jorge Rivero, and Sergeant Tuscurero,
played by Christopher Mitchum. McNally is not so much angry at the
Rebels for what they did, which he regarded as their duty as soldiers, as
he is bent on revenge against those of his own troops who sold the information of the train's schedule to the Rebels. McNally teams up with the
discharged rebel soldiers, now veterans, to seek the identities of the traitors.

Screenplay for Rio Lobo was by Burton Wohl and Leigh Brackett,
from a story by Burton Wohl. McNally encounters a woman of spirit by
the name of Shasta Relany, played by Jennifer O'Neill, who was ill-cast in
the role. Shasta leads McNally and his allies to Rio Lobo, where they are
helped by a man named Phillips, who is played with scene-stealing bug-
eyed mad intensity by Jack Elam. They are forced to deal with a band of
bad men who are deputy sheriffs, the leaders being the ones who sold the
news of the Union army gold shipment.

In this film there is much heroism delivered with gusto and terse one-
liners. When a man is hit on the head he is always conveniently knocked
unconscious. When cowboys are shot they fall like sacks slowly tottering
from rooftops. Revenge is achieved by the Mexican girl, Maria (Susanna
Dosmantes), who has been scarred in the face by the vicious sheriff. She
shoots him, face to face, and McNally blandly congratulates her, asserting
the code of justice in the Hollywood western: "If you hadn't a done it,
somebody else would have."

Rio Lobo represents the Southwest that was populated by veterans of
the U.S. Civil War. Hawks and John Wayne are a Hollywood team that
communicated values of manly toughness that was yet respectful of
humane values. Passions ran high and death and suffering were accepted
as part of the picture to be endured with tight lips and grim determination. John Wayne was nearing the end of his career in this filming. He looks
his age. In his younger years he played many a fighting figure, be it western or combat. He stands alone as an icon of U.S. manliness, personify-
ing the values of toughness and fairness. Wayne, who, himself, avoided
military service during World War II, is most often cited as the icon that
deceived boys going to Vietnam into believing that fighting in war was
heroic.

Gardens of Stone, 1987

An example of the war veteran as professional soldier is found in Francis Coppola's excellent *Gardens of Stone*. Released in 1987, the plot concerns soldiers in the elite Old Guard of the army's Third Infantry Division, which has the responsibility for the ceremonies taking place at Arlington National Cemetery. The film was shot on location at Fort Myer, Virginia. *Gardens of Stone* begins and ends with a funeral. Considered the "most strack unit in the army," the NCOs are veterans of wars in Vietnam and Korea. James Caan and James Earl Jones portray believable veterans of the Old Guard. Caan plays Tech Sergeant Hazard, a veteran of two tours in Vietnam, who wears a Combat Infantryman Badge with a star, indicating that he also fought in Korea. Jones plays Sergeant Major Nelson who, together with Sgt. Hazard, takes on a new private, Jackie Willow, played by D.B. Sweeney, who is the son of a career sergeant with whom they fought in Korea. The two crusty veterans take to the private with easy camaraderie.

The crux of the plot concerns Private Willow's ambition and desire to fight with the infantry in Vietnam and win his CIB. The two old sergeants downplay Vietnam and do not think of it as a war. Hazard says of Vietnam, "Nothin' to win and no way to win it." Young Willow argues with them. He wants to believe in the army and the cause.

Screenplay was by Ronald Bass, from a novel by Nicholas Profitt. Angelica Huston plays Sgt. Hazard's love interest, Samantha Davis, who is a liberal reporter for the *Washington Post*. Dick Anthony Williams plays the first sergeant, Slasher Williams, who is a master of the mock tirade. Dean Stockwell plays the company tough but sympathetic CO, Captain Thomas.

In the background, throughout the film, are the bodies of war veterans being buried. "Burying is our business," says Sgt. Hazard, "and our business is better." He is referring to the catch phrase of soldiers in combat, "our business is killing, and business is good." Sgt. Hazard wants to be transferred to a unit where he can train troops going to Vietnam. "We once hoped we could help a few come back standing up."

Many career military men during the Vietnam War spent their time between tours in Vietnam escorting bodies coming back and training recruits on their way over. Either task had its load of guilt, especially for those who could sense death as lurking like a vulture over the young men as they trained.

Before leaving for Vietnam, Willow, now promoted to buck sergeant, is sent to OCS and on to the war as a second lieutenant. The girl he courts is the daughter of an army colonel, who is resistant to the liaison because she is marrying below her family rank. Mary Stuart Masterson plays Rachel, who expresses the fear, based on her experience of her girlfriend's husband, who "came home different. Men come home crazy and broken and cold." Jackie Willow reassures her that that won't happen to him; indeed, his is the final funeral scene.

The funeral details are mixed with military marches and ceremonies. The slow precision of the soldiers' funeral cadence is machine-like. Funerals are called drops. One soldier remarks that they do 15 drops a day. "We're just a bunch of toy soldiers," says Sgt. Hazard. He explains to Willow that the steel plates they wear on their shoes are for sound effects, as in show business.

Gardens of Stone is rather ineffectively interspersed with newsreel footage of the war in progress. The real impact of the film is in the contrast established between the bodies being buried and the anguish of the war veterans burying them.

Lethal Weapon, 1987

Action movies featuring war veterans as protagonists also feature duty as drive. *Lethal Weapon*, released in 1987, was popular as an action movie starring Mel Gibson as Martin Riggs and Danny Glover as Roger Murtaugh, contrasting Vietnam War veteran cops.

Glover's Roger is a conservative, African-American, middle-class, family man, whose redundant lines are a variant of "I'm too old for this, shit," when he has to put up with his new partner, wild-haired, intense, non-conformist Martin. Roger is a staid character, an ex-army grunt, while Martin was a sniper for the anti-guerilla Phoenix Program: "When I was 19, I did a guy in Laos from a thousand yards out in high wind. It's the only thing I was good at."

In this movie, the antagonists are also former army intelligence operatives of a notorious group called the Shadow Company, which is now smuggling heroin. "It goes all the way back to the war." The plot action begins with the death of the daughter of one of the Shadow Company, who has a duty-bound relationship with Roger: "he saved my life in the Ia Drang Valley." Quickly the wired Martin (a state Gibson plays well) saves Roger's life, which binds them to each other. "You saved my life, thank you," says Roger.

An important subplot to this war veteran movie is the fate of the veterans' daughters. The Shadow Company daughter was poisoned and dies in an erotic apparent suicide that begins the action movie credits. The teenaged daughter of Roger is kidnapped and stripped to her underwear,

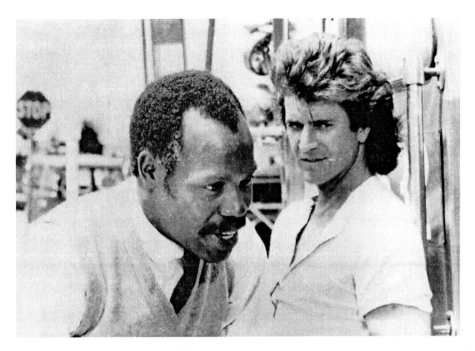

Wild-haired Mel Gibson (right) plays Martin Riggs and Danny Glover (left) plays the conservative Roger Murtaugh, two Vietnam War veteran cops in *Lethal Weapon* (MGM, 1987), an action movie directed by Richard Donner with a comic twist of odd companions bound to each other.

forced to witness violent deaths, as well as the torture of her father, and escapes one jam after another, only to appear smiling at the movie's end, as if unscathed.

Lethal Weapon was directed by Richard Donner as an action movie with the comic twist of odd companionship. The movie proved popular enough to spawn several sequels, deriving energy from the dynamism of the pair of opposites engaged within a struggle with outside forces. Early in the movie, to size up their potency, the pair verbally compare their firearms: a "9mm Baretta" to a "4 inch Smith."

Gibson's Martin establishes his character first by a mad, comical drug bust in a Christmas tree lot, then by a suicidal night in which he, in a series of close-ups, loads his 9mm and chambers a round, removes the safety, and tearfully sticks the weapon in his mouth. We learn that he has lost his wife to a traffic accident. He then establishes that he is willing to die and seems to draw energy by near death experiences. When he intervenes in a suicide attempt by a man standing on the ledge of a building, Martin steps out on the ledge with him and slaps handcuffs on the man's arm and on his own wrist. "Do you really wanna jump — do ya?" Martin explains it later to Roger, "A lot of guys have trouble during the silly season." The film introduces titles with "Jingle Bell Rock" and Christmas season decor. The drama gives its all to action, including heroic torture and escape scenes, leaving the characters behind in a rush of excitement. In a shameless scene, as Roger and his daughter are trapped in the torture chambers, Roger says to his daughter, "There are no more heroes left in the world," just as Martin crashes in and rescues them.

War Veterans on Trial

Two war veterans-on-trial movies deserve comparison at this point, because they similarly present the war veteran as the product of his loyalties and commitments. In *Anatomy of a Murder* (1958) the veteran on trail, Manny (Ben Gazzara), is a worldly wise guy, a veteran in more ways than one, who committed murder avenging the rape of his wife. The war veteran in the 1999 production of *Snow Falling on Cedars* is a Japanese-American who is a victim of social circumstances, and is accused of murdering to get his stolen land back.

A major difference in the two movies is the emphasis on the war veteran atmosphere. Manny, the veteran of World War II and the Korean War, is something of a loner, an anomaly in society. When the psychologist talks about him on the stand, it is as if he were a psychiatric case. The emphasis of the film is more on Manny's wily character, creating an ambiguity in that he *could* be lying about his motivation. In *Snow Falling on Cedars* the war veteran defendant is charged with killing another war veteran, and the reporter covering the story is also a war veteran. Mixed into the plot are the biases generated and kindled by the friction of war. A major contrast between the two films is the sense of cultural assimilation of returning veterans in *Snow Falling*, versus the isolation and virtual encapsulation of Manny's war activities.

The prosecutor in *Snow Falling* preys disingenuously on the jury's anti–Japanese sentiment. The judge finally chides him. "Shame on you!" In *Anatomy*, the prosecutor is clipped and efficient, like a university psychiatrist showing off his polished technique on stage. Both cases are made, however, on the predilection of the war veteran, who is experienced in killing, to kill again.

Snow Falling slides into a dark mood that it never escapes. Even with the right verdict, the film ends with a fade into gray. *Anatomy*, which maintained a jazzy humor, finishes with deviling ambiguity. It seems that justice was served, *even* if Manny knew exactly what he was doing at the time and willed it to happen.

The War Veterans' PTSD and the Next Generation

The roles of children in war veteran families are complicated by the so-called intergenerational transmission of PTSD, often transmitted less directly than it was to the daughters of veterans in *Lethal Weapon* and *The Visitors*. Three very good examples of this are *Desert Bloom*, *The War*, and *In Country*. Other films deal with the family contagion. The serious *Ulee's Gold*, *The Presidio*, and the lightweight *Meet the Parents*, also look at the veteran father-offspring bond, while the middle-aged war veteran daughter in *Straight Story* seems to have benefited from her father's abiding loyalty. The problem of the war veteran's abandonment of his children is taken up in *Distant Thunder*.

There are essentially two ways that PTSD can be transmitted to the next generation, and sometimes they are combined. A traumatized parent can traumatize a child directly, through physical abuse, sexual abuse, neglecting care, or placing the child in harm's way. Also common is the indirect transmission of symptoms of PTSD to the child by close association with the traumatized parent. Guilt, fear and paranoia, anger, racial hatred, revenge, the sense of having no future, can be transmitted even if the child is not directly traumatized. Danieli (1997) has studied the intergenerational transmission of PTSD in Holocaust survivors and others, and has shown the second generation more vulnerable than others to PTSD under conditions of overwhelming stress.

Desert Bloom, 1986

Eugene Corr directed *Desert Bloom*, which was released in 1986. It is set in the era of the Korean War in the as-yet-undeveloped Las Vegas, Nevada, of 1950, where Jon Voight plays Jack, a disabled combat veteran from the World War II Battle of the Bulge, who operates a gas station on the edge of town. He has a problem with alcohol and social isolation, and develops a problem with repetition compulsion as the movie progresses.

The film is partially narrated by Jack's stepdaughter, Rose, played beautifully by Annabeth Gish. She gives us a wonderful sampling of a 13-year-old girl's complex life. These are the early days of the atomic bomb testing and Jack is unnerved by increased military presence in the area. He does not yet know about the plans to detonate a test bomb in the desert.

He loses his balance through a series of alcohol-needy searches for booze, episodes of abusive and misdirected discipline, and a flashback, where he is completely dissociated, crawling down a dark hall under attack. In perhaps the most poignant moment in all war veteran films, Jack is seen sitting on the front porch at night, wearing his great coat, his rifle across his knees, waiting for attack, while his family is inside at a party singing "Somewhere over the Rainbow." The film's final scene, however, is not downbeat, but has a note of friendly reconciliation between the Rose and her stepfather.

Added treats in *Desert Bloom* are the delightful Ellen Burstyn, playing the glamorous Star, Jack's sister-in-law, and multi-layered JoBeth Williams as Lilly, Jack's wife and mother to Rose and her two younger sisters. As the tension builds around the A-bomb test, the references to its paradox bombard the plot. The school children are lectured and drilled with civil defense exercises. The kids are given blood tests and issued dog tags. In one striking scene, the warning sirens start to wail and all the kids in the school yard fall to the ground, protecting their heads with there arms, as instructed, and as they all lie still and the prolonged siren wails, a tether ball repeatedly circles the pole.

The A-bomb becomes a daffy cultural theme in Las Vegas, where there is a Miss A-bomb beauty contest. "Hey, hey, too hot to handle."

Jack tries to track what's going on with his short-wave radio. "I'm set up to monitor everything," he declares. He listens to the McCarthy hearings and rants about Jews and Communists in the Defense Department. The tension focuses on Rose's coming of age at 13 and her need for freedom, and Jack's need to protect and monitor. When he "disciplines" her with scolds or slaps, she pouts and broods. Lilly tries to motivate her daughter with guilt, when she pouts during the celebration of "Daddy" being released from the hospital alcohol ward: "He's been through hell and all you can think of is yourself." Rose states her ambivalence in voiceover when her stepfather is in the hospital, "I was happy he was gone and afraid he wouldn't come back."

When Jack rages and smashes furniture, Lilly takes on the task of reassuring everyone that "it'll be all right in the morning." In the end, however, even Lilly begins to unravel and fights with Star and Jack. When the three are struggling in a hands-on brawl, it is 13-year-old Rose who has to intervene with Daddy's rifle. Lilly screams at Jack for kissing Star, "Big war hero shooting blanks!"

Rose's neighbor and friend is a boy named Robin. He repeatedly asks Jack for jobs to do. His father was killed in the war, and he defends Jack when a girl laughs at Jack's awkward fall because of his stiff leg.

The tight, complex screenplay by Eugene Corr is from a story by Corr and Linda Remy. The 1950 Las Vegas life is well-produced nostalgia. Lilly's rah-rah sayings have an ironic zing as she tries to paint a happy face on every calamity. When Jack goes into the hospital after his drunken flashback, Lilly explains, "Its his nerves, he's shot. Even heroes have to rest." In a rare moment of candor and frustration she confesses to Star, "I have a husband in the house, who still thinks its World War II." Even when she's trying to be stern and realistic, she cannot avoid the hearty aphorism salad, and as she preps the girls for Jack's return from the hospital, she assures them that things will be better. "Daddy's coming home. But promises don't butter the bread. The proof is in the pudding."

We get an ominous ring of foreboding when Jack assesses his post-hospital recovery. "I know I'm not the easiest person to live with. A lot's happened. My standards are too high. That's why I drank. From now on I'm going to be easygoing."

Voight's Jack is played as a rigid, dull-minded man who struggles to be righteous and is proud of his intellectual discipline. He announces that

Korean War veteran Jack (Jon Voight) lectures his wife, Lilly (JoBeth Williams), about kitchen cleanliness, when what he really wants is to find his bottle, in Eugene Corr's *Desert Bloom* (Columbia Pictures, 1985).

he reads *True* magazine and subscribes to the "Great Thinker Series." He has a room of his own where he keeps his short-wave radio. The camera tracks along the wall where there are clippings from the Battle of the Bulge, Patton, and Korea, as well as campaign medals, a Purple Heart and Bronze Star. As he listens to the radio, planes fly over from nearby Nellis Air Force Base and Jack becomes anxious. He searches for his bottles in various places where we've already seen Rose and Lilly discover them. His frustration turns to anger. When he finds dirty dishes in the sink he focuses his anger, smashing the plates and yelling. He then drags Rose out of bed and makes her kneel on the floor in front of the mess.

Rose says in voice over, describing Jack's erratic mood swings, "Jack was like tossing a coin, you never knew which side was coming up." In the best Hollywood knack for creating meaningful coincidences, Rose runs away on the night of the A-bomb test (packing a can of cream of mushroom soup in a neat little understated joke), while her war veteran stepfather is sitting on the front porch guarding against attack by an unknown force, his rifle across his knees, a cigarette in his mouth, and a whiskey bottle on the table, ready.

But in the end we see something grudgingly realistic. Jack promises to try harder. He tells Rose that he is proud of her and thanks her for her help. She gives him a tight little smile, but it is her first for him.

In the final scene Lilly rouses the family, "Rise and shine, its A-bomb time!" They assemble in the early morning in front of their house watching the atomic cloud mushroom in the distant sky with a phosphorescent glow. A radio breaks in, "Morning survivors."

Distant Thunder, 1988

The war veteran living in exile usually has the romantic sense of *The Sun Also Rises* or the exotic *Saint Jack*, or the wild south-of-the-border scenes in *Born on the Fourth of July*. The 1988 release *Distant Thunder* gives us a sense only hinted at in other films, like *Spitfire Grill*, or parodied in *O.C. and Stiggs*, of the veteran in exile in his own land, the legendary "bush vet." *Distant Thunder* features the Vietnam War veteran, Mark Lambert, played by John Lithgow, as a pained and saddened man living in the mountainous Olympic Peninsula of Washington State. He gathers ferns and associates with two other veterans, Harvey (Reb Brown) and Larry (Dennis Arndt). We see their friend, Louis (Tom Bower), commit suicide in the beginning of the film by walking on the Burlington Northern tracks until a freight train takes him out. Mark tries to dissuade him. Louis has just had a fight with his wife and shouts, "it don't mean nothin', man," just before the train hits him.

Vietnam War veteran Louis, played by Tom Bower (left), awaits the suicide train as another veteran, Mark, played by John Lithgow (right), looks on helplessly in the Northwest drama *Distant Thunder* (Paramount Pictures, 1988). (Photograph by Jack Rowand.)

We understand that Mark was on a long-range combat operation into North Vietnam when they encountered an ambush with Mark the only survivor. He feels responsible for one man's death when he tried to keep him from making noise, having him die in his arms as they huddled in the water beneath a bush.

Mark decides to give up his exile and go into town and find work at the local mill. He is befriended by Char, played by Kerrie Keane, whose father died in Vietnam. Char encourages Mark to write to his son, whom he hasn't known for all these years and is now graduating from high school and celebrating his 18th birthday. His letter prompts his son to drive across country to visit his dad. Jack, Mark's son, as happens in movies, is the 4.0 student and valedictorian of his class. He is played with gravity by Ralph Macchio.

Char cuts Mark's hair and tries to help him prepare for meeting his son, but the anticipation of the meeting is overwhelming. Mark goes to a bar and gets in a fight with Char's jealous lover and then flees to his mountain refuge. Jack arrives and Char leads him up the mountain after his dad. In their mountainous isolation, the veterans get in a shootout with each other, triggered by the pursuit of the jealous boyfriend, who is stabbed by one bush vet, only to be saved and evacuated by the others.

The overriding emotion in Mark is sadness. He is cut off from life and unable to forgive himself for his Vietnam actions. Ironically, the "civilization" that he avoids is the fibrous carnage of the logging yard, where logs are dumped in the water and loaded aboard barges. Mark goes about getting a job there while avoiding everyone's gaze.

Distant Thunder was directed by Rick Rosenthal from a screenplay by Robert Stitzel, adapted from a story by Stitzel and Deedee Wehle. The film begins with an LRRP insertion and the night ambush, so that we know clearly what keeps Mark suffering. This portrayal is in contrast to comical or stereotypical representations (e.g., *O.C. and Stiggs*) that exaggerate to parody the bravado and aggression, but give us no sense of what the avoidance is all about.

The fool in *Distant Thunder* is the character Larry, who wears a boonie hat with a Combat Infantryman Badge, and who howls with mockery of life. We see him first lying in the mud in the heavy rain, drunk, singing as Mark tries to help move to shelter.

> Drop your napalm in the schoolyard
> watch the kiddies run and shout
> as they try to put it out [my paraphrase and structure].

When Jack asks him why the barbed wire, Larry replies, "We got it from the VA." And laughs, whooping like a fool.

When Mark and his son finally meet, the relationship doesn't quite work for them. They are awkward, avoiding each other's gaze. They argue and finally fight. Mark tries to explain and the son asks, "what about what I went through?"

In Country, 1989

Adapted from a novel by Bobbie Ann Mason, *In Country* was directed by Norman Jewison and released in 1989. Set in a rural Kentucky town, the film stars Bruce Willis as Emmett, the vet, and Emily Lloyd as his niece, Sam. Her father, Dwane, died in Vietnam and she tries to get her uncle to talk about what happened. Willis' Emmett will associate with other Vietnam War veterans, but otherwise is a social isolate. "They all act like there's some big, deep, dark secret," laments Sam. Willis is so believable that he

The final sequences in the Vietnam War veteran movie *In Country* (Warner Bros., 1989), feature a prolonged visit to the Vietnam War Memorial Wall by Sam, played by Emily Lloyd (right foreground), who has come to memorialize her father, by Mamaw, played by Peggy Rae (center foreground), who has come for her son, and by Emmett, played by Bruce Willis (left foreground), who has come for his lost brother and himself.

seems lost in the part. He has a vivid flashback during a thunderstorm in the beginning of the film.

In Country is perhaps the most emotionally evocative and true of all war veteran films. The core of the drama concerns the daughter's search for her father's identity and the stonewalling about the secret that combat is so horrible that it is not fit for innocents.

Sam is seen jogging through the town in her running shorts and "walkperson" radio, then graduating from high school, with her family gathered. Jewison uses Sam's running as a transitional image that weaves the scenes of the rural Kentucky town together. She discovers her father's letters to her mother. Her mother, played by Judith Ivey, is off in the city tending her new baby with her new husband. Sam is living with her uncle and refuses her mother's invitation to live with her and attend college.

Where *Desert Bloom* was coming of age in the '50s, *In Country* has captured the rural Southern culture of the eighties. In her romanticizing about her father, Sam laments that he never got to have those special life experiences, like attending a Bruce Springsteen concert.

The local Vietnam War Veterans organization holds a dance, which Sam attends. There is a scuffle between the vets over philosophical differences, living in the past versus repressing. Both vets end up being held back, pumping up excessive adrenaline. Ironically, the wizened vet who advocates not living in the past is the one wearing the Vietnam War paraphernalia. Sam goes home with one of the vets, Tom, played by John Terry. It appears that he is unable to consummate their sexual relationship. When Sam urges him to talk, he says, "My mind takes me where I don't want to go."

Gradually Sam learns some of the horrible stories of her father's combat. She acquires her father's journal from her grandmother, played by Peggy Rea, (who manages to steal all of her scenes). Sam drives into the swamp, and spends the night there, reading the journal by flashlight. As she reads, the scenes are acted out in a swampy area, where combat veterans appear and are finally ambushed. At times we see Sam reading in the distance as the troops advance through the swamp.

When Sam wakes up next morning, Emmett is waiting beside her. He asks her what she was doing, and she replies that she was out "humpin' the boonies." Emmett responds, talking roughly at first: "In country, every second you're on guard or you die. When I come back here everybody's weak. Over there everybody you care about gets killed, one after the other. After a while you just quit feeling." As Sam embraces him from behind, he says, "I ain't got nothing left. There's something wrong with me. There is a hole in my heart out there with them. I'm already half dead."

The prolonged final scene of the movie is the family visit to the Vietnam War Memorial. They drive there, Emmett, Sam, and Mrs. Hughes, Dwane's mother, who brings a potted geranium. She is given the remarkable lines of the film. Regarding the Wall, she says, "Lord, it's black as night." And as she climbs the ladder to touch her son's name, she looks down anxiously, "You don't think anybody can see up my dress, do you?"

In Country captures the intrafamilial tragedy of war. Where the daughter searches for the father she never knew, where the war veteran uncle, who knows the story, is remote, where the daughter's mother wants to move on with her life, and where her grandmother idealizes her son's contribution to society. Emily Lloyd as Sam is a casting coup who does justice to Bobby Ann Mason's novel, faithfully adapted for the screen by Cynthea Cidre and Frank Pierson. The finale, if not the plot itself, jerks tears consistently out of all but the most resistant of lachrymal glands

The War, 1994

The War is an unpretentious depiction of a rural Mississippi war veteran who is trying to raise two kids. Kevin Costner plays the Vietnam Marine veteran, Stephen, having a major problem with guilt-driven nightmares. He told his children that he was off job-hunting, but in fact was in the veterans' hospital being treated for PTSD. We see him sleeping in his bed, having just returned home. His son, Stu, played by Elijah Wood, who got top movie billing, comes in to wake him. Stephen is sweating with his shirt off, and we see a large C-shaped scar on his torso. When his son shakes him Stephen grabs the boy by the throat and pulls him down.

Stephen teaches his kids to abjure violence, yet they end up in a "war" with neighboring poor kids, who live in a junkyard. *The War*, a poor choice for a movie title, was directed by Jon Avnet, and released in 1994. Mare Winningham plays Stephen's wife as a heartfelt countrywoman, Lois, and Lexi Randall plays Lida, his 12-year-old daughter, who narrates the film. Lida remarks, "Ever since he came back from Vietnam things haven't been just right." "Mom says the war destroyed our lives." "If it hadn't been for the war, we'd still have our house."

The War is one of the few films that deal with PTSD by name and with candor. The family is poor. Stephen remarks that PTSD gets in the way of his keeping a job. When he is hired as a school janitor, he is immediately fired when it is learned that he was in a psychiatric ward. "Why?" Stu asks. "I went nuts for a while and the docs call it posttraumatic stress. Remember how I used to do things that didn't make much sense. I landed three jobs after the war and I lost each one because of dreams—it wasn't cause I couldn't do the work." The fact that Stephen never mentions hav-

Kevin Costner (left) plays Stephen Simmons, a Vietnam War veteran in *The War* (Universal Pictures, 1994), who talks to his son, Stu (Elijah Wood), about his philosophy of non-violence. (Photograph by Richard Felber.)

ing a service-connected disability in PTSD is appropriate, since war veterans were not always advised of their filing rights, even as they were treated.

Stephen later describes the source of his guilt. Himself wounded from being stabbed in hand-to-hand combat, he is forced to leave his wounded and dying friend in the field when the helicopter can only take one more man aboard.

Stephen finally is able to repeat his traumatic conflict when he is working in a waterlogged mine with his new friend and work partner. They are trapped under rock following a cave-in. Stephen doesn't leave this time. Instead, he pries his friend loose with a crowbar, only to be trapped himself. He later dies of his wounds.

Costner comes across in a fashion similar to Peter Fonda's Ulee, in *Ulee's Gold*. He is a war veteran who has become a peacemaker. He advocates non-violent solutions when his kids engage the junkyard kids in a contest over a tree house. There is an attempt to make the "Dead End Kids" theme contemporary with swear words, some tough violent poundings, and scenes of kids playing poker and smoking cigarettes, but the film retains a series of corny exchanges. Stephen, in a saintly gesture, offers

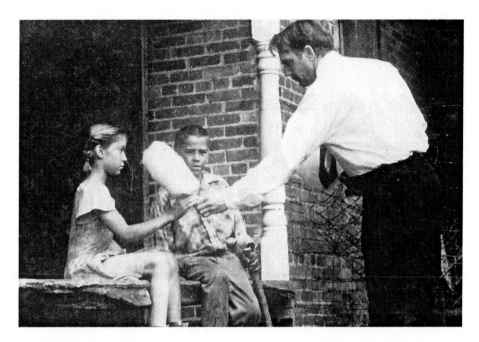

Stephen (Kevin Costner) offers cotton candy to the junkyard children (Jennifer Tyler and Lucas Black), who are at "war" with his son and daughter in *The War* (Universal Pictures, 1994). (Photograph by Richard Felber.)

cotton candy to two of the junkyard kids, Ula (Jennifer Tyler) and Ebb (Lucas Black), who are the children of the redneck Mr. Lipnicki, played with squalor by Ranor Scheine.

Stu, after his father's death, breaks into his father's locker and finds his Bronze Star, a photo of Stephen and his friend, dog tags, and a U.S. flag. He dons his father's fatigue jacket and becomes a kind of trickster in the kids' "war" over the tree house.

Lida has the final lines as voiceover narrator. "War is like a big machine that no one knows how to work and gets out of hand."

The War was written by Kathy McWorter and features a sixties soundtrack that includes Credence Clearwater Revival's "Who'll Stop the Rain." The film unfortunately but adroitly dodges the issue of when one may fight to defend his own. When the ornery Mr. Lipnicki becomes aggressive toward Stu, Stephen counterattacks and takes him down with his hand gripping his throat and demands they both apologize. Yet the film maintains the pacifist stance without coming to grips with the exception.

War Veterans and Their Treatment

Not many films realistically tackle the effects of war on the psyche and the mundane, undramatic, dogged perseverance to become well that involves psychotherapy. *The War*, discussed earlier, and *Mrs. Dalloway*, tackle the social and cultural prejudice against the war-troubled veteran. Many of the action films to be discussed exploit the war veterans' vulnerability to anger and flashbacks. *Jacob's Ladder* incorporates the veterans' hospital into the horror sequences with increasingly gross distortions, while *Article 99* frontally assaults the Veterans Affairs hospital treatment of veterans. Perhaps the most hideous tale of wounded veteran treatment comes from *Born on the Fourth of July*. *Desert Bloom* gives us a sense of the veteran going off for VA alcohol treatment, then returning, full of resolve, but with limited insight, only to lapse back into pathology. In *The War*, the veteran returns from the VA hospital after having disappeared while looking for work. He explains PTSD to his children. In *Heroes*, the veteran has run away from the hospital, no doubt with the encouragement of everyone he left behind. *Fleshburn* and *Blackenstein* show the war veteran patient gone mad and endeavoring to murder those who were involved in his treatment. *Private Duty Nurses* shows a Vietnam War veteran who may well kill his nurse, as he takes her motorcycle riding without a helmet.

Film director John Houston made, as part of his war effort, a film about the treatment of psychiatric problems arising from war exposure. *Let There Be Light* was, as Houston described it in his autobiography (1980), a staged documentary. Houston constructed sets around actual army screening of incoming patients at a Long Island hospital. He filmed real doctors and patients. What he did, however, to dramatize the documentary, was to create a Hollywood ending, showing the emotionally traumatized veterans cured by hypnotism, counseling, and recreation. We see at the end of the film busloads of cured veterans leaving the hospital waving from windows, while a few veterans remain in treatment. The film, as Houston points out, was shelved by the army and re-shot by other directors, who removed racial minorities. It was released ironically, according to Morgan (1997), as *Shades of Gray*, using actors as patients and doctors.

In reality, chronic posttraumatic stress disorder is not highly responsive to treatment. It is at best understood and managed in ways that minimize its influence. Morgan points out that the army, in its remake of Houston's relatively realistic film, produced a movie that downplayed the role of combat in creating psychiatric problems, and laid the blame instead on poor parenting, specifically poor mothering. *Shades of Gray* contended that symptoms of mental illness were rife in the U.S. population. Morgan also observed that the timing of *Shades of Gray* was coincidental with a major push on Congress to fund the training of more mental health professionals. *Shades of Gray*, as a final product, however, is entirely consistent with the philosophy of the U.S. cinema censorship at the time (Doherty, 1993b), which minimized any reference to the deleterious effects of war on the veteran.

Several authors, in their critiques of the post–Vietnam War era, notably Dean (1997) and Lembcke (1998), have criticized the mental health professions for riding the tails of a social issue for its own gain. It can be argued here, however, that this is not at all new. The authors seem to view the actions of such professionals as compromising the integrity of the subject, as if PTSD were a questionable diagnosis because it had never been called that before, and those professionals who argued for the creation of a diagnostic category were doing so to push other agendas, including professional gain. One could similarly question the role of sanitation, when Florence Nightingale began to campaign for the subject after witnessing the horrible losses of the Crimean War.

Treating war veterans for PTSD over 20 years means that I have personally talked intimately, individually and in groups, with combat veterans from a number of wars. I have developed some feeling for the universality of certain emotions and sentiments. I have known some veterans who served in more than one war and have benefited from their perspective on the differences. Most of my knowledge comes from this clinical skew, however, although I have read accounts of war veterans, met veterans socially, and viewed others on TV, who appear to be free from the clinical diagnosis of PTSD or other war-related psychopathology. It is also true that war veterans may have posttraumatic stress symptoms without qualifying for the disorder as catalogued by the diagnostic manual, and it has been shown that the more symptoms one has, the more likely that there will be other concurrent disorders, both emotional and physical (Marshal, et al., 2001).

It is my opinion that once PTSD becomes chronic, after about six months post trauma, it is a disorder whose symptoms remain, if not manifest, always in potential. As a stress-sensitive disorder, PTSD can manifest in a person long after it has been quiet, although I observe it more like a disquieting mood than a volcano in terms of management. The feeling that the veteran has of PTSD awakening, however, may be quite different given *his* frame of reference. Port et al. (2001) document the worsening of PTSD symptoms in some war veteran POWs five decades after their repatriation.

Private Duty Nurses, 1971

Three student nurses walk together on a Southern California beach during the romantic opening titles. Written and directed by George Armitege, *Private Duty Nurses* attempts to present a romantic, sexy plot in which each nurse finds a lover who is attached to a cause. One nurse hooks up with a ecology-conscious doctor, who tests the ocean water. One nurse attaches to a black activist doctor and participates in a sit-in occupation of the hospital director's office, while the third nurse, Spring, is assigned to help a wounded Vietnam War veteran patient, played by Dennis Redfield. The doctor informs Spring that the veteran has been nicknamed "Domino." The doctor explains that he has just put a plate in Domino's head and a fall or blow could be fatal. Domino has been a problem as a patient because he went out and raced motorcycles.

When Spring meets Domino, he is sitting in the examining room wearing his motorcycle helmet. When she asks Domino if he was in Vietnam, he replies affirmatively. "Wanna see my snapshots of Bob Hope?"

Private Duty Nurses was released in 1971. It is badly scripted and the acting is usually flat, except for Domino, who has his moments. Meant to be a sexually titillating movie, it is not even that. It attempts to ride three relevant and controversial issues: racism in medical training, pollution of the environment, and the return of the Vietnam War veteran. It manages to attach scenes of heterosexual copulation with each issue, as if to make the issue easier to examine. None of the issues is given much explication. For example, can a well-meaning helper save this self-destructive war veteran? Spring smokes a joint with Domino between laps as he practices on a racecourse. Domino takes a drag and says, "it's what kept me alive in Nam." He goes on to say that he hates the ones who stayed and the ones who sent him there. "We were alone over there and that's just the way it's gonna be back here. One mistake from death." Spring says to Domino, "you see death in everything. Why not life?"

Domino crashes his motorcycle in a race and emergency surgery is performed. Actually the surgery scenes are the most convincing scenes of the film. The fall seems not to have killed him at all. In fact he recovers in a quite articulate fashion and predicts that vets like him will some day run the country, "just like the vets from World War I and World War II. One stoned killer from Nam on TV."

Ironically, *Private Duty Nurses* ends with Spring riding off on the back of Domino's motorcycle, neither of them wearing helmets, riding into the glowing sunset that obscures the closing titles. The message we get is that the helper has been drawn into the war veteran's psychopathology and is participating with him in some sort of *folie-à-deux*. Which is not a trivial note. The power of the war veteran's experiences has the potential for creating an attraction for others who endeavor to help the veteran in his return. Instead of renewing the veteran, the helper is drawn into the veteran's far more dark and dangerous world.

Blackenstein (*The Black Frankenstein*), 1972

Directed by William Levey, *Blackenstein* was created during the Vietnam War and released in 1972. The plot concerns a Dr. Stein (John Hart) who practices in a mansion in Southern California. Dr. Stein is the winner of the Nobel Peace prize. He experiments with sizzling, flashing, arcing electric gadgetry putting humans together again. He is visited by Dr. Winnefred Walker (Ivory Stone) who holds a Ph.D. in physics. Seems her fiancé, Eddie, was wounded in Vietnam. He lost both his arms and legs when he stepped on a land mine. We see Eddie, played by Joe De Sue, at the VA hospital lying in a bed, covered with a sheet, like the veteran in *Johnny Got His Gun*. A mean hospital orderly is taunting Eddie. "What the hell did you go for?"

Winnefred says to Dr. Stein, "I love Eddie. As soon as he's well, we're going to be married." Dr. Stein agrees to treat Eddie with a DNA formula. Eddie is transferred to Dr. Stein's mansion. Dr. Stein tries to buoy Eddie's spirits. "You've been through a lot and you've done remarkably well." Dr. Stein, it seems, was awarded the Nobel Prize for "solving the DNA genetic code." He urges Eddie, who is without arms and legs, "Don't throw out the possibilities. You must be willing to help yourself."

Unfortunately an assistant to Dr. Stein, Malcolm, becomes jealously in love with Winnefred, and when she rejects his advances, he switches DNA samples, so that Eddie is injected with the DNA of a madman.

After his injection, Eddie falls asleep and wakes up growling, with a deformed forehead, wearing stylish go-go boots. Deviating from his treatment plan, he goes directly back to the VA hospital and eviscerates the taunting orderly. But then Eddie goes awry on a tangent. He begins to attack women in a series of bodice-ripping assaults. Cops are eventually brought in and search for "a patient from the veterans' hospital." They do not reach him, however, before he rips Winnefred's nightgown and kills Dr. Stein amid the sparks of the operating room. Finally, Eddie is attacked by dogs and himself eviscerated. Winnefred is taken away by an African-American cop who has an affectionate, protective arm around her shoulder. Winnefred is black. So is Malcom, and so is Eddie. However, no mention is made of their race in the film. Eddie is indiscriminate regarding his victims—he eviscerates caregivers and sexy women without regard to race.

Written by Frank Saleti, who also produced this odd mixture of unintended satire, *Blackenstein* is a war veteran exploitation film regarded as a period example of black exploitation. Some B-movies are made with a low budget but a respectable level of competence. But for some, the filmmaker must wake up and say, along with Eddie, "What have I done?"

It appears most of the budget of *Blackenstein* was spent creating electrical arcs in Dr. Stein's lab. (*The Black Frankenstein* title is only on the title track of the film itself. *Blackenstein* is the title on the video package.) Despite the obvious production failures, the film has some pertinent messages. The VA hospital orderly is the only staff person to be seen on the ward. He taunts the armless, legless Eddie when he asks for water. "Get it yourself," he says. Such a scene represents a common perception of the VA hospitals, although such behavior from any hospital or nursing home staff is not so uncommon, where doctors and nurses dislike or disregard their patients. In government institutions incompetent or misbehaving personnel are hard to fire. Aids who are paid at a low level need their jobs. In this film, the orderly feels that he has to explain his non-veteran status, and grows angry at the disabled veteran who put himself in harm's way. Eddie is virtually mute, but when he returns as a growling monster, the orderly is the first to taste his revenge. If Hollywood's job is to act out our fantasies, doing the things we'd never do ourselves, *Blackenstein* doesn't fail us.

Heroes, 1977

Heroes was released in 1977 and does not wear well with time. It was intended to be a quirky road comedy with cheery Sally Field and silly Henry Winkler, in an updated version of Ann Rutherford and Mickey Rooney, as the wacky war veteran who takes a bus across country carrying earthworms in a box. The worms are intended to start a worm farm business. Seems he and the other vets on the hospital ward thought up this plan. Seems he was placed on the ward after interfering with an army recruiter, protesting the Vietnam War that he had just come back from. Winkler plays the veteran who most of us would rather not meet. He's identified with the archetype of the trickster in his worst form, the hypomanic fool with a box of earthworms. (A more objective review of this so-called screwball comedy directed by Jeremy Paul Kagan can be found in Walker, 1991, pp. 110–111.)

Fleshburn, 1984

A nightmare for those who treat war veterans in psychotherapy or counseling is that one may turn psychotic and angrily blame the therapist for his or her dilemma. It is the fear that has the therapist awake at 4:00 A.M., watching for the psychotic with combat training to peer through the window. *Fleshburn* acts out that nightmare when a Native American Vietnam War veteran is arrested. The introductory statement fills in the background.

> In 1975, Calvin Duggai deliberately abandoned five men to die in the desert because of an argument involving tribal rivalry and the powers of Indian witchcraft. Four psyhchiatrists testified that Duggai was not capable of distinguishing right from wrong and recommended he be institutionalized.

The first scenes then show Duggai, played with silent fury by Sonny Landham, escaping from the institution and killing the driver of a truck who offers him a ride. The truck driver was also a Vietnam War veteran, but said he was stationed in "Dang Pang" and wasn't in combat.

Once free, Duggai then proceeds to overpower and capture each of the psychiatrists. Two are married to each other and he captures them in the middle of a quarrel. The psychiatrists are played by Steve Kanaly, Karen Carlson, Macon McCalman and Robert Chimento. Periodically we see Duggai's flashbacks to Vietnam, but their meaning is left unclear.

Fleshburn is a story of the doctors' struggle for survival after Duggai drops them off, bound and barefoot, braking one doctor's leg. Directed by George Cage, the screenplay by George and Beth Cage was based on a novel, *Fear in a Handful of Dust*, by Brian Garfield. The writers keep the film from the exploitation category. The dialog is intelligent and the acting credible. The plot, however, has too many improbables. One psychiatrist, Sam, left his profession, because of his doubts, to become a park ranger. He is described as part Native and he is the one who instructs the others on desert survival. The flashback scenes for each of the doctors aren't very helpful. The Native American Vietnam War veteran, Duggai, isn't given any character depth. We only see him as a vengeful man, but don't understand his madness other than, as the film states, that he was in combat for three tours in Vietnam.

The role of the truck driver seems to repeat in Vietnam War veteran films and they seem to all be compulsive talkers. We have the above truck driver who served in Dang Pang. There was the truck driver in *Death-dream*, also murdered for his act of charity. There was a very interesting Vietnam War veteran truck driver in the about-to-be-reviewed *Alamo Bay*. The truckdriver in these films is the stagecoach driver of the Westerns; he's the ferryman, who takes the hero from one land to another. He usually has something important for us to hear or notice about the protagonist.

Jacknife, 1989

Jacknife was released in 1989 and features a fairly real situation of one Vietnam War veteran (Robert De Niro) visiting another at the start of fishing season, as they had once promised to. De Niro's veteran, the polynomial Joseph, nicknamed Megs, or Jacknife, has been in treatment for PTSD. The vet he's visiting, Dave, played by Ed Harris, was in his outfit in Vietnam, and is now alcohol dependent.

A tender love story develops between Dave's sister, Martha, played with charm and warmth by Kathy Baker, and De Niro's Joseph. A flashback scene, fueled by alcohol, shows Dave raging through the trophy hall of his high school during a school dance, which Joseph and Martha are chaperoning. Martha is a teacher at the high school.

Joseph and Dave were part of a trio of friends in Vietnam who fought together, and the major flashback concerns a helicopter assault that went bad. Dave breaks his leg jumping out. Their friend, Bobby, is killed trying to rescue Jacknife.

Jacknife is a story of blue-collar truck drivers. Joseph's courting of Martha has the affection and awkwardness of people touching worlds they

Jacknife (Kings Road, 1989) presents a fairly realistic portrait of Vietnam War veterans. From left to right are Dave, played by Ed Harris, his sister, Martha, played by Kathy Baker, and Robert De Niro as Jacknife, which is an ominous nickname for a trucker.

are unused to. Dave doesn't want them dating, because Megs (aka Jacknife and Joseph) is a loser.

The film makes a good case for the group psychotherapy treatment for war veterans. It also slaps us with the contrast between the high school, amateur sports, romantic heroism, and the course of suffering set up by combat experiences. Dave, drunk, staggers through the high school hallway lined with trophy cases, smashing the glass and shouting ambiguously "Bullshit! We should have stayed put!" The ambiguity of that statement comes from the observation that their friend was killed because of their actions, and that perhaps they all "should have stayed put" and never gone to war.

The dramatic monologues in the group therapy are examples of acting that isn't authentic, but lends anyway to the drama of the story. What gives the film its sense of realism is the work of one war veteran cajoling another into getting off the booze and into treatment. This theme that highlights the ignominious aspects of substance abuse, also shown in *Desert Bloom*, stands in contrast to the jovial alcohol dependency and abuse in the earlier John Ford movies (*Fort Apache*, *The Sun Shines Bright*, *She Wore a Yellow Ribbon*).

Jacob's Ladder, 1990

Jacob's Ladder, is also an urban war veteran drama, but this film is also solidly in the horror genre. Directed by Adrian Lyne and released in 1990, *Jacob's Ladder* stars Tim Robbins as Jacob, a New York City mailman and Vietnam War veteran. His sultry wife, Jezebel, is played with passion by Elizabeth Peña. This film is a unique war veteran film depicting the "flash forward" that is hard to conceptualize unless one has read *Incident at Owl Creek Bridge*. A squad or platoon is given an experimental hallucinogenic drug that causes them to become killing animals. The survivors of the carnage congregate as war veterans after one of them is mysteriously killed in a car explosion.

Periodically in the film we are greeted with horrific surprises, the sort that sends chills up even suspecting spines. Worms come out of a nurse's head at the VA clinic, or are they horns? A queasy feeling is generated in the viewer, that this is a huge metaphor for the toxic nature of psychological traumas. It is as if the soldier, dying on the operating table in the field hospital, sees his whole life flash before him, even that part that he has yet to live. In one nightmarish scene Jacob is strapped on a gurney and rolled through the bowels of the hellish hospital, each corridor more insane and disgusting than the last.

Jacob is married to Jezebel, yet seems also connected to a marriage

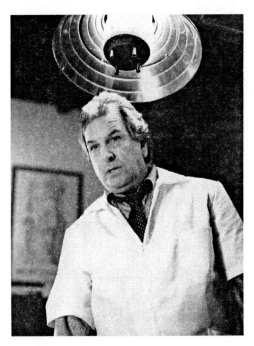

With the light framing his head like a halo, Danny Aiello plays the chiropractor, Louis, in *Jacob's Ladder* (Tri-Star Pictures, 1990). His role seems Hermes-like in that when he treats Jacob, the Vietnam War veteran, he causes sudden, remarkable memories to manifest.

that took place before the war, which led to the death of his son in an accident. Seen in brief flashbacks, the son is played by Macaulay Culkin in an uncredited part. Jacob also flashes back to Vietnam, sometimes due to the bone-crunching jerks of his wise and kindly chiropractor, played dreamily by Danny Aiello.

The veterans huddle on a rooftop, talking after a funeral. (By the way, it was a rare situation for people from the same geographic area to be in a squad in Vietnam.) They seem to have no memory of the carnage caused by the drug. Yet they are all dogged by a guilt that springs upon them like demons. They agree to seek some information from the army and try to hire a lawyer, but all of them, including the lawyer, back out quickly. acting scared and ashamed, leaving Jacob alone. The hallucinogenic fevers that Jacob experiences give the viewer the sense that he is gradually dying, and when he finally dies, we realize that he hasn't lived since Vietnam.

The theme of something happening in combat, which is repressed as a memory, yet influencing the war veteran unconsciously, is played out also in *The Manchurian Candidate* and *Conspiracy Theory*. All three of these films create scenarios in which the veteran is faced with influences he does not understand that seem to be playing out in the world around him, which is a great metaphor for the psychological problem of unconscious projection. C.G. Jung observed that we tend to encounter our own unconscious content first outside ourselves as projection, which is often the first step toward integration of the unconscious content (e.g., repressed memories) into consciousness.

Article 99, 1991

Article 99 takes place at a fictional veterans' hospital. It begins with the arrival of a farmer (DD-214 tucked in his pocket), who drives his pickup to the hospital at the same time a new doctor arrives to take up his training position. (The movie was filmed in Kansas City.) Both arrive as a veteran, denied services, goes berserk and drives his pickup through the hospital front entrance and fires his M-16 around the lobby. He is finally subdued by a team of medical guerrillas, reminiscent of *M*A*S*H*, who hustle him off to psychiatry. (Don't let anyone be encouraged by that event. Such a terror attack in real life would land the perpetrator in chains in federal prison, regardless of his pathology.)

Pat, the farmer, played by Troy Evans, has a heart attack during the fracas and has to be revived. The new doctor, Peter Morgan, played by Kiefer Sutherland, happens to be a neophyte heart surgeon who learns that there isn't equipment to do heart surgery. Seems there is an oppressive hospital director who would rather use precious resources to fund the primate research.

In *Article 99* there is a group of doctors who are intent on supplying medically needed services by stealing equipment and moving patients through authorized procedures to keep them in the hospital until medical help is available. They operate on the sly and in defiance of authority in order to serve a higher order of care. The plot develops mainly around relationships and romances between the doctors, and the initiation of Dr. Peter, who allows himself to *care* for a dying World War II veteran of D-Day, played by Eli Wallach.

Article 99 was directed by Howard Deutch, written by Ron Cutler, and released in 1991. The doctors and staff, who genuinely care about the patients as veterans, have to operate in defiance of the rules. The film has a downbeat ending that suggests that even though the callused hospital director was exposed in the end, his replacement is a carbon copy.

Kathy Baker plays Dr. Diane, a psychiatrist who cares. She has a sign on her office door, which is a little white life preserver with two geese at the bottom with their bills kissing. The words around the preserver are "Home is where you hang your heart." Dr. Sturges (Ray Liotta), the leader of the guerrilla doctors-who-care, develops a romance with Dr. Diane.

The film is quite condemning of the VA hospital system, with direct statements about malpractice as the doctors walk through the patient morgue. (VA doctors cannot be sued for malpractice.) For the purposes of drama, the patients revolt as the doctors perform unauthorized but necessary open-heart surgery to insert a pacemaker in the farmer vet, who

was seen in the opening credits. The hospital staff join the patients, lock-
ing arms to keep the federal police from entering. A patient in a wheelchair, Luther, is the ringleader of the rebellion. He is played by Keith David
and dressed as a veteran whose identity is stuck in the Vietnam War, with
paraphernalia about his person, badges, jewelry, and medals of the war.

Article 99 is shallow in its casting and plot. The admitting nurse who
coldly denies services is rude and ugly. The hospital director is a shallow
"suit" who has no saving grace. It exaggerates to the extreme what in reality in VA hospitals are problems far more complex, subtle, and difficult
to correct. Not all the VA staff who dislike veterans are ugly and rude, nor
are all the caring ones necessarily tops at their professions. There is truth,
though, in the bitterness expressed by one nurse, that the new intern,
referred to rudely by the charge nurse as a "tern," will skip through his
duties quickly and be on his way to a lucrative practice, while she has to
work with the same obstreperous system year after year. The farmer-
patient's story that ties the movie together, arriving at the beginning, having a heart attack, and then being saved by emergency surgery at the end,
is just that. We have no sense of who he is amidst the overcrowded plot,
other than a farmer with a bad heart and a distressed wife. A heftier plot
would have given Article 99 some more memorable characters and message.

It is true that a veteran once drove through the front entrance of a
VA hospital in rage over the poor federal treatment of veterans. The veteran who does so in the opening scenes of Article 99 is called Shooter (Leo
Burmester). He wears a boonie hat and refers to Vietnam place names
between bursts of his M-16. He tells the new patient just before he goes off
that he has "posttraumatic stress or some bullshit." The plot would have
thickened nicely if we had been given more of his story, too.

The so-called "turfing" of patients refers to the arrangements made
for necessary care through the bending of rules and shuffling of records.
The tactic, as mentioned, has the trickster spirit of M*A*S*H, McHale's
Navy, and Catch-22, when madness, war, and juggernaut government
bureaucracy mix in a confluence of funky comedy. In the serious reality
of the federal government's betrayal of veterans it *does* renege on delivering promised services both in a broad systematic policy of decisions, and
in small individual acts of bureaucratic sabotage by spiteful, jealous man-
agers, rude technicians, and underpaid clerks. Article 99 points out to us
that it is the poor and working middle class veteran who suffers from the
betrayal. Unfortunately, the film does not have the power to make the valid
point register with effect. Good people operate within, not so heroically,
but personally, making extra efforts to get something done, advocating for

a veteran's need for this examination or that, expressing warmth to an estranged veteran visiting from out of town. And it's not that the VA hospital is better or worse than the city's general hospital, it's that the veterans were promised that if they put their lives on the line, their country would take care of their health care needs. Such a contract seems to be only amendable at one end.

CHAPTER 3

Returning in Disguise

The veteran who returns so changed that no one recognizes him is a theme begun in Homer's *Odyssey*. At the end of his ten-year voyage following the ten-year war, Odysseus is landed on his home shore by Phaeacian sailors while he is sleeping. Athena appears to him and disguises him as an old traveling beggar and in that form he returns to his home.

The symbol of the disguise is a complex one. It is a cliché to point out that participating in combat irrevocably changes people, but to be changed beyond recognition is a more demanding criterion. Adopting a mask, or having a mask imposed by combat, can be a literal development. The triptych caper movie *Dead Presidents*, yet to be reviewed, puts so much emphasis on the concept of the war veteran in disguise that the masks (white face on dark skin) become images so striking they are exploited as the film's advertising icon. The masking in *Dead Presidents* is a reversal of the usual action cliché of masking with black mud on white face which occurs in a number of action films (e.g., *Ruckus*, *The Park Is Mine*).

Another kind of disguise, one so common it is universal, is the disguise of ignominy, Bearskin's pelt, the whiskey coat, which hides the memory of war. Substance abuse and the war veteran will be discussed later. What is discussed here specifically is the hero hidden behind a mask or guise following his homecoming, which is a repeating theme in war veteran movies.

Ulysses, 1954

Italians should never be trusted to portray the Greeks' own *Odyssey*. For one, most of the names are changed. Odysseus becomes Ulysses. Poseidon becomes Neptune, although for some reason Athena gets to keep her Greek name. *Ulysses* (*Ulisse*), released in 1954, was a lavish Italian production by Carlo Ponti and Dino De Laurentiis, directed by Mario Camerini. Screenplay credits require a directory. Seven writers are listed, including notables such as Irwin Shaw and Ben Hecht, but all the king's horses failed to salvage the wreck of a script. A film of Homer's *Odyssey* that depicts the fully developed archetypal character of the war veteran really requires a series rather than one movie. To further abuse the subject, the international cast of actors in this *Ulysses* speak in dubbed English, which is only convincing when their heads are turned away. Portraying gods and heroes is tough on actors, anyway, even in the operatic tradition of the Italians. In this *Ulysses* the actors are so stiff that they seem like Monty Python cartoon figures with their mouths moving. Kirk Douglas plays the war veteran and Anthony Quinn plays Antinoös, the chief rival among the suitors. The script does violence to the story with horrible distortions and plot compressions. For example, when Ulysses is washed ashore at Phaeacia, he has no memory of his adventures or his own identity. As his memory returns, we see the story unfold, such as it is. This dramatic ploy deprives Ulysses of his chief attribute, his *metis* or ability to deceive. When the Sirens sing their song, it is Penelope's pining voice, not the enchanting song of the hero's exploits. There is no bed built into the tree, and therefore no last test placed upon Ulysses by his wife.

In the end, Ulysses promises to "make up for it" and live out tranquil years of wedded bliss. Kirk Douglas, for his part, made a passable adventurer, but here he would have been better off to have traded roles with Anthony Quinn. Kirk would have made a great Antinoös and Anthony Quinn has the sturdy build that Homer attributed to Odysseus.

The Stunt Man, 1980

One of the most complex films of this category is the independent film *The Stunt Man*, directed by Richard Rush and released in 1980. Starring Peter O'Toole, Steve Railsback, and Barbara Hershey, *The Stunt Man* is a comedy-drama about a Vietnam War veteran who happens into a movie set and causes the death of a stunt man, who he thinks is about to run him over on a bridge with an antique Dusenburg motorcar. The war veteran (Railsback) is on the run from the law after the whimsical opening credits that set a circus tone. The death of the stunt man comes with a jarring whine of ruptured bridge cables. The war veteran has unknowingly happened into a war movie, directed with imperial grandiosity by Peter O'Toole's Eli Cross. The clever screenplay is by Lawrence B. Marcus, based on a novel by Paul Brodeur. Interestingly, Brodeur (1970) had the veteran a deserter who was on his way to basic training.

In a scene that captures the archetypal moment, the war veteran, now Bart the stunt man, emerges from the makeup room, where he has had a makeover disguise. Instead of the ragged fugitive, he is a blond surfer boy, his suffering now hidden from view.

The movie, set in a beachfront resort, is about a World War I pilot who is shot down and escapes from German imprisonment. Many of the stunts involve keystone cop chases over rooftops with death-defying leaps to joyful calliope tunes. The delightful musical score is by Dominic Frontiere.

Railsback plays the young veteran who becomes Bart, the stunt man. He gives his character a blue-collar wariness, untrusting, bewildered, scrambling, ready to adopt a disguise and play a role if it will get him by. The director is a god-like artist who floats on crane or helicopter, expounding his exasperation about the limits of the

Steve Railsback plays a Vietnam War veteran who has been done over and emerges as the stuntman Bart, in Richard Rosh's *Stuntman* (20th Century-Fox, 1980), a movie about a war veteran who plays a risky role in a movie about war.

form. In a convoluted point of view, this is a movie about the making of war, where the war veteran again puts his life on the line for the whimsical wishes of those above him.

The Stunt Man is a unique work in the war veteran tradition of films that describe themselves in action. It is also an important example of honing a film for the sake of popular appeal, stripping it down to simpler and simpler formats. The author, Brodeur, as we noted, had the deserter on the run from the military, while the screen adaptation turned him into a Vietnam War veteran on the run.

Bart's explanation about why he came to be an outlaw did not make sense. It seems he can hardly be trusted to tell an honest story. Having a war veteran adopt a disguise in order to fit in, and then get caught up in repetitive episodes of survival, appeals to the Odyssian archetype. Odysseus, after all, was related to Autolycus on his mother's side, a demi-god who could well have been selling aluminum siding and was himself descended from the god Hermes. And when we talk about Hermes, we think of shape-changing disguises adopted as a matter of form and as easily as slipping through a keyhole.

Ivanhoe, 1998

To be changed in a way that cannot be directly seen or experienced is perhaps more common for the war veteran. The archetypal proportions are seen in a film rendition of *Ivanhoe,* in which the veteran, Ivanhoe, returning from the Crusades, dons the disguise of a traveling pilgrim. Ivanhoe's noble King Richard is late returning from the foreign war because of his capture while traveling home. Contrary to historical accuracy, *Ivanhoe's* Richard finally returns disguised as a black knight, known as the Sluggard, doing battle against the forces of his brother Prince John. Richard is aided by a band of outlaw war veterans, yeomen led by Robin of Locksley.

Sir Walter Scott (1820, 1996), who placed his fictional character at the end of 12th century England, exploiting folk legends of the time, wrote *Ivanhoe* as a novel. Wilfred of Ivanhoe is the son of a Saxon nobleman, who returns home from the Crusades dressed as a pilgrim. There is friction between Normans, who hold the central power with the help of the King's brother John, and the indigenous Saxons. King Richard has placed his land in his brother's care while he is away fighting the Muslims for control of the Holy Land. In Scott's version of history, Richard returns in disguise, dressed in black, and enters jousting contest as the Black Knight.

In a jousting tournament before the Prince and his Court, Norman knights fight Saxon knights, and Ivanhoe, still anonymous, known only as the Disinherited Knight, wins the day, but is himself severely wounded. He is nursed by Rebecca, daughter of Isaac the Jew. Ivanhoe is captured by the Normans, along with Rebecca and Isaac.

Technically they were Anglo-Normans, as this takes place about a 130 years after the Norman Conquest of 1066. Norman colonizers of England were speaking English within two generations, although French remained the court language. It was Norman beef on the table, but Saxon and Celtic cattle in the pasture.

Richard and the outlaws, organized by Robin, combine to lay siege to the Norman's castle, holding the wounded Ivanhoe, Rebecca, Isaac, and others hostage, and eventually win the day.

The key for the war veteran is not just the return in disguise. Ivanhoe's mission is to restore his name and reputation, besmirched by lies about his loyalty, so much so, that Ivanhoe's father has rejected him and betrothed his ward, the golden-haired Rowena, to a noble but hairy Saxon prince.

Scott gives a hard look at the hypocrisy of justifying war with religious rationalizations, the condemnation of the righteous by the conniving dishonest. Although Richard's crusading zeal taxed the people of England, it was probably not questioned as policy. It was the duplicitous Prince John's government that was labeled as unjust. According to historian John Gillingham (1999, p. 122), Prince John did indeed have that reputation and was not a popular romantic leader like his brother, Richard the Lionhearted.

The strong character of the Jewish Rebecca represents an impressive acknowledgement of the exotic influences on the troops of the Muslim and Jewish populations of the Middle East. The dark, sadistic Knights Templar, who ally with Prince John, are also veterans of the Crusades, who appear to have been hardened by too many years of service overseas.

The most recent film version was the made-for-British-TV movie, adapted by Deborah Cook and first shown in 1998. (A previous U.S. version was released in 1952, directed by Richard Thorpe, with Elizabeth Taylor memorably as Rebecca and Robert Taylor, unconvincing as Wilfred of Ivanhoe. Another version was filmed in 1996, directed by Douglas Camfield, with James Mason as Rebecca's father, Isaac of York.) The 1998 British version was directed by Stuart Orme and stars Steven Waddington as Wilfred of Ivanhoe, Susan Lynch as the strong and passionate Rebecca, and Victoria Smurfit as the glamorous Saxon Lady Rowena. In this version it is the weaseling Prince John, played delightfully by Ralph Brown, who gives the production its brightest moments. The crucial next-to-the-last words were uttered by Rowena when she finally allows herself to accept Ivanhoe, after being assured by generous Rebecca that she was never loved by or in love with Ivanhoe: Rowena kisses Ivanhoe and says, "Welcome home."

In parallel to Homer's *Odyssey* there are two Saxon servants who ally with Ivanhoe, the pigherd, Garth, played by Trevor Cooper, and the Fool, Wamba, played by Jimmy Chisholm. Scott, with direct reference to *The Odyssey*, expresses his opinion about Christianity by having the Fool disguise himself as the friar-confessor, heroically sneaking into the Norman castle as it is under siege.

The Mask of Doubt: The War Veteran's Return as Existential Dilemma

Probably the most interesting and common war veteran theme in movies is the man whose values and identity have so changed that his postwar existence presents a challenge of personal philosophy. This is a not-uncommon theme in the war veteran whose belief system and values were harshly challenged and compromised in combat. For some, the dropping of illusions due to combat can be a gift, a benefit of combat, but for others, the loss of illusion caused by combat can lead to loss of meaning. The question of meaning can be a dangerous question for a combat veteran when the abstract ambiguity invites projection of the veteran's guilt and disappointment.

The Razor's Edge, 1946

The Razor's Edge was directed in 1946 by Edmund Goulding, and in a 1984 remake by Don Byrum; both versions were adapted from a novel by Somerset Maugham. Tyrone Power played the World War I veteran in the first movie, and Bill Murray in the remake. The story relates a war veteran's wandering search for life's meaning after his experiences in war crushed his values. Murray does more than modernize the role. He and director Byrum give the war veteran a connection with the war and its traumas. Both Murray and Power have the wooden intensity that works for the role, while Murray has the added blessing of his inherent self-mockery. That wooden intensity comes from the rigidity of holding too much in, but should not be mistaken for emptiness.

The Man in the Gray Flannel Suit, 1956

The Man in the Gray Flannel Suit was directed by Nunnally Johnson and released in 1956. A World War II airborne infantry veteran, Thomas Rath, played by Gregory Peck, is plagued by flashback memories of the war that captivate his attention while he's riding the train to his job on Madison Avenue. Adapted from a popular novel by Sloan Wilson, the movie depicts the clash of values when the veteran is required to choose between family and career, while haunted by his wartime past.

Peck's Rrath has flashbacks which allude to his work as an infantry officer during battles of the European Theater. In one scene his wife, Betsy, played by Jennifer Jones, taunts him for not having the guts to get ahead. On the train into work, he recalls a scene in flashback sequence in which he kills a German with a knife, so that he could take his warm coat. He next recalls an affair he had with an Italian girl, Maria, who is played persuasively by the exotic Marisa Pavan. In the next sequence, he is participating in the assault on the island of Okinawa. Here he kills his own sergeant when he throws a hand grenade at a machine gun emplacement in a bunker. Unable to believe the sergeant is dead, Thomas carries him back to medics and begs them to help.

Nunnally Johnson has laced in scenes with references to death. Chickenpox strikes the house and the Rath's kids become humorously morbid. They are watching television cowboys fighting and in make-believe they shoot at each other. Gregory Peck's Rath is repressed and withdrawn. His wife alludes to his remoteness as a loss of intimacy. He is preoccupied and Johnson's direction lets us in.

The compromise achieved by the film gives us the feeling that Peck's Rath is doing the mature and right thing by supporting his wife and children. He has, after all, consciously struggled with his wartime memories and dealt up front with the temptations of the material world, and now he is ready to settle down. One definitely gets the sense that Rath has set his heart aside with Maria and made a pact to live out his life responsibly — and he will make the best of the present, although it is not nearly as interesting as the past.

Buried in the plot is a moving scene in which Thomas meets the elevator operator in the office building, who turns out to be a war veteran sergeant from his unit. Their meeting is awkward as they are both surprised at meeting out of the context of war, and the scene captures the relatively common occurrence of war veterans meeting conjuring stunning memories of combat closeness from another world. War veterans' military unit reunions have that element of both relishing the camaraderie and dreading the memories that are stimulated. In the case of *The Man in the Gray Flannel Suit* the dreaded memory relates not to trauma, but to love. Wartime creates a romantic yearning for a return to the good life, yet, as Beauty discovered when the Beast transformed into a Prince, she misses her scary, primitive former companion.

> Thomas Rath says to Betsy, "I don't know,… I guess I expected peace to be nothing but a time for sitting in the moonlight with you like this, and I was surprised to find that this isn't quite all there is to it."
> "I disappointed you."
> "Of course you didn't. I was my own disappointment. I really don't know what I was looking for when I got back from the war, but it seemed as though all I could see was a lot of bright young men in gray flannel suits rushing around New York in a frantic parade to nowhere. They seemed to me to be pursuing neither ideals nor happiness— they were pursuing a routine. For a long while I thought I was on the side lines watching that parade, and it was quite a shock to glance down and see that I too was wearing a gray flannel suit" [Wilson, p. 300].

The Seventh Seal, 1957

The Seventh Seal, released in 1957, established director Ingmar Bergman in a filmmaking class of his own. The stark film concerns the

Death (Bengt Ekerot, right) draws black in the chess game with the Knight (Max von Sydow) in Ingmar Bergman's *The Seventh Seal* (Janus Films, 1957). "Very appropriate. Don't you think?"

Knight, Antonious Block, played by Max von Sydow with brilliance, returned from the Crusades and dogged by doubt, disillusionment, and, literally, Death. He is accompanied by his servant, a man of the earth, who, in playing off against the intellectual Knight, creates a duo reminiscent of the king and his jester, along with a number of other adventuring hero-and-sidekick pairs. This squire, Jons (played by Gunnar Björnstrand), however, is a strong and serious character as well. Bergman offsets a small group of nomadic, childlike minstrels, who eventually travel with the Knight, against the mad plague sufferers with their mean and desperate clergy. The Knight contemplates a gaunt crucified God of suffering and confesses to a voyeuristic Death, disguised as Father Fate mocking God's design.

    The Seventh Seal is a classic of war veteran films. The war survivor Knight playing chess with Death. (What a way to mate!) His squire sums up the ten-year effort in the Holy Lands. "Our crusade was such madness that only a real idealist could have thought it up." The Knight mourns his survival. When he approaches Death, whom he mistakes for a priest, at the confessional, he declares that his heart is empty.

> Through my indifference to my fellow men, I have isolated myself from their company. Now I live in a world of phantoms. I am imprisoned in my dreams and fantasies."

(Note: The wording of dialog differs between the movie subtitles and the screenplay published in the 1960 *Four Screenplays of Ingmar Bergman*, translated by Lars Malmstrom and David Kushner. This quotation was taken from page 149 and is approximately what was translated on the screen.)

In the course of their journey to his castle, the Knight picks up fellow travelers, the minstrels and their infant son, symbols of innocence, and other survivors, a cuckolded blacksmith, and a woman saved from rape and death by the lusty squire, Jöns.

On the way they encounter a witch, a girl tied to a cross and about to be burned. The Knight endeavors to talk to her and discovers that she indeed believes she sees the devil. She tells him she is 14. He gives her an anesthetic drink that knocks her out before she is burned. Jöns says, "She sees what we see."

Jof, the juggler (played by Nils Poppe), who has visions, describes the final scene on the hillside: Death leading the party, the Knight, his wife, the servant, etc.

> He tells them to hold each other's hands and then they must tread the dance in a long row. And first goes the master with his scythe and hourglass, but Skat dangles at the end with his lyre. They dance away from the dawn and it's a solemn dance toward the dark lands, while the rain washes their faces and cleans the salt of the tears from their cheeks [Bergman, p. 201].

For the war veteran life is the dance of Death, the chess game. When he looks at success he thinks it will be taken from him. Even when he is happy, he cannot lose his grip on Death's hand.

Some Came Running, 1958

Some Came Running, directed by Vincente Minnelli, was released in 1958 and has the feel of that era. The cast of Frank Sinatra and Dean Martin reinforce the period mood. Adapted by John Patrick and Arthur Sheekman from a popular novel by James Jones, the movie deals with a veteran's return from the war. As the movie opens with the intrusively loud score by Elmer Bernstein, the protagonist, who we learn is Dave Hersh (Frank

Sinatra), is riding in army uniform on a Greyhound bus with remarkably clean windows. He arrives asleep in his hometown, much as Odysseus arrived in Ithaca awakening in a fog, only Dave has passed out and been placed on the bus by his drinking buddies. As he awakens, he searches for his possessions. He gropes into the crotch of his pants for his hidden wad of money.

As Frank steps off the bus, he invites the driver to have a beer, but the driver declines. Back inside the bus, Ginny Morehead awakens. Ginny is played by Shirley MacLaine in her breakthrough role. Dave's prankster friends have placed Ginny on the bus with the unconscious Dave. Ginny carries a white bunny purse with floppy ears, which aptly describes her personality. Dave gives her 50 dollars from his money clip and tells her to get lost.

He rents a hotel room and the clerk recognizes his name as the same as the owner of the jewelry store across the street. Dave unpacks, revealing his love of literature: books of selected works by William Faulkner, John Steinbeck, Thomas Wolfe, F. Scott Fitzgerald, and Ernest Hemingway. Although it seems odd, there is a kind of nomadic soldier's sense about carrying great works in efficient compendiums. Dave also extracts a worn and tattered unnamed manuscript authored by himself. He demonstrates his ambivalence toward writing by tossing it impulsively into the trashcan and then digging it out and tossing it into a dresser drawer. He then settles down to drinking whiskey and looking out the window at this brother's store.

The scene changes to Dave's brother, Frank (played by Arthur Kennedy), arriving at his store to learn that his brother is back in town. Frank visits Dave in his hotel room and we learn that Frank was forced to send Dave to a foster home after their father died. Dave sounds as though he is bitter that Frank, the older brother who was just married, would opt to place Dave in "Mrs. Dillman's Home for Little Boys."

Through the opening scenes Dave wears the uniform of an army enlisted man with no stripes or other insignia. Only a Combat Infantryman Badge and a few campaign ribbons. He never refers to his role in the war. Throughout the film, no mention is made or reference given to the war or army life. Frank asks, "Know what you're going to do now that you're out of the army?" Dave replies, "Sure, never to go into it again." There is pressure on Dave from Frank to get on with his life, materially at least, and as far away from Parkman as possible. Dave, however, is playing the role of a shadow character who doesn't watch the clock when he drinks. His return is unwanted and inconvenient for Frank. The theme is similar to that of the 1956 film *The Man in the Gray Flannel Suit* and to

Ginny Morehead (Shirley MacLaine) steps off the Greyhound bus carrying her bunny bag behind war veteran Dave Hirsh (Frank Sinatra), still in uniform, but without rank, in Vincente Minnelli's *Some Came Running* (MGM, 1958).

that of 1960's *From the Terrace* in which the veteran is confronted with a choice between material ambition and independence, and individual integrity.

Drinking and smoking dominate the film. Dave goes to a bar, Smitty's, where he meets his soul brother, Bama Dillert, played with panache by Dean Martin. They will eventually partner up, playing poker in the towns around Parkman, Indiana, even as far away as Terre Haute. The rapport established between the veteran and the gambler is based on having a common hip, cynical, bitter, sarcastic, unvarnished, and boozie view of life.

Dave is invited to dinner by his brother, whose wife, Edith (Nancy Gates), is angry at Dave for past affronts alluded to in his fiction writing. Also invited are Dave's former professor and mentor, the tediously discrete Robert Haven French, and his daughter, Gwen, played with riddled ambivalence by Martha Hyer, an admirer of his writing and professor of literature herself. Gwen quickly finds that her admiration is mistaken as sexual attraction, and Dave Hersh is aroused enough to make repeated passes at her, which she spurns with passionate, persistent, yearning discipline.

Dave, the veteran emerging from the war that is without reference, abruptly stops drinking and carousing with the likes of bumptiously charming Ginny Morehead, now a worker at the local brassiere factory. He dons a business suit and goes for the allure of the literary professor, who has lovingly prepared his manuscript for publication and sent it off to the *Atlantic* magazine, where, of course, it is immediately accepted.

Still, however, the fickle Gwen spurns Dave's affections. He begrudgingly marries Ginny on the rebound. The dénouement takes place in a loud, jazzy, neon red, crowded carnival scene, when Ginny's old boyfriend resurfaces and shoots first Dave, then Ginny, killing her as she throws her body over Dave's. Dave survives and Ginny dies, and we wish it were the other way around.

Ginny's death is called collateral damage in war. A woman who will take a bullet for a man must love him dearly. Sinatra's Dave Hersh is truculent as a rejected lover with Ginny, while she absorbs the punishment and keeps on giving, because she wants so badly to enjoy life. Sinatra's is a tight, tense role of a man who has buried his feelings in denial and self-discipline. Once he takes off one uniform he dons another and the pressure is on to get on with life.

Yet finally the story is about death. The death knell for Bama Dillert, who has diabetes and won't stop drinking. The death of Ginny Morehead, the slow and generous factory girl. The turn comes when Sinatra's Hersh, who cannot separate sex and romance from his artistic gift of writing, begrudgingly chooses life with Ginny Morehead.

The failure of *Some Came Running* to relate to the war just fought gives the whole move a sense of shallowness, as though the soul of Dave Hersh was in the war and his humanity is dying with his bacchanalian friends. There seems to be an inevitable relationship between denial of death and collateral damage.

Ashes and Embers, 1982

Ashes and Embers, released in 1982, is an African-American polemic about a Vietnam War veteran who struggles with his readjustment. The film has some interesting flashback sequences and some moments of artful beauty, but it shows its low budget roots by being poorly edited, scripted, and produced. The film was directed by Haile Gerima and stars John Anderson as the vet and Evelyn Blackwell as his grandmother. The

remarkably interesting music is by "Brother AH and the Sounds of Aware-
ness." Most of the sequences are allowed to run too long and there is too
much political proselytizing, which detracts from the movie as an art form.
The veteran describes his shame and ambivalence about fighting the white
man's war. He says, "Grandma, I'm not home. I mean, I've come home,
but I'm not. I'm confused." He confesses to her with anguish, "I rode on
a road of bones helping the white man." To his girlfriend, in an over-long
sequence, he acts out the scene following combat, picking up body parts.
He warns her, shouting angrily, "You see me comin', you better lock your
shit up."

Powwow Highway, 1989

Powwow Highway deals directly with the Native American war veteran on the reservation, his relationship to his own culture and the greater
U.S. culture. The Vietnam War veteran is Buddy Red Bow, whom we soon
learn is something of a firebrand in the Lame Deer, Montana, Cheyenne
tribal counsel. Buddy, played cockily by A. Martinez, has also been an
American Indian Movement activist. He learns that his sister, Bonnie,
played by Joanelle Nadine Romero, has been arrested, with her two young
daughters, in a drug bust, transporting a bag of marijuana. She is interned
in the Santa Fe Jail. Her two daughters are placed in a children's home.
Buddy enlists Philbert Bono, played as an enchanted wise fool by Gary
Farmer. Philbert wants to become a warrior. He has the ability to trans-
pose his spiritual reality and the reservation reality of his existence. He
buys a rust-bucket car for a bag of marijuana and calls it Protector, his
war pony. Philbert agrees to drive Buddy to Santa Fe. He drives instead,
while Buddy sleeps, in the opposite direction, toward the Pine Ridge Reservation in North Dakota.

A very significant war veteran scene takes place at a Pine Ridge powwow in which Buddy confronts the corporation-hired goons. Someone
from the grandstand throws a knife that, sticking suddenly in the wall
between them, convinces the goons to back away. The knife thrower, the
voiceover explains, "was in Nam with Buddy." He "spent 31 months in a
tiger cage" and "has just about every medal there is." Buddy goes up and
sits with his veteran buddy, who is clearly suffering. He stutters and struggles and finally insists that Buddy go dance with the others. Buddy is com-
pelled to obey and we see him gradually warming to the Native traditional
ways as his cynicism recedes. Earlier, to set up the powwow scene, we see
Philbert remark about Buddy's throat choker necklace, which is of Cheyenne design, with a military Purple Heart. Buddy nonchalantly explains,
"I thought I'd put the tin to some use."

Buddy and Philbert finally rescue Bonnie and her daughters. Philbert does this, it seems, in a state of delusion. He ties his "pony" to the bars of the adobe jailhouse window and pulls the bars out of the wall, releasing Bonnie. Bonnie's daughters, played by Chrissie McDonald and Sky Seals, do a fine job fending for themselves.

Philbert seems delusional, or at least enchanted. However his consciousness, he draws Buddy into believing in his culture again. Buddy's decision is made easier when the whites are portrayed as either bumbling, vain, or menacing. Two great white characters with style are Texan Rabbit Layton, played with spark by Amanda Wyss, and the coffee shop waitress (Leigh Opitz), who fields her position convincingly.

Powwow Highway was directed by Jonathan Wacks from a screenplay by Janet Heaney and Jean Stawarz, adapted from a novel by David Seals. Although at times the acting seems stiff, there is also a stillness that seems appropriate. One senses Jay Silverheels in the background whispering, hey, man, get it right. Act natural.

The War Veteran
Who Refuses to Fight Again

The first and second literary works to make it into print in the Western world are about war and the war survivor: *The Iliad* and *The Odyssey*, by Homer. These works made the leap from oral tradition into print as soon as there was an alphabet to work with and a wealthy tyrant willing to put scholars to work as scribes (Nagy, 1996). These two works were already favorites as disparate songs in oral tradition. No filmmaker has yet to *successfully* take on the mythic magic of Homer's *Odyssey*. Several movies, however, have paid homage to the archetype of the taunted and debased hero. Frank Sinatra's character Dave Hersh in *Some Came Running* returned unconscious to his home town after the war, asleep on the bus, greeted not by enchanted shepherd boy, Athena, but by the earthy Ginny (Shirley MacLaine). Clint Eastwood's *Firefox* presents an airplane that can read the pilot's mind, as could the mythic Phaeacian ships. Humphrey Bogart portrays a returning soldier in *Key Largo*, similarly taunted by gangsters (admittedly a lot classier in the being of Edward G. Robinson and his boys) and hobbled by his vow never to fight somebody else's war again.

The war veteran who refuses to fight again is a derivation of the existential theme of Odysseus taking a place as a beggar at the door of his own palace, while his wife's suitors engage in revelry. He is the veteran who has had his fill of war and killing, who is disillusioned about the need for war and what it has accomplished, the veteran who simply felt used as cannon fodder to get other men medals and protect unappreciative fat cats at home. Kevin Costner's Marine veteran, Stephen, in *The War*, discussed earlier, feels the futility of fighting as an overwhelming commitment to non-violence.

Key Largo, 1948

Film critic Pauline Kael wrote during the era of *Key Largo*, "It's an old Warner Brothers trick: you identify with Humphrey Bogart, the cynic, who sneers at hollow patriotism; then he comes through for his country and his girl" (1954, p.65). *Key Largo* is the classic of the war veteran tradition. Directed by John Huston and released in 1948, the movie features an all-star cast, with Humphrey Bogart as the war veteran, Frank McCloud, who travels to Key Largo to visit the parents of his war buddy, George, who died while talking on the field phone with Frank from a forward position. When he arrives at the Hotel Largo, run by his buddy's family, he finds the place is invaded and controlled by a gangster, who has returned from court-ordered exile in Cuba.

Edward G. Robinson plays Rocko, the gangster with the style of an unctuous, vein, psychopathic tough guy. He taunts the veteran, contemptuously calling him "Soldier." Bogart's McCloud clenches his teeth and avoids fighting the gangster and his toughs. He has vowed never to fight another man's war again.

Lauren Bacall plays George's sister and Lionel Barrymore plays the wheelchair-ridden, obstreperous Mr. Temple, George's father. Claire Trevor rounds out a cast of strong supporting characters as Gaye Dawn, Rocko's girl friend, a has-been showgirl singer. Gaye is alcohol-dependent and made by the taunting Rocko to sing a truly pathetic song in order to get a drink: "Moanin' low, my sweet man I love him so.... He's the kind of man needs the kind of woman like me." At the end of the song, Rocko refuses her a drink because she wasn't good enough. Ironically, in a gesture of sympathy, Frank goes quietly over to give her a glass of whiskey. And gets as thanks three quick slaps from Johnny Rocko.

The plot is driven by a hurricane that increases in ferocity and then wanes with musical accompaniment. A plot complication, and an odd twist, is the plight of local Seminole Natives. Two brothers have escaped from jail, we learn at the beginning. Later a group of Indians paddle in canoes to the shore, driven in by the hurricane, but are kept out of the hotel during the storm by the heartless Rocko. Jay Silverheels plays Johnny,

Tough guy gangster Rocko (Edward G. Robinson, right) sticks his pistol in the stomach of the tough guy war veteran who won't fight, Frank McCloud (Humphrey Bogart, left), in John Huston's *Key Largo* (MGM, 1948).

one of the escaping Osceola Brothers, in an uncredited role. The investigation of their escape involves the sheriff's deputy, who is beaten, held captive, and finally shot and killed by the gangsters. The sheriff then comes out and kills the Osceola brothers, after being told by Rocko that the Osceolas killed the deputy.

When Mr. Temple and Nora urge Frank to fight the gangsters, Frank replies, "I fight nobody's battles but my own. Me, die to rid the world of Johnny Rocko, no thanks. One Johnny Rocko more or less won't make any difference." Finally, of course, with the assistance of Gaye smuggling him Rocko's gun, Frank fights and kills all the gangsters, because, as Mr. Temple shouts out with rooting encouragement, "If you're a fighter, you can't walk away from a fight."

The significance of this film is that it reflects the attitude in the late '40s of fatigue from the war, and at the same time the realization that conflict was still threatening. As Mr. Temple says of Johnny Rocko: "Nobody's safe in the world, Nora, so long as he's alive."

Key Largo was adapted by Richard Brooks and John Huston from a 1939 play by Maxwell Anderson, which set the scene just *before* World War II. In the Anderson original, the protagonist, King McCloud, leads a band of leftists to fight the Fascists in the Spanish Civil War. When the cause is lost and the loyalists are retreating to a negotiating position, McCloud's squad is left in a rearguard action, meaning certain death. McCloud advocates abandoning their position, but the others, whom he had recruited, opt to stay and fight to the death.

The Anderson play highlights survivors' guilt as McCloud goes to each of the families involved and apologizes to them, saving the father and sister of his dead friend to last. This version also, by the way, gives much more dignity and cause to the Seminole Natives, their exile to Oklahoma, and their resistance, as represented by Osceola, to White domination.

The concept of survivors' guilt is retained in the film, but represented by the sentiment and values of Frank McCloud, who refuses to once more fight another man's battle. By 1948 it was not politic to represent the Spanish loyalists and their American volunteers as in any way heroic. Bogart's McCloud is an infantry veteran of the Italian campaign. He mimics helplessness but bides his time to take advantage of the cramped confines of a fishing boat, far from collateral damage. The theme we are left with is that strong men act weak when they stop caring.

Ulee's Gold, 1997

An independent gem, *Ulee's Gold* attempts to tell the *Odyssey* story sequel, speculating about Odysseus as an unromanticized Vietnam War veteran after he has settled in for a time. Helen is a junky and "Telemachus" is in jail, and Ulee (short for Ulysses, which is Latinized Anglo-Irish for Odysseus) has been so affected by his experience in Vietnam as a sole survivor of his squad, that he has vowed to abjure violence, thus providing the plot its dramatic force.

Ulee's Gold, directed and written by Victor Nunez, is more than just an updated variation of *Key Largo*. *Ulee's Gold* picks up the returning war veteran some years later. Ulee is a Florida beekeeper and producer of tupelo honey. His son, Jimmy (played by Tom Wood), is in jail for larceny. His daughter-in-law, it turns out, is addicted to drugs in Orlando in the company of local rabble, and Ulee himself is caring for his granddaughters. The plot is driven by the quest for a hidden cache of robbery money. The loot has been hidden by Jimmy, and Ulee is lured into the plot when his son's accomplices hold his daughter-in-law, Helen, played convincingly by Christine Dunford. Ulee's wife, Penelope, has been dead for six years, and we learn from Helen in a spiteful exchange with Ulee during her painful drug withdrawal, that Ulee has suffered from the loss of his wife. She shouts, "You stuck around in your body, but your heart left a long time ago. Maybe you never cared."

Peter Fonda plays Ulee, the limping war veteran. He reveals his military history by talking with his granddaughter, ten-year-old Penny (played by Venessa Zima with great heart), in his work shed, where he has his Cav patch and campaign ribbons pinned along with a picture of his squad (ten grunts). "They're all dead," she asks, "every last one, except for you?" He affirms that that is the case. She asks, "have they been bad to deserve dying?" He replies, "No, they were good guys. Your grandpa was tricky — lucky. That's why I made it out."

Significantly for Homer devotees, Penny is playing with a toy horse as she talks to Ulee. The horse is a replica of antique design, suggestive of the Trojan horse, Odysseus' invention that brought down Troy and led to the return of Helen.

Ulee's trickiness is tested again when the bad boys from Orlando, Jimmy's former crime partners, Eddie Flowers (Steven Flynn) and Farris Dooley (Dewey Weber), contact Jimmy, informing him that they have Helen in their apartment. Ulee drives down to pick up Helen, and Eddie and Farris inform him that they are really looking for the loot Jimmy has hidden.

Ulee returns with Helen, who is all but comatose with drugs. He has to restrain her and a neighbor, a nurse renting a cottage from them, is called to help. Patricia Richardson plays the nurse, Connie Hope. Ulee's teenaged granddaughter, Casey, played by Jessica Biél, manages to transform herself in a few scenes from rebellious to cooperative, as if the crisis has given her purpose.

Just as Helen recovers, Farris and Eddie show up and demand that Ulee lead them to the money. They threaten Ulee's family in the process. He resolves this crisis in a manner not dissimilar to the method chosen by Frank McCloud in *Key Largo* — though with much less bravado. Fonda's Ulee is quiet. He is less in conflict, but overworked and very tired. His chief problem is resolving his dilemma without resorting to murdering the men.

Eddie taunts Ulee after they've gotten their money and are about to leave. "You're chicken, that's it. You haven't done much with your life, have you Mr. Jackson?"

A footnote to the drama is Ulee's distrust of the local cop who arrested Jimmy. Apparently they were once friends. But even when he has to confront the robber, Ulee refuses to call in the police. He places family loyalty above the law. It is the sheriff, played by J. Kenneth Campbell, who

Peter Fonda plays Ulee Jackson, a hard-working beekeeper and Vietnam War veteran in *Ulee's Gold* (Orion Pictures, 1997). The net that hangs from his hat acts like a shield between him and anyone who comes near. (Photograph by John Bramley.)

finally makes amends to Ulee, in a gesture that seems symbolic of forgiveness in the post–Vietnam War era.

The Patriot, 2000

The Patriot was released in 2000 in time for Independence Day. As a movie, directed by John Emmerish, it made every effort to find popular and commercial payoffs. Withal, however, the movie's production was exquisite, with consultants from the Smithsonian advising on the design of costumes and sets. The "look" of the movie was worth the price of admission. It gave us an authenticity that virtually carried the drama's popular characters.

Mel Gibson plays a veteran of the French and Indian War who participated in what we now call atrocities, or abusive violence. He participated in the mutilation and dismemberment of enemy dead as a terror tactic to influence the Indian allies of the French. He has vowed not to fight again and refuses to volunteer to fight with the rebels against the English. When he is finally forced to fight to save his family, he engages his children in the battle and organizes a band of "militia," who raid British forces from their swamp-island retreat. The movie has the ballad-popular appeal of Robin Hood stories, with the various characters making up the band, including the slave who fights for his Master and then volunteers when freed, and the Episcopal minister who converts to military life to fight for liberty.

The war-veteran-who-refuses-to-fight theme illustrates important cultural differences between the post–World War II era and the post–Vietnam War era. In *Key Largo* (1948) and in *Ulee's Gold* (1997), the war veteran is threatened by criminals. In the former, the criminals are gangsters who have been exiled to Cuba and the veteran (Humphrey Bogart) was an infantry officer, who is modest but disillusioned by his combat experiences. *Ulee's Gold* presents the war veteran also as a modest man who disavows violence as a result of his war experiences as an infantry enlisted man. The dramatic difference, profound for the comparison of the eras, is that Bogart's veteran resorts to violence only after he is safely away from collateral damage, whereas Peter Fonda's Ulee is non-violent to the point of self-sacrifice, relying on the Odyssean trickiness to cope with the criminals. Frank McCloud also has his deceptions, but violent solutions are not out of the question. He is only recently back from the war, whereas Ulee has been back over 20 years. The post–World War II period was the era in which the threat of another international war was still vivid. The Soviet Union was not mentioned, but the left-wing sentiments of the original stage production had been expunged from the film. The philosophy reflects the era's tension in which violent retaliation is a hole card to be played when the time is right. By the 1997 release of *Ulee's Gold*, there was no credible enemy of the United States, only terrorists, menacing, who seemed not very well equipped.

The Fake War Veteran

The Odyssean subject of the "fake" war veteran becomes very complicated as soon as it is examined. For example, there are different categories of fake. There are men who are not veterans at all who claim to be war veterans to exploit sympathy or seek fraudulent benefits. They are relatively easy to detect in the therapist's office because they usually have an absence of real identity and are often borderline-psychotic in personality style. Then there are men who are real veterans of the military who claim to have been in combat when they were not. They are harder to detect because they know the jargon and provide a vivid account, often retelling true stories related by authentic combatants. And then there are the complicated combat veterans who claim to have done more than is factually true. The character, Roger, in Wellman's aptly titled *Heroes for Sale*, is an excellent example of the fake war veteran taking credit for another's deeds. Often unsure of their own memories, combat veterans may be motivated to exaggerate or distort for reasons that are complex.

A different version of the fake war veteran is seen in *The Man Who Wasn't There*, that of the veteran who spent the war in a safe job, but claims to have been in combat.

Le Retour de Martin Guerre, 1982

Two films, one inspiring the other, arise from an interesting (and, to some, fascinating) story of Martin Guerre. Recorded for posterity by a sixteenth century jurist who was part of a tribunal of officials trying the case, the record became something of a popular sensation at the time and has remained in print in some form or another to this day. The best current book on the subject is by Natalie Davis, *The Return of Martin Guerre*. And by far the best film on the subject is *Le Retour de Martin Guerre*, directed by Daniel Vigne, and starring Gérard Depardieu as the trickster Pansette, the fake Martin, and Nathalie Baye as Martin's enigmatic wife, Bertrande. The premise is that when Martin Guerre left his wife many years before, there was no record of what he looked like. His mother and father had died in the interim and, since Pansette resembled Martin, and Martin had described his friends and neighbors to Pansette while they were campaigning together, Pansette, creates the ruse. The irony is that Bertrande knows he is not Martin, but goes along with the pretense because she prefers the new version of Martin. He is nice to her and a good lover, whereas the original Martin rejected her. The only record of Martin's physical appearance is in the form of a mold of his boot kept by the village cobbler. He notes that the pretend Martin's foot is smaller after his return.

All goes well for the new Martin until he demands compensation from the family elder for the profits of his land during his absence. When a vagabond appears in the village who recognizes Martin as Pansette, his cover is blown and he is tried and convicted of fraud, and ignominiously hanged before gathered villagers.

Set in 1542 in Artigat, a French village on a plain near the foothills of the Pyrenees during the reign of Francis I, the beauty and the difficulty of the film is its devotion to period authenticity. The sets and costuming are remarkable for realistic feel. The peasants are unwashed. The rooms are dark, lit by streams of daylight or weak candles. The peasants eat with their fingers.

The enchanting music for *Le Retour de Martin Guerre* was composed by Michel Portal, and contributes to the sense of plaintive authenticity. It is not until Gérard Depardieu takes up his own defense during the trial that the film has a sense of dramatic acting.

Hidden behind the fraud is the problem for most returning war veterans, which is that they have changed so much they do not feel and often do not behave like the same man who left. The longer the time spent in combat conditions, the more that change takes place for the combatant. The veteran remembers his neighbors, relatives, and friends, but he cannot relate to them as he related to them before. It is not that they have changed. Very little changes people's personalities. Repeated psychological traumas, such as are common in combat, change personalities so much that the combat veteran returns as an alien in his own home.

Sommersby, 1993

The Return of Martin Guerre was rewritten and transformed into a U.S. Civil War story and film, resulting in *Sommersby*, released in 1993 and directed by Jon Amiel in a French–U.S. production. The adaptation retains much of the complexity of the original, in that the fake veteran is a more appealing and a better person than the original. Richard Gere plays the fake Jack Sommersby like a politician seeking office. He is vague and ingratiating. Unfortunately, he is also flat of voice and expression. Jodie Foster plays his wife, Laurel. Whereas Nathalie Baye had to work within the restricted role for women in the 16th century, communicating with her eyes and gestures, and her Mona Lisa smiles. Jodie Foster has a broader character to convey the need for a man to love and to help her survive. Gere's fake Sommersby is a con man, the very sort who would creep into a therapist's office seeking support for a contrived service-connected disability.

The film alludes to Homer's *Odyssey* when the fake Sommersby returns with his hand wrapped in a rag, and when Sommersby's faithful hound, Jethrow, sniffs the stranger, he smells his master's scent. This film plays the irony further in having the real Sommersby guilty of murdering a man for which the fake Sommersby must hang, unless he confesses to his fraud. Then in a kind of Celtic twist, it seems that the fake Sommersby has been defending the right of the former slave to own land and fostering a kind of post war communal sharing of labor and materials. He is confronted by hooded KKK and drives them off, only to have them show up in court, without hoods, as witnesses to the alleged Sommersby murder.

The character of Odysseus in the original *Odyssey* is assisted by the god Hermes, whose realm is the borderland, the realm of transitions and transformations. When Odysseus meets strangers on his return to Ithaca, he tells them stories pretending to be a survivor of some calamity, war, or slavery. He never reveals his true identity on an initial encounter with familiar figures. He even tricks his grieving father for a time before he claims his true identity. When the goddess Athena met him on the shores of Ithaca, he tried to fool her with a story, to which she responded with a laugh.

> "Any man — any god who met you — would have to be some champion lying cheat to get past *you* for all-around craft and guile! You terrible man, foxy, ingenious, never tired of twists and tricks— so, not even here, on native soil, would you give up those wily tales that warm the cockles of your heart!" [Book 13, lines 329–334, Robert Fagles' trans.].

The protagonists in Martin Guerre and his U.S. Civil War imitator, Sommersby, are Hermes-like dissemblers. They have a conman's feel for what it takes to win someone over into believing in them. They have the politician's gift of turning a shambling lie into a positive contribution to society.

In *The Odyssey* we see Odysseus' wife, Penelope, present an enigmatic, tight-lipped face vis-à-vis the old man claiming to be her husband. Even with a little sprucing up from Athena, he does not convince his wife until he tells her about how he made their bed in the boughs of an olive tree, a secret shared only by them. Penelope's enigma is that she may have known from the first the beggar was her husband, but went along with the ruse because she liked the result. In *Le Retour de Martin Guerre* and *Sommersby*, Penelope's enigma is reversed, for the abandoned wife may know the man is *not* her husband.

The veteran's punishment for posing is execution. The delectable complexity of the plots of the different versions is presented to us as a warning tale about the dangers of pretending and then falling in love with the character of the pretense. But we know that a trickster cannot be trusted. Although he seems like a likeable character, we never know that his personality won't again shift when the wind changes.

The Man Who Wasn't There, 2001

The Coen Brothers have a history of inserting whimsy and dark humor into plots that are delightfully complex and scenes that surprise. In *The Man Who Wasn't There* Billy Bob Thornton plays Ed, the barber, in a stultifying performance. Through a fog of boredom and cigarette smoke he learns that his wife is having an affair with her department store boss. Ed's wife, Doris, is played by Frances McDormand with a seething intensity. She is the perfect foil for the barber. The barber's customer, a weasily salesman, claims to have a great business deal that fell through for lack of $10,000. The barber goes for the offer and blackmails the department store boss to get the money and revenge.

Doris' boss at Nirdlinger's Department Store, Big Dave (James Gandolfini), is an overbearing man who describes himself as a combat veteran of the Battle of Okinawa, a notoriously bloody campaign. Through a series of mistakes, Big Dave discovers the source of the blackmail and attacks the barber, who fatally stabs his assailant in the neck. However, it is the barber's wife who is prosecuted. Her defense lawyer, Freddy (Tony Shalhoue), hires a private detective to investigate Big Dave's background and it is discovered that he spent the war in a naval shipyard and never left the States.

The Man Who Wasn't There is a well-acted gem of deadpan humor. Just when it seems fit to end, the plot takes an unexpected turn, and minor characters become significant. The barber's hapless scheming gets him implacably further and further into jams until it seems the movie can't go on, we've had enough, and then another surprise turns the tale again. Scarlett Johansson plays Birdy, the sweet girl who plays a mechanical Beethoven and can cause an accident by showing her gratitude.

The Man Who Wasn't There was written by Joel and Ethan Coen. The film takes place in 1954 in Santa Rosa, California, then a small town in rural northern California.

It is a source of continued irritation to combat veterans when they hear boastful men like Big Dave claim combat experience. There seems to be a negative correlation between amount of combat and the boastfulness of the combatant. It is also observed by those who practice psychotherapy that there are those men who will claim that combat and its emotional consequences explain their aggressive or explosive behavior, when in fact they are men with personality disorders who didn't need combat to be angry. On the other hand, the use of the law enforcement background check is a convenient cinematic plot device to discover the truth, as in *Mr. Majestyk*, *First Blood, Absolute Power*. Just as the modest picture on the bulletin board in the shed, *Ulee's Gold*, or medal in a frame in *The Desperate Hours*, subtly reveals the combat history.

CHAPTER 4

The War Veteran as Social Symbol

The war veteran is presented frequently in cinema as representing the damage done to society by the war. He walks the streets on crutches. He stands in the background as society rattles around him. He becomes a living symbol of sacrifice that offsets other values.

The war veteran is a social symbol for every postwar society. Generals, pilots, PT boat commanders, and even former artillery captains run for President of the United States. The war veteran comes to symbolize the war for many, playing the scapegoat or benefactor, depending on the attitude toward the war. *Dances with Wolves* presents a picture the U.S. Civil War veteran seeking the furthest frontier after his brush with death on the battle line. While the U.S. had its western frontier, England had Ireland, with its garrisons for peaceful R&R, except for the anger of its occupied citizens. The popular sensation of fairies in post–World War I England presents a picture of a nation seeking a spiritual connection between the war dead and the millions of citizens and veterans in grief. The other side of the post–Civil War picture of veterans is presented in John Ford's mundane romantic comedy about gathering war veterans, *The Sun Shines Bright*; in it, the veterans use their war veteran status as a springboard into community social life.

The war veteran as hero or anti-hero was played out in the movies first in the Depression era films of the '30s and then in a category the French critics identified as *film noir*. (See Selby, 1984, for an annotated index of *noir* films.) This genre was already established and waiting for the Second World War veteran to stumble into it like a dark alley. *Film noir* was a theme that adapted easily to the war. Probably the most dominant images of *film noir* are the negative, dark shadow with dialog marked by distrust and hatred. Hirsh (1981) writes:

When he surfaces in *noir*, the returning soldier has the disconnectedness of an ex-con; he seems both amnesiac and somnambulistic. The crime dramas absorb the soldiers into the *noir* world rather than focusing directly on such problems of the immediate postwar situation as demobilization, the severely shaken economy, the loss of Roosevelt and readjustment to a new President (p.21).

The Sun Shines Bright, 1953

This 1953 film by director John Ford features a romantic slice of life in Kentucky, some time after the U.S. Civil War. Veterans on both sides of the war populate the town and meet with their organizations in opposing halls. The film concerns Judge Billy Priest, a Confederate war veteran, played by Charles Winninger, who is running for re-election and facing a moral dilemma, whether or not to honor the death-bed request of a wayward woman who has returned home to die. He chooses the honorable and righteous alternative and participates in her funeral on Election Day. The townspeople are won over to his righteous path and all ends well. His opponent for the judgeship speaks to the crowd, referring to the veterans' voting bloc. "It is a great day in Kentucky when no longer — no longer can an empty sleeve or a gimpy knee serve as a blanket to smother the progress in the 20th century."

Ford directs with his usual sense of ethnic humor, ribbing the pompous and the hillbillies. He has his brother and former silent screen director Francis playing an alcoholic vet with a coonskin cap and an ever-present jug. Stepin Fetchit plays Jeff, the judge's servant, with his whiny, gawky, bug-eyed behavior. African Americans sing and play banjos with smiles as the proud, stiff whites parade and dance. The United Confederate Veterans and the Grand Army of the Republic (the Union Army veterans), gray-bearded and hobbling, wear mix-and-match pieces of uniforms. Tunes on the soundtrack recall sentimental romantic aspects of war: "We're spending the night on the old camp ground." Men who rode and fought together recall their abiding loyalty. As the general says with straight sincerity to the judge, "You'll loom large in my memoirs."

The film has Ford's favorite repertory characters abounding, and is said to have been the director's career favorite. *The Sun Shines Bright* is from a screenplay by Laurence Stallings, drawn from stories by Irvin S. Cobb. The comic stereotypical treatment of African Americans is quite consistent with his comic stereotypical treatment of war veterans as they age and outgrow their uniforms. Ford himself maintained formal ties with many of his World War II cronies. He continued long after the war to meet and booze with the old boys of his Field Photo group (McBride, 2001).

The Big Chill, 1983

The Big Chill was released in 1983 and was popular as a film that summarized the sixties from the perspective of the eighties. This warm, affiliative ensemble movie features seven friends from the University of Michigan who gather for the funeral of one of their group, Alex, who has committed suicide. They spend the weekend at the house where he died, which happens to the large, rural, colonial structure of Harold (Kevin Kline) and Sarah (Glenn Close). The movie was filmed on location in Beaufort, South Carolina. Also present at the weekend is Chloë (Meg Tilly), who was Alex's girlfriend. Meg (Mary Kay Place), Michael (Jeff Goldblum, at his comic best), Sam (Tom Berenger), and Karen (JoBeth Williams). The Big Chill was directed by Lawrence Kasdan, and written by Kasdan and Barbara Benedik.

The gathering of mourners in The Big Chill (Columbia Pictures, 1984). Seated in the center is the Vietnam War veteran, Nick (William Hurt), surrounded by his friends from college, who are gathered for the funeral of their mutual friend. The only person not an old college friend is Chloe (Meg Tilly), seated at Nick's right. She was the dead man's girlfriend and becomes a muse for Nick. From left to right, they all are Sarah (Glenn Close), Harold (Kevin Kline), Chloe, Nick, Sam (Tom Berenger), Meg (Mary Kay Place), Michael (Jeff Goldblum), and Karen (Jobeth Williams).

One of their group, Nick, played by William Hurt, served in Vietnam. We never learn what happened to him in Vietnam, or, for that matter, why he was there. Did he enlist or was he drafted? It seems to be suggested in one line that he was experience-hungry at one time. It is never clear that he was in combat, however. We see him compared to his peers at the gathering. Nick drives an old battered Porsche. He uses drugs copiously, pills, marijuana, cocaine, and alcohol. Hurt's Nick is largely flat in affect. We see him awake at night watching TV while everyone around him is asleep. We see Nick sitting alone in an old, vacant cabin as he starts at a bird sound. When he is followed in his Porsche by a cop for running a red light he is belligerent. He talks of being alone, that everyone is alone, an ironic statement coming is this movie that savors affiliation. He sums up his depression as they are all gathered in the living room talking about Alex: "It's not why, but why *not*, kill yourself."

The most prominent implied effect of Vietnam on Nick is his sexual impotence, which he repeatedly refers to with insouciant acceptance. "Did I ever tell you what happened to me in Vietnam?" Ironically he manages, by the film's conclusion, to make the most upbeat statement of them all, when he announces that he is staying with the gamine Chloë to work on the deserted cabin. Tilly's Chloë is a study in the Guiletta Musina school of acting. Together Chloë and Nick form a mime couple featuring sad silence, although Chloë is given the best line of the movie. When asked about whether Alex was ever happy, she replies succinctly, "I haven't met that many happy people to know how they act."

Nick apparently has had a series of jobs, including working as a radio psychologist in the San Francisco Bay area. He seems haunted, vacant, sad, stoned, but perseverant. "I'm not cynical about dessert," he states.

Part of the movie's continued popularity is the sound track, which comes on periodically with undue amplification, featuring the rock bands and songs of the sixties.

As social symbols go, the war veteran usually takes his place as the man who haunts his society. *The Big Chill* has a double entendre as title, standing for both the colloquial slang for friends gathering for a relaxing weekend, and the chill that Nick carries for them all, the chilly isolation of the posttraumatic bell jar. "Wise up, folks," he retorts. "We're all alone out there."

Choose Me, 1984

Keith Carradine plays the curious role of a Vietnam War veteran jet pilot, Mickey. Geneviève Bujold plays Dr. Nancy Love, a radio talk show psychologist, who rifles through Mickey's suitcase as he's bathing, discovering his war history in a box of ribbons, newspaper clippings, pictures, and an Air Medal award. At first Mickey presents himself as just released from a mental hospital, but we don't know if he's straight about his story.

Alan Rudolph wrote and directed this romantic melodrama, released in 1984, in a stylized, jazzy, noir kind of mood. Lesley Ann Warren plays Eve, who runs Eve's bar (not the original Eve) on a romantic, stagy street where in the neon and shadows strut beautiful prostitutes and sporty hipsters. Dr. Love on the "Love Line" talks to Eve about love at the same time they are both having sex with Mickey and sharing the same house. Mickey has asked them both to marry him and travel with him to Las Vegas, where he has money. If Mickey is sincere, he must be desperately lonely. The slickness of the style gives a sense of fate pulling them all along some inevitable slide.

When Mickey turns out to be a real air force veteran, a man of genuine combat, he becomes not a crackpot on the loose, but a romantic character falling from high, grasping at women for warmth who have none to give.

Dances with Wolves, 1990

Kevin Costner directs his own lead in *Dances with Wolves*, which was released in 1990. He is saved by the magnificent photography of Dean Semler and the Black Hills of South Dakota. Costner's acting, with his unflappable flat voice, is saved by prolonged and welcomed periods of silence. With half the remaining dialog spoken in Lakota Sioux, Costner, as Union army veteran John Dunbar, is much more convincing.

Dances with Wolves opens with Union officer John Dunbar, on the surgeons' table, surrounded by evidence of numerous amputations and instruments of the grossest form of surgeries. The doctors cut off his boot, but leave him unconscious on the table, themselves exhausted, to take a break. Dunbar, rising from the table, painfully puts on his boot and rides away. Battle lines are drawn, but neither side is aggressive until the fatalistic Dunbar rides into no man's land and challenges the Confederate marksmen. When they fail to shoot him down, the Union troops are rallied and charge to rout the opposition. Dunbar is declared a hero and given the assignment of his choice. He chooses the farthest outpost on the western frontier.

Once he arrives, he discovers the post abandoned and takes up residence, dutifully restoring the structures and defenses. Gradually he meets a curious wolf and a nomadic tribe of Sioux, the latter in the area waiting for buffalo. Dunbar befriends the Sioux and falls for a white woman, Stands

With Fist, played by Mary McDonnell, whom they have adopted as an orphan. She is now a widow. Dunbar is renamed Dances with Wolves and learns the Sioux customs and language. As one army sergeant says when he returns to the white culture, "Turned injun, didn't ya?"

Dances with Wolves was adapted for the screen by Michael Blake from his own novel. Costner directs with a love that displays gorgeous pictures of the life of plains Natives. Graham Greene plays the thoughtful Kicking Bird, and Floyd Red Crow Westerman plays the elder, Ten Bears.

We don't have a strong sense of why Dunbar chose the isolation and dangers of the Western frontier, although he seems to take to it when he finds it. Connecting his quest to his war experience, and particularly his brush with death on the operating table, leading to his suicidal behavior, might have given us much needed understanding of his motivation to seek the borderland. By beginning the movie on the operating table, we have no sense of Dunbar before he was wounded, and therefore there is no depth of character.

A Dangerous Man: Lawrence After Arabia, 1990

This film about Lawrence of Arabia is subtitled *Lawrence After Arabia*. It stars Ralph Fiennes as Lawrence. Although a smaller man in stature and power than Peter O'Toole who portrayed the legend in David Lean's *Lawrence of Arabia*, Fiennes plays well the brilliant trickster figure. His brilliance is shown brightest when he reads an ostensive translation of Prince Feisal's letter from Arabic into English before the post World War I ruling board, composed of English and French victors, and when challenged by Clemenceau, spontaneously with flourish translates the letter into French, obviously having memorized it.

A Dangerous Man is part of the war veteran life of T.E. Lawrence, the man who fought with Arab princes to defeat the Turks and capture Damascus. In doing so we know how he was traumatized, through direct hands-on killing, and through sodomizing rape and torture while a captive.

We see Lawrence here without power, obliged to help Feisal through loyalty to a comrade of war, losing ground to the betrayal of the Arabs, a betrayal that has the inevitable force of glacial movement by the officious powers of England and France.

Lawrence stands for many war veterans who fought passionately and with great sacrifice for a cause that they later felt was betrayed. He finds that hero worship has disrupted his relationship with Feisal and bogged the proceedings. It shows him having no recourse but to use his prestige and popularity to publish the story of the betrayal in a newspaper. He is sacked as an army officer and shuttled off to do research on Arab castles, which is where he began. In the final frame, the story of T.E. Lawrence is summed up: "From 1922, Lawrence spent his remaining years in the lowest ranks of the air force and army. He died in 1935, after a motorcycle accident. He was 46."

Directed by Christopher Mensaul and released in 1990, *A Dangerous Man* was written as a screenplay by Tim Rose Price. The plot establishes that the French and the British seek the Arabian oil. The Emir Feisal (played with deep emotion by Alexander Siddig) is finally given the kingdom of Iraq. Lawrence says to Feisal repeatedly, and Mensaul makes it the last word of the movie, "It's not over."

Throughout the movie we see Lawrence as admiring working men and women with fetish fascination. He shows the scars of torture on his back. He confesses to the beautiful Madame Dumont (Polly Walker), who is lying in his bed naked waiting for him, "I cannot respond to you as you'd wish. It's simply not within my power to do so."

Fiennes, like Peter O'Toole before him, does a skillful job of conveying a man of well-developed discipline, who has been traumatized by war and cannot give up on the cause that he fought for. Fiennes plays Lawrence as a shy man of dauntless courage and fierce loyalty.

Wild at Heart, 1990

In *Wild at Heart* the war veteran is a rotting symbol and decadence pockmarks the character. Bobby Peru, played by Willem Dafoe, is the Vietnam veteran whose laughter makes one feel sick. He is consistent with the theme of *Wild at Heart*, released in 1990, in that the entire movie is a series of symbols describing a decadent quest, done in camp and high satire. Sailor, played by Nicolas Cage, and Lula, played by Laura Dern, are on a lusty, low-down, sensual ride from Cape Fear, through New Orleans, to Big Tuna, Texas.

To best describe the quality of Big Tuna, Texas, the film's director, David Lynch, focuses on the graffiti of the backside of the sign: "Fuck you." Lynch begins the film with flame, and flames describe the destruction throughout the film, beginning with Sailor beating a man to death on the staircase of the ballroom, while Lula looks down thrilled and horrified from above, and Lula's mother, played with disgusting soap opera affect by Diane Ladd, who hired the man to kill Sailor, watches her agent die with disdain and chagrin. Sailor sings to Lula on the dance floor his repertoire of favorite Elvis Presley hits. He takes pride in his imitation of Elvis, and in his snakeskin jacket, which he says is his symbol of individuality. He later refers to himself as a robber and manslaughterer, after his release from prison. On his odyssey after his release, riding with Lula in his

T-bird convertible, Sailor meets Bobby Peru in Big Tuna. There in Big Tuna, Bobby talks Sailor into participating in an armed robbery of a feed store, which appears to be a farmers' co-op with thousands of dollars.

Just before they set out on the caper, Bobby menaces Lula, who is sick in her hotel room with early symptoms of pregnancy. Bobby delights and even flaunts his rotten teeth. Willem Dafoe plays Bobby with "USMC" tattooed on the back of his hand. He talks about spending four years in Chow Bin, Vietnam, wherever that is. His rotten teeth are obviously fitted over his good teeth in a Halloween-like prosthesis, causing his mouth to have a swollen mushy bulge of a prizefighter. Bobby is shot by the sheriff after gratuitously shooting the feed store clerks with his shotgun during the robbery. Sailor is finally captured after Bobby shoots his own head off to end the melee.

Lynch gives us no surcease. Each scene is played with such high campy humor that the viewer is left unable to criticize, but sick of the sight nonetheless. After Bobby shoots his head off, the camera shows the clerks lying inside the feed store in a heap of carnage. One of them searches for his missing hand. The other encourages him, saying it can be sewed back on. Then we see a dog running out the door with the hand in his mouth, a tribute to Sam Peckinpah's *The Wild Bunch*.

Lynch plays other film tributes. He features a running gag, not only of sappy country-western romanticism, but of the *Wizard of Oz*. Lula clicks the heels of her red shoes together after Bobby leaves her room and Lula's demented mother appears riding a broomstick as the Wicked Witch. When things are at their worst for Lula, she cries out in mock despair, "The whole world's wild at heart and weird on top!"

To cap off the macabre, Isabella Rossellini appears as Perdita, a perverse but gorgeous spider woman, who is somehow affiliated with Bobby Peru and drives the getaway car.

Dafoe's Bobby Peru is a disgusting character in this low-class mockery of the working class that seems both posed macho and oblivious of its own destructiveness, and in fact seems to delight in its decay. Director Lynch adapted *Wild at Heart* from a novel by Frederick Elmes. Film aficionados love the insider references to *Cape Fear* and *Bonny and Clyde*, but the war veteran statement seems sleazier than even bad taste would suggest, because it seems to mock what most horrifies the war veteran who knows that carnage is not camp.

Troubles, 1993

Ian Charleson plays Major Archer, who is first seen reading a letter from his fiancée in a bunker during artillery shelling. His taciturn nature is demonstrated when a nearby explosion brings dirt down on him and he casually slips his helmet on and goes on reading. The content of the letter is narrated by his fiancée and we see her rather tongue-in-cheek speech directed into the camera. We next see the major leading an assault with pistol and whistle as the Tommies climb out of their trenches. He is wounded by a blast and we see him lying in a shell crater under another body. When he tries to move the corpse on top of him, the bloody arm comes off. In the next scene a hospital nurse is reading another letter to him; she looks impressively like his fiancée, and invites him to visit their home at the Majestic Hotel in Ireland. In voiceover, we see the major as a civilian (throughout the movie he is called Major), speaking the most profound war veteran words as he expresses his ambivalence about visiting. "I seem only at ease in the company of strangers." As he is sitting on the train looking at the other passengers, he says to himself, "how easily they can come apart." When he reaches the hotel, there is no one about in the lobby and he strikes a gong, which makes a reverberating sound that causes a flashback to the memory of his being hit through his helmet. When asked about the war, the major says, "There hasn't been a single night that I haven't dreamt about it."

Troubles was directed by Christopher Morathan, from a screenplay by Charles Steeridge, adapted from a novel by J.G. Farrell. The title should have been "The Majestic Hotel," for the focus was as much on the crumbling structure as it was on the major and the Irish revolutionary "Troubles." Released in 1993, the film was evidently made for TV and didn't make it to the Masterpiece Theater circuit. As a drama it has its own troubles. The rundown hotel is full of quirky characters, not the least of which is the owner, Edward Spencer, played by Ian Richardson, who is an English gentleman. The crumbling, overgrown condition of the hotel seems to symbolize the decline of the post-war British Empire. *Troubles* was released in a two-volume video and is overlong.

When the major arrives, he is unable to talk intimately with his fiancée, and concludes that their relationship is over, but that is before she dies suddenly, apparently of boredom. However, an exotic Irishwoman, Sarah Devlin, played by Emer Gillespie, captures his fancy.

The plot quirkiness provides little room for character development. We have vague ideas about IRA activity which followed the First World War. The local Irish are seen as common folk, but not nearly as strange as the occupying British. The British citizens are portrayed as either mad or prejudiced against the Irish, who they regard as a lower form of humanity. The major refers to the British as blackguards. He is himself criticized by Sarah as too repressed and polite. She rejects him when he proposes, saying she wants a man who expresses his opinions. "You're not the man I want, that's all there is to it." It seems that the taciturnity of the major is exactly the character trait that leaves him finally without romance, or even connection to the world of his culture.

The Spitfire Grill, 1996

The war veteran fits very well into themes about outsiders. *The Spitfire Grill* pairs a hermit Vietnam War veteran with an ex-con girl, Percy, played by Alison Elliott, who is trying to rehabilitate by working in the remote town of Gilead, Maine. The Gilead town diner is the eponymous Spitfire Grill. Percy learns that the hermit, Eli, played mutely by John M. Jackson, is the son of the grill's owner. Eli took to the woods after he returned from the Vietnam War. Eli, it is explained, was a "four year all-state" champ who enlisted in the army. "The whole town saw him off."

Hannah Ferguson, Eli's mother, the arthritic owner of the Spitfire Grill, is played by Ellen Burstyn. Eli is elusive, hiding even from his mother, in the wooded mountain slopes above the diner. Percy takes over the task of filling a food sack for Eli after Hannah falls and injures her back. Eli comes in the night for the sack that is left by the woodpile. As a hermit, he becomes an enigma for the girl and she dubs him "Johnny B." She sings, "Johnny B. never knew what hit him. Do you suppose if a wound goes real deep, healing will hurt as much as the wound?" Percy, it is revealed later in the film, had a baby she had named Johnny. Percy was molested by her stepfather from age nine, and became pregnant at age 16. Her stepfather attacked her when drunk, with a knife, and killed her baby, then kidnapped her later from the hospital and took her on a wandering trip that ended up in Maine. She was sent to prison for manslaughter for killing her stepfather with a razor. The story makes her motivation seem justified, in the just war conception of killing.

To further the archetypal connection, Percy is reading a ragged copy of Homer's *Odyssey*. She reads a line that is a signal, when the "rosy-fingered dawn rose upon the sailors and they started on their journey."

Here the Vietnam War veteran becomes the symbol for the wounded and the outcast of the society. Restoring "Johnny" to society becomes a way to reintegrate the wayward wounded girl. Percy's fascination and pursuit of the elusive veteran she names "Johnny B." leads her to an idyllic waterfall, the presence of which causes her to feel her grief. She in turn lures the isolated war veteran by sitting in a dell and singing, like a siren of feeling.

Part of the charm of this movie is its set location in Peacham, St. Johnsbury, Vermont. It was directed and written by Lee David Zlotoff and

The war veteran is not in this scene, as he is elusive in most of *The Spitfire Grill* (Castle Rock Entertainment, 1996). Gathered in a thoughtful pose are, from left to right, Percy Talbott (Alison Elliot), the young woman just released from prison, Hannah Ferguson (Ellen Burstyn), mother of the war veteran and owner of the grill that was named after the English World War II fighter plane made famous in the Battle of Britain, and Shelby Goddard (Marcia Gay Harden), who grows more independent as the movie progresses. (Photograph by Eric Lee.)

released in 1996. There is a layering in war veteran movie tradition — it is suggested in the voiceover narration that the father of Hannah is a World War II veteran and that the name of the grill comes from the English fighter plane.

Percy is befriended by Shelby, played by Marcia Gay Harden, who is married to Hannah's nephew, Naom, played with righteous prejudice by Will Patton. Shelby is a passive, insecure woman who develops a sense of individuality and defiance of her husband as the result of her contact with Percy. Naom was a childhood friend of Eli's. Naom is righteous but paradoxically dark in character, whereas Eli is the ragged hermit, paradoxically light. Eli fashions bird sculptures in the woods.

This film is faithful to the repeating theme that the survivor of psychological trauma is attracted to restoring the life of another survivor, and, in following this fascination, trying to cope with her own trauma and save herself. In the final moment of the film, as Hannah is walking into the grill in the early dawn hours looking for her dog, there sits Eli, in ragged woolens, returned finally from the war.

It is more poetically true that a psychologically wounded girl like Percy would be a better healing resource for the emotionally wounded veteran than the sexy hospital volunteer that Jane Fonda played in *Coming Home*. In *The Spitfire Grill*, the town's abandoned church becomes a symbolic sanctuary where Percy tells her story. The return of spirit for Hannah and Shelby comes with the return of Eli and the sacrifice of Percy.

Fairytale: A True Story, 1997

Another example of this collective open cultural wound phenomenon is found in *Fairytale: A True Story*, a 1997 film in which two children are caught up in a collective contagion of wishing for something that is innocent and spiritually pure. Directed by Charles Sturridge from a screenplay by Ernie Contreras, based on a historically factual story by Albert Ash and Tom McLoughlin, the film features two girls who, just at the end of World War I, live in the house of an amateur photographer. They are playing about with fairies and take their father's camera to record their fairy friends.

The exterior scenes are also, as in *Mrs. Dalloway*, scattered with wounded soldiers on public streets and trains. The girls play cats cradle with a soldier on the train who is terribly wounded in the face. He tells them of seeing fairies and later in the film appears to defend them.

The news reports of the girls' fairy pictures grows into a public sensation and prominent citizen experts become involved, including Sir Arthur Conan Doyle, played by Peter O'Toole, and Harry Houdini, played

Elizabeth Earl plays Frances in *Fairytale: A True Story* (Paramount Pictures, 1997). Frances knows something we don't know. The film thankfully leaves us with a playful sense of ambiguity about the existence of fairies and their connection to the afterworld. (Photograph by Framestore.)

by Harvey Keitel. Although the story seems to be officially debunked, it is clearly the film's intent that we are left with lingering doubts about the existence of fairies.

In the final scene of this endearing film, the girl's father makes his entrance, finally returning from the war to the background music of Handel's "See the Conquering Hero Comes." The girls' father, in woolen brown uniform, is none other than Mel Gibson in an uncredited cameo appearance.

Photographing Fairies, 1997

Another 1997 British film concerning the curious connection between fairies, children, and war veterans is *Photographing Fairies*. The movie was directed by Nick Willing, with a screenplay by the director and Chris Harrald, from a book by Steve Szilagyi. The plot also concerns a World War I British veteran, but while focusing on the veteran, it shifts our attention away from the enchanted girls and onto a story of a man affected by a pre-war trauma, the death of his newlywed wife during a snow storm in the Swiss Alps. Toby Stephens plays Charles Castle, who, after surviving the snowstorm, is next seen in the trenches as a war photographer, taking belabored pictures from a box camera on tripod of corpses lined in a row. An incoming artillery shell sends everyone scrambling for cover except

Charles, who casually keeps on working even after the shell lands, in a surrealistic shot from the point of view of the shell itself, right next to the photographer. In a comical scene, his assistant, Roy, played by Phil Davis, urges Charles to come into the fortified trench, which he finally does only after he is finished with his work. The shell explodes after he has casually settled into the cover of safety.

The war veteran Charles is then in another comical scene photographing a middle-aged couple who apparently lost their son. "Life goes on, doesn't it?" the woman says. Charles photographs them with a model dressed as a soldier. Later he will doctor the photograph and insert the face of their dead son. Charles then goes to a Theosophical Society lecture and debunks a trick photograph of children with fairies. Sir Arthur Conan Doyle is present and challenges Charles to seek the truth. Sir Arthur is played by Edward Hardwicke, a familiar figure who played Watson in a recent British Sherlock Holmes TV series.

Charles gives out his card promoting his photography studio at the lecture. A lovely woman takes a card and later comes to his studio with photographs of her two daughters with fairies. Charles first scoffs at the pictures, but then examines them closely and finally, in a dramatic sequence reminiscent of Antonioni's *Blow Up*, enlarges them until he can see fairy images in the girl's eyes.

Photographing Fairies takes a bizarre twist, as it seems the girls have discovered a magic flower that grows in a huge old tree. Eating the flower, which Charles discovers on his investigation, causes a kind of hallucinatory vision in which fairies come fluttering into view. The film fairies are the quaint creations of special effects animator, Ron Mueck.

Throughout the film, Charles has repeating surreal dreams of his wife's death, falling into a crevasse that opens in front of her. It is clear that he has remained as numb after the war as he was during the war.

Frances Barber plays the girls' mother, Beatrice Templeton. The girls' father is the village reverend, played by Ben Kingsley. The wide-eyed and clever girls are Clara, played by Hannah Bould, and Ana, played by Miriam Grant. Their mother is killed in a fall from the tree, chasing down fairies. Reverend Templeton goes berserk when Charles tries to set up equipment to photograph the fairies; he cuts down the tree and smashes and burns the equipment, and when the two grieving widows fight, the reverend is accidentally impaled on an upturned camera tripod. Just prior to this scene, Ben Kingsley's quirky, intense reverend tries to console Charles by telling him, ironically it turns out, "you can get over anything if you try." Even though it was in fact an accident, Charles confesses to murdering the reverend and is put to death on the gallows.

The role attributed to fairies is that they are caught between two worlds, having a Hermes-like connection with the land of the dead. Charles, it seems, wishes to rejoin his wife, and in the last scene, following the release of the gallows trap door, he pulls her from the snowy crevasse.

Photographing Fairies is a good example of unfinished business proceeding from traumatic grief. And an example, too, of how a man may go *into* combat already numb with posttraumatic stress disorder. The English pastoral scenery is a great treat. Erotic nightmare scenes of Charles with his dead wife come sensuously alive, unfortunately restrict the film to a mature audience.

The post–World War I sensation in England was the photographic evidence of the existence of fairies. Their psychopomp function involved connections to a spirit world or afterlife and made the sensation understandable in a nation that had lost millions of its men to warfare. *Fairytale: A True Story* plays with the reality of the fairies, while *Photographing Fairies* takes a quasi-literal slant in trying to create a psychedelic flower that allows one to view fairies. The war casualties are more prominent in the former film, while they are virtually non-existent in the latter, *Photographing Fairies*. The sentiment, however, of unfinished grief turning into survivor's guilt, was very much real in England after their catastrophic war.

Mrs. Dalloway, 1998

The war veteran in *Mrs. Dalloway* is a haunting symbol interwoven through the mind of an upper-middle-class woman ruminating about her upcoming party. English society in the 1920s and 1930s was wounded by the loss of its men, far more than I think the post–Vietnam War era, when the moneyed classes were able to avoid service. This was still an era when the English rich had values that demanded service. Adapted by Eileen Atkins from Virginia Woolf's novel, *Mrs Dalloway* was finally filmed and released in 1998. It was directed by Marleen Gorris with a largely Dutch crew. The wonderfully expressive Vanessa Redgrave plays Clarissa Dalloway. The movie is set in London in June of 1923, when the country is still in acute adjustment to the open wound of World War I. Men in uniform, amputees on crutches, pass along the streets. Clarissa, on her pleasant morning walk to order flowers for her party, looks out the shop window at the sound of a car backfire to see a startled face of a frightened man looking in from the street. He is a war veteran of the Italian campaign, Septimas Warren Smith, played by Rupert Graves. He turns on the sidewalk and cries out to his wife, "I'm stuck!" We have already seen him before the opening credits in a trench shouting as his friend, Evans, is blown to pieces.

Septimus Warren Smith (Rupert Graves), a fated, suffering World War I British veteran, looks off furtively, his gaze alert for threat, as his wife (Amelie Bullmove) looks on in *Mrs. Dalloway* (First Look Pictures, 1998).

Later Clarissa will see him again framed in a windowpane of her home, an apparition, a kind of translucent afterimage. Scenes shift in Ms. Woolf's famous novel, like the scenes of a Robert Altman movie, with segues of seamless passing coincidences. We see an old friend of Clarissa's visit, Peter Walch, played by Michael Kitchen. Just back from India, Peter was once in love with Clarissa and proposed to her. After he leaves her house, he walks through the park and becomes a flashback cue to Septimus, who is sitting in agony on a bench. We see Peter transform in Septimus' eyes into Evans and explode on the park lawn.

Still later, the doctor, who will subsequently appear at Clarissa's party, is called to treat Septimus, who is talking about suicide and acting very distraught. Dr. Holmes learns from Septimus' wife, Reeza, played by Amelia Bullmore, that Septimus believes he is guilty of some terrible crime. Dr. Homes tells her that it is a case of delayed shell shock and he needs rest, "away from loved ones." He tells Reeza that Septimus has served with distinction. However, the veteran insists, "I've failed. I have committed a crime. I cannot feel. I did not care when Evans was killed."

During the preparations to take Septimus off to a country hospital, the veteran leaps out the window and impales himself on an iron fence spike. Then we are back at Clarissa's party and we see Dr. Homes appear, apologizing for being late and telling the story of Septimus' suicide. Clarissa is disconcerted and cries out in voice over, "Don't talk of death in the middle of my party." The guests, all high level men in government, talk of the idea of sending war veterans overseas to Canada or Australia. Dr. Homes replies that politicians are not really interested in shell shock. Clarissa muses, "he threw himself out a window. Why? Why? He's thrown his life away. He will always stay young—we've grown older." "That young man killed himself. I feel very like him—less afraid."

Mrs. Dalloway is a film directed and produced by women, with women in several key production roles, including director of photography. It was adapted from an important novel written by a woman who lived in the time of its action, when post-war England felt the loss of a generation of young men.

Gosford Park, 2001

There is only one remarkable war veteran in Robert Altman's *Gosford Park*, which was released in 2001. He is Lord Stockbridge, played as a stiff and distant figure by Clive Owen. We hear remarked in the opening scenes that Lord Stockbridge lost much of his hearing in the trenches.However, as it is set in 1932, still much distinction is made between those who did and didn't serve in the war. Fourteen years after combat, doing one's duty was still a measure of manhood—or was it courage? "Not everyone was cut out to be a soldier," the countess remarks at the dinner table in a tart rebuke of one who didn't serve. "You didn't fight—thank God for Raymond [Lord Stockbridge]." The butler, we learn in another scathing rebuke from a fellow servant, was a conscientious objector. Lady Stockbridge wears a dog tag as a piece of necklace jewelry, but we never learn whose dog tag it is.

Gosford Park is the latest in a career of ensemble works by director Altman and is a delightfully fast-paced, funny movie. It was written by Julian Fellows (who won a richly deserved Academy Award for his work) from an idea credited to Altman and actor Bob Balaban, who plays Morris Weissman, a Hollywood producer of Charley Chan films. Weissman arrives with a host of others at the country estate of Sir William McCordle (Michael Gambon), who has made his money running factories. The host has also exploited his female workers, one of whom had a child by him that was given up for adoption. Not coincidently, that child has grown up to become Parks (Alan Bates), butler to the visiting Lord Stockbridge. The humorous film flows smoothly from character to character, with a gifted cast consisting most notably of Maggie Smith, as the bigoted and saucy Constance, Countess of Trentham, and Helen Mirren, as the sad, dedicated housekeeper, Mrs. Wilson. Jeremy Northam plays the famous actor and matinee idol Ivor Novello, who is also visiting. Northam has a beautiful voice, singing for the household as the servants listen rapturously in the hallways and on the stairs.

The pheasant hunting scene in *Gosford Park* is a tribute to the great bird hunting folly portrayed in Jean Renoir's classic 1938 *Rules of the Game*. It has dead pheasants falling like hailstones. Gentlemen shooters blazing away, fortunately into the air, as their gun bearers look on with respectful silence. Lord Stockbridge, a stiff old war veteran in tweeds, bags his bird. The allusion to *Rules of the Game* is significant because *Gosford Park* is about the crossing and blurring of boundaries that separate the classes. In the opening scene the Irish maid must walk and stand in the rain as the countess walks under an umbrella to enter the waiting automobile. And when, enroute, the countess cannot open her thermos, the maid must step out of the car in the rain, walk around, and stand in the rain to open it.

Gosford Park centers around the countess' new personal maid, Mary, played with soul by Kelly Macdonald. It is Mary who connects all the flowing parts together by pursuing her curiosity. Through her we see the blurring of class boundaries, that was partly caused by the war. When a maid speaks out of place at a dinner party, there is a stunned silence and everyone assumes she'll be sacked, as she is. The maid, by the way, was the current paramour of the owner of the estate.

A "gentleman" (Ryan Phillippe) poses as a servant and is scorned by the servants when they discover his pose. He visits Lady Sylvia (Kristen Scott Thomas) in the wee hours to help her with her sleep disturbance. At the downstairs dinner table of the servants, he asks who among the service staff had parents who were in service. Most raise their hands. They seem aware that the war has changed all that. They can all feel it. No class in England escaped the devastation caused by the war, and into the vacuum of the vacated lives trooped a new wave of residents.

The Legend of Bagger Vance, 2000

The sports star whose career was interrupted by the war is a parable for many men who are unfortunate enough to come of age at the time of war. Such men do not profit from the war, rather they are, at best, a ways behind the profiteers. For a baseball fan, Ted Williams was the most famous star to don a uniform of his country and fight in combat. Robert Redford produced and directed *The Legend of Bagger Vance* about a young golfer, ripe with potential, having won a prize in a Georgia tournament.

Rannulph Junuh was the pride of Savannah. Played by Matt Damon, Rannulph enlists in the army.

The film begins on a golf course. An old man, played by Jack Lemmon, narrates as he walks alone toting his golf cart. He has a heart attack and rolls on the ground. We are informed by his regretful but unalarmed voiceover that he's had these before. The film in flashback picks up the old man as a child, Hardy, played by J. Michael Moncrief, in his first role. Hardy is a golf lover and in 1928 in Savannah, he sees Rannulph Junuh return from the war, after having disappeared for ten years. We see the combat action, a trench assault with catastrophic casualties, and learn later that he was the sole survivor of his company.

The Legend of Bagger Vance is from a screenplay by Jeremy Leven, based on a novel by Steven Pressfield. Being ten years late returning after a war is a theme with an archetypal ring. We see, through Hardy's gaze, Rannulph returning to Savannah in hobo clothes. Rannulph's fiancée, Adele, has been waiting. Played by Chartize Theron with a comic grace, Adele has inherited a golf course and country club from her father, who committed suicide after the stock market crash. Adele wants to hold a golf tournament for the rich to attract business. She seductively invites the two reigning golf stars of the time. However, the citizens of Savannah, at a town meeting, want a local contestant, and the boy, Hardy, impudently makes a plug for Rannulph Junuh. The boy is then given the task to recruit the reclusive war veteran. Hardy finds Junuh in his abandoned estate playing poker with local men in trashy surroundings. The men are drinking whiskey and "killing the memory cells."

Reference to *The Odyssey* continues as Bagger Vance shows up one night as Rannulph is practicing his rusty golf swing. Will Smith plays Bagger in the Athena role with an enigmatic smile. Bagger appears mysteriously from the shadow of the field. He speaks wisely to Rannulph Junuh, the Zen-in-golf wisdom, and even seems to contribute magic in the flight of the ball, the way Athena assisted Odysseus invisibly.

In introducing the contestants in the celebration opening the golf tournament, Adele awkwardly mentions that Rannulph was decorated in the war after most of his company were … "defeated."

Significantly, Rannulph Junuh doesn't win the tournament, but he ties with the great golf stars for first place, and that is a victory. Bagger walks off before the final shots, and then mysteriously reappears on the golf course to complete the flashback, as the dying Hardy gets up and walks off with him.

Robert Redford has taken on in his career the task of beatifying sports. Baseball, horse breaking, and fly fishing, to name three. He emphasizes

Angelic Will Smith (left) as Bagger, the caddy, smirks knowingly at the war vet-eran golfer, Rannulph Junuh (Matt Damon), while between them, like Hermes, stands Hardy (J. Michael Moncrief), the boy whose initiative brings the two together in *The Legend of Bagger Vance* (DreamWorks Pictures, 2000). (Photo-graph by David James.)

the aesthetic appeal of the sports by trying to describe the spirit or soul. *The Legend of Bagger Vance* also gives us a formula for healing war veter-ans disabled by traumatic survivor's guilt. By Rannulph taking up a sport that he loved and was gifted at, he is able to recapture the remnants of his prewar identity.

Redford has created a film center outside Hollywood, but his dramas have all the studio system's romantic panache. The alcohol abuse is put aside. Bagger advises Junuh about "confronting his demons." The intru-sive combat memory in the woods on the final day of the tournament only briefly distracts from Junuh's concentration. Bagger says, "come out of the shadows, Junuh, it's time for you to choose."

For most war veterans with those kinds of traumas in their experiences, the choice is never the facile A *or* B, then *or* now. The decision is more in the mundane task to try to find a place to carry A, while pursuing B. The choice for Junuh to return to golf and give it his full concentration means that he has to relate to his "demons" in a different way. It is not that he does not have them anymore, but that he is giving other things his attention.

The Legend of Bagger Vance has a staging that gives it an old-fashioned look of a Hollywood musical. The scene of combat gives us an understanding of why Rannulph Junuh is crushed. "Fate plays funny tricks...." His recovery is a hero's return to light with the assistance of a spiritual sports adviser.

Part of the stagy quality of the film is the subject of period race relations, which is completely ignored. African-Americans are on the golf course, but they are not players and certainly not members of the country club. Bagger refers to Junuh as "sir" with the benign condescension of Jeeves to Wooster, and then Hardy refers to Bagger with the same respect. It seems as though racial prejudice is too complicated an issue for a story of divine guidance. This is not the same kind of candid look at racial stereotyping as John Ford's *The Sun Shines Bright*, but rather a soft-focused wash of the problem.

The War Veteran as Comic Figure

The war veteran as comic figure comes out of the working class and minority sub-cultures as satires of quirky behavior. This is not the glamorous figure, although certainly glamorous war veterans have their comical twists, as Mel Gibson's manic quirkiness in *Lethal Weapon* testifies. We are more likely to see the comical war veteran in cultures where many war veterans reside, all around, as co-workers, neighbors and friends.

Comedy, usually a good forum for social criticism, does not work well with war veterans, because it requires *exaggeration* of symptoms, a device which can be viewed as cruel, or at least insensitive to many of those touched by the problem. When the Korean War veteran Kirby in *Dead Presidents* beats a man with his prosthesis after it is pulled off in a fight, all the action is within character and a fine use of comic relief. Whereas in *Nothing but Trouble*, the mock war veteran's wounds and prostheses are part of the overall grotesque attempts at comedy. *The Big Lebowski* straddles the border of good taste when the war veteran flaunts his grief while spreading his friend's ashes.

The best of war veterans can find themselves in funny situations and sometimes their circumstances as war veterans add to the humor, such as Alex Cutter's drunken shenanigans in *Cutter's Way* and the return of Italian-American veterans to the town they liberated in *Machine to Kill Bad People*. And of course the old startle response can generate a laugh, except for those first seconds, when it is all very real. Bill Murray's war veteran in *Rushmore* exploits his sad social alienation for laughs when he walks out onto the diving board. For a moment he is Buster Keaton in Budweiser shorts.

Machine to Kill Bad People, 1948

Roberto Rossellini directed *La Macchina Ammazza Cattivi* (*Machine to Kill Bad People*). Released in 1948, the film is about humorous circumstances that arise when Italian-American war veterans return to a town where they fought the German occupation. The two Italian-speaking veterans, Joe and Bill, with their wives and suitcases, pause at a vista before they enter the hilly town in southern Italy. "This is where Joe and I landed with thousands of Americans to fight against Germans," Bill explains to their wives. "Remember how nervous you were, Corporal?" Joe retorts, "How about you, Sergeant? I had to shove you ashore." They are visiting on a business trip with hopes of buying a rocky peninsula where there is a ruined castle and town cemetery. They have an idea of moving the cemetery and turning the land into a resort. One says, in the spirit of American enterprise, and symbolizing the influence of U.S. values on the war-torn land, "Listen 50,000 Americans landed on this coast, and another 50,000 claim they did. Now add their wives...."

The veterans are not central to the plot, but rather a chorus that passes through the scenery, as they change houses. Bill's wife is a pretty woman whose dress and appearance generate voyeuristic curiosity among the town's males, young and old. The crux of the plot has to do with the devil appearing disguised as Saint Andreas, the patron of the town. The devil dupes the local photographer by giving his camera a power that kills the person whose photo he snaps for enlargement. The photographer sets out on a course to rid the town of evil people, but as the drama develops, the good turns evil and the evil people don't seem so bad after all.

Machine to Kill Bad People is a gem to watch for the view of authentic post-war Italy and the innovative directorial skills of Rossellini. It is essentially an ensemble piece in the style later developed by Robert Altman, capitalizing on the processions of faith, celebrating the patron saint, and describing the delicate balance of power in the town around which the comedy gambols. It begins like a folk tale, with the war veterans hitting the old man with their car; he appears suddenly and then disappears, so that they are not quite sure it happened. We next see the old man walking in a procession through the town with celebrants holding aloft a statue of Saint Andreas, looking disconcertingly similar to the ragged old man.

Up in Smoke, 1978

The motorcyclist, Strawberry, is a Vietnam War veteran who has a flashback as he drives Cheech Marin, as Pedro, in his antique, camouflaged Harley Davidson Electraglide with sidecar, in *Up in Smoke*. Strawberry (played by Tom Skerritt) is taking Pedro to score "some of that good Nam smoke." Strawberry starts shouting about paddies and claymores and driving his motorcycle erratically. Pedro, helpless in the sidecar, can only shout out with anguish, "You flipped out on one of your Vietnam trips, man?"

Finally Strawberry jumps off the motorcycle, leaving Pedro to continue on until the motorcycle, with sidecar and passenger, crashes into a building. *Up in Smoke* was released in 1978 and directed by Lou Adler as the vehicle for the stoned comedy of Cheech and Chong. The scene of Pedro haplessly locked into the course set by the hallucinating survivor of Vietnam is a stark enactment of the plight of many partners and mates who are tied to the war by their attachment to the veteran.

In the throes of a flashback, Vietnam War veteran Strawberry (Tom Skerritt) transports hapless Cheech Marin in his motorcycle sidecar in *Up in Smoke* (Paramount Pictures, 1978), a great sendup of the fates of many partners of war veterans.

O.C. and Stiggs, 1987

Robert Altman, a World War II veteran and a U.S. film director who is leaving a remarkable legacy of fine, unique films, directed *O.C. and Stiggs* as a bald satire of middle-class life in the air-conditioned sunbelt of Arizona, where life is re-created as an imitation of reality. One of his lesser-known films (released in 1987, but filmed in 1983) this would pass for a comedy about two cut-up teenagers, O.C., for Oliver Cromwell Oglevie (played by Daniel H. Jenkins) and Mark Stiggs (played by Neill Barry), both of whom are living with odd, pathetic families. They take on a local insurance salesman, Randall Schwab (Paul Dooley), who has all the style and class of a low class, racially bigoted used car salesman. Jane Curtain plays his alcoholic wife, Eleanor. It seems that the insurance company represented by Mr. Schwab has reneged on the claim of O.C.'s grandfather, who has become senile and should be receiving full-time nursing care. (Gramps is played with hilarious deadpan wit by Ray Walston.) The teenagers, in achieving their revenge, hatch a number of outrageous plots designed to wreak havoc on the Schwab household, who are in the course of marrying their daughter to a young man of Asian ancestry, much to Mr. Schwab's chagrin. Mr. Schwab is a blatant racist and part of the teenagers' revenge is to harass his household with a parade of winos who sport Schwab T-shirts, and an African band, King Sunny Ade and his African Beats.

The Vietnam War veteran angle is also played for laughs when the boys enlist two survivalist vets. Dennis Hopper gives a satirical portrayal of his role of the crazed photojournalist in *Apocalypse Now*. "Are you guys veterans?" asks O.C. "Does Ho Chi Minh eat Rice Crispies?" retorts the veteran. The boys buy a loaded automatic weapon from the veterans for a joke gift for the Schwab's stupid son and cajole him into shooting up the wedding party. The veteran cautions the boys when he gives them the weapon, believing it's going to be a wedding gift. "Tell her to try it out on a dog first to get the feel for it."

Later, for the movie's finale, the veterans come to the boys' rescue in a camouflage Huey helicopter, with, of course, Wagner's *Valkyries* on the soundtrack. They pick up Schwab in the helicopter and dump him off into his own pool, as if he were a Vietnamese prisoner being interrogated. "It's real," shouts the veteran. "Everything gets to be sooner or later."

This comedy of chaos, which has the seeds of some of Altman's great later movies, was not successful at the box office. It was based on a story from *National Lampoon Magazine* that was written by Tod Carroll and Ted Mann, with screenplay by Donald Cantrell and Ted Mann. It also features another fine film director, Melvin Van Peebles, as Wino Bob, and a flaming gay high school drama teacher, Garth, played by Louis Nye.

Compare this exaggerated parody of the survivalist war veteran to the more realistic portrayal of the so-called "bush vet" in *Distant Thunder* and we see the awkward ambivalence toward the war itself and the way it affected its veterans.

There is always something interesting in Robert Altman's films, not least in *O.C. and Stiggs*. In this film he manages to salvage scenes that seem outrageous or adolescent, and make them work. He turns the Fred Astaire–Ginger Rogers dance scene with O.C. and his newfound love, Florence (Tina Louise), at the Schwab wedding, into an incongruous magical moment. As a B-24 pilot, Altman, at age 19, flew 46 missions over Borneo and the Dutch East Indies (Harmetz, 2000, p. 15). He would have been the perfect director for Joseph Heller's *Catch-22*, surely capturing the same spirit of anti-authoritarian incongruity that he captured in *M*A*S*H* and to a lesser extent in *O.C. and Stiggs*.

Men at Work, 1990

Men at Work features Vietnam War veteran Louis (Keith David). Louis is the brother of the owner of a garbage disposal company. He wears an army field jacket with staff sergeant stripes and is assigned to escort two garbage men who are misbehaving in their job. The garbage men pick up a corpse, and Louis decides, because of a comical complication, to help them dispose of the body. This attempt at a comedy was directed by Emilio Estevez and stars Estevez and his brother, Charlie Sheen, playing the garbage men in a fictional California seacoast town, Los Playas. It was released in 1990. Estevez also wrote the original screenplay.

These young cut-ups-as-garbage men get involved in a murder of a local politician, who was trying to expose a local chemical polluter. Leslie Hope plays the curly-haired love interest. The combat veteran has a few funny lines, as when he cows two comic cops with a threat, "I thrive on misery. In the jungle, it's all misery." He has a funny flashback when he sees the kidnapped hapless pizza delivery boy as a VC in black pajamas and conical hat. "Back in Phu Bie, he'd a been killed."

Men at Work is a good example of a bad movie employing a Vietnam combat veteran who menaces for laughs. A certain poetic psychological truth, now called the Patty Hearst Syndrome, is when the pizza boy prisoner helps his captors defeat the henchmen of the polluter.

The flashback, by the way, like the startle response, is never funny for the war veteran unless in retrospect. Only the voyeur could laugh when a man acts out his terror.

Nothing but Trouble, 1991

Nothing but Trouble is an absurdist, gothic, slapstick farce, on the order of Beetlejuice. The film is directed by Dan Aykroyd, who stars as Alvin Volkmyer, an overage maniac in a grotesquerie of stage makeup, who lost his leg and his nose, and perhaps his mind, in the First World War. He happens to be the justice of the peace in an abandoned coalmine junk-yard wilderness, into which Chevy Chase and Demi Moore, two urbane travelers, stumble when they stray off the trafficked highway. Released in 1991, this farce features constant grotesqueries that actually save it from being totally lost as entertainment. Aykroyd, as the justice of Valkenva-nia, removes his prosthetic nose and leg before retiring. He appears on the judicial bench wearing his medals. John Candy plays his son, the deputy. Aykroyd plays another character that is an indescribable juvenile blob. The late rap star Tupac Shakur appears as another of the unlucky traffic stops. The story is by Peter Aykroyd, and the nepotism shows in this undisci-plined, but fortunately laughable farce.

The Big Lebowski, 1998

In The Big Lebowski, the comic Vietnam War veteran is the bowling partner and longtime friend, who happens to take issues a bit too far. The movie was directed by Joel Coen, who has been noted for giving his films an odd twist (Fargo, Blood Simple) and co-written by Joel and Ethan Coen. The brothers made their film into a sentimental mockery of a Raymond Chandler–type LA detective film, using an odd, comic pair: the aged hip-pie, Dude ("or Duder, or His Imperial Dudeness") played lovingly by Jeff Bridges, and the Vietnam War veteran, his bowling partner, Walter, played with gusto by John Goodman.

The plot revolves around Dude as a hapless victim of mistaken iden-tity. An attempt is made to extort a supposedly wealthy man, also named Lebowski, played with angry pomp by David Huddleston, and also a war veteran, wounded in the Korean war, and now disabled in a wheelchair. "Some Chinaman took them [his legs] away." The big Lebowski, however, is also something of a fake, in that he really doesn't have his own money, except for an allowance his daughter gives to him. The big Lebowski is an opinionated, intolerant, angry paraplegic in a wheelchair. He tries to make up for his immobility by officiousness. In an attempt to "out" the big Lebowski as a fake veteran, Walter lifts him out of his wheelchair and tries to make him walk, but finds that he is indeed paralyzed when he collapses in a heap. For Walter, it seems, intuition is often wrong.

Dude, whose name is also Lebowski, is mistakenly assaulted by dumb

Jeff Bridges (left) plays the other Lebowski, who prefers to be known as the "Dude," seated in the waiting hall of the Korean War veteran Lebowski, in the Coen brothers' *The Big Lebowski* (Gramercy Pictures, 1998). Seated beside Dude, is his friend, bowling partner, and Vietnam War veteran, Walter (John Goodman). (Photograph by Merrick Morton.)

thugs. The action then involves Dude trying to make sense out of the events. Dude is a man dedicated to not working, collecting welfare, and smoking dope. He barely remembers his college days of the sixties when he majored in occupying the administration building. His one gift of quality seems to be his dogged perseverance.

Goodman plays Walter Solchek, a well-meaning Vietnam War veteran who tries to do the right thing, but manages to make every situation worse with his hyper-aroused dramatics. He over-reacts in a bowling alley, pulling a semiautomatic pistol out of his bowling bag while arguing a technical point, chambering a round and taking aim, all to assert his position. Walter continues to wear his dog tags, as if they were medals. Everything seems to associate to Vietnam. When he scorns someone, he shouts, "I got buddies lying face down in the muck, so that you can enjoy your freedom!" One gets the feeling that he's subjected many persons to such scorn in a similar manner. When their mutual bowling partner, Donny, played by Steve Buscemi, dies of a heart attack, they take his ashes to the California beach in a coffee can. As Walter dumps the ashes, he talks about

Donny as a good boy, a surfer, and then segues into remembering all those young men who died at Kay Sahn, and Hill 364. As he casts the ashes into the wind, they blow back and besmirch the Dude.

In a tribute to *Saint Jack*, Ben Gazzara plays the pornographic film maker, Jackie Treehorn, who has cast the big Lubowski's fun-loving wife, Bunny (played by Tara Reid), in one of his movies, *LogJammin'*. John Turturro also has a bizarre character part as Jesus Quintana, a svelte bowling opponent who taunts the Dude's team with graphic gestures and gesticulations. "Don't mess with Jesus."

Voiceover narrative for *The Big Lebowski* is performed by Sam Elliott, intoning a mellow western yarn to the tune of "Tumbling Tumbleweeds." The movie is, in its inspiration by the Coen brothers, a tribute to LA style. Elliott renders a tribute to folks like the Dude, who contribute so much to culture in their own way. When Lebowski's daughter, Maud, played by the articulate, piquant Julianne Moore, a feminist graphic artist on a flying trapeze, wants to conceive by a man who will not contest paternity, she trysts with the "all-abiding Dude."

Rushmore, 1998

In *Rushmore* the war veteran is Harold Bloom, played by Bill Murray, who happens to be a self-made, wealthy manufacturer, who drinks and/or smokes continuously, and who accepts the oddball kid protagonist as if he were normal, and who yearns for an intimate relationship that seems unobtainable. Fifteen-year-old Max Fisher, played by Jason Schwartzman in a strong performance, is a kid who doesn't fit in, it seems even with himself. His father is a barber, but Max claims he's a neurosurgeon. His mother died when he was seven. Max is admitted to Rushmore Academy, an elite boys' school, on a scholarship after writing a play. There, however, he turns out for (and even creates) so many student activities, including clubs for beekeeping and fencing, that he performs poorly academically and is threatened with expulsion. Max meets a grade school teacher, Rosemary Cross, played by Olivia Williams, who has lost her exceptionally talented husband. Max becomes infatuated with her at the same time he makes friends with Mr. Bloom. Bloom, who endows the school, likes the kid's unique, daring, innovative audacity. Bloom, however, also falls in love with Rosemary.

Murray's Bloom has a perpetual scowl on his face. He fights with his snotty, oafish twin sons, who are on the wrestling team. We see him at a pool party, drinking, smoking, and sitting alone, across the pool from the party. He climbs up to the high diving board, showing off his Budweiser beer shorts and, cigarette in mouth, dramatically walks to the edge, pauses

Vietnam War veteran and school patron Mr. Bloom (Bill Murray) dances with Max's girlfriend, Margaret (Sarah Tanaka), as Max (Jason Schwartzman) and Miss Cross (Olivia Williams) look on in *Rushmore* (Touchstone Pictures, 1998). (Photograph by Van Redin.)

and jumps inauspiciously into the water, as if making some sort of social statement. When he makes a graduation address to the Rushmore student body, he uses analogies that are at best maladroit: "Take dead aim on the rich boys, get them in the crosshairs, and take them down."

Bloom attends one of Max's plays, which are well-received gangster dramas, and seems to be attracted to Max's grasp of reality. Shortly after they meet, Max asks Bloom if its true he was in Vietnam. Bloom confirms the fact. Max asks with his deadpan mimic of adult style, "Were you in the shit?" Bloom responds affirmatively.

Bloom, a married man, soon comes into competition with Max for the love of Rosemary. They even start to fight, resorting to a series of dirty tricks, Max setting off bees in Bloom's hotel room — the room rented after his wife sues for divorce, which she proceeded to do after Max snitched about the affair. Bloom retaliates and runs over Max's bicycle. Max cuts the brake line on Bloom's car. Bloom has Max arrested.

Finally they reach a truce and, in the funniest scene in the film, Max and Bloom are riding in a hospital elevator after visiting the beleaguered Rushmore school director, played with humor and suffering by Brian Cox, who has had a stroke. Bloom and Max are facing the camera standing in the elevator. Bloom feeds whiskey into a soft drink can. He has one cigarette in his mouth and, as they talk about Rosemary, Bloom lights a second cigarette, saying that Rosemary is "too fucked up." And as he exits the elevator with two lit cigarettes between his lips, Max asks if he's all right. Bloom pauses and then admits that maybe he's a little lonely.

Directed by Wes Anderson and released in 1998, *Rushmore* seems to be developing a cult following. Anderson keeps a flat, deadpan humor working, which seems to balance Max's audacity. *Rushmore* was written by Anderson and Owen Wilson.

In the dramatic finale of the film, Max presents a play about the Vietnam War that manages to incorporate strings of clichés and jargon generated in the war. The play has a corny outcome of the U.S. hero, played by Max, himself, and the VC hero, played by Margaret Yang (who was in turn played by Sara Tanaka), in a Mexican standoff, now made cliché-famous by Quentin Tarantino. The GI says to the VC, will you marry me? Just earlier Rosemary had asked Bloom if he liked the play. Yes, he said, "Let's hope it has a happy ending."

There is a certain truth in Bill Murray's Bloom as Vietnam War veteran. He is clearly not enjoying his life. There is a comic meanness to him. When he walks through a school playground, where small kids are playing basketball, he spontaneously leaps blocking a little kid's shot. Rosemary thought that he hated himself. Max replied, in his deadpan, cliché-ridden truth, "War does funny things to a man."

Meet the Parents, 2000

Meet the Parents was released in 2000 and features Robert De Niro as the implied Vietnam War veteran, a former POW, who has retired from the CIA. This romantic comedy stars Ben Stiller as Greg Focker, who wants to propose to his girlfriend Pam, played by Teri Polo.

Pam invites Greg to visit her parents, implying that it is wise to ask her father about the marriage first. Her sister, Debbie, played by Nicole De Huff, is going to get married, which is the occasion for their visit. What is interesting about this little collection of jokes directed by Jay Roach and written by Greg Glienna and Mary Ruth Clark, is the veteran motif, described frequently in the therapy office, of the overprotective father, who clings so closely to his daughter that he drives off her suitors. De Niro's Jack Byrnes is a regimented man who uses his intelligence contacts to gather information, and who indulges his paranoid need for control by

Robert De Niro (second from left) plays Jack, the overprotective war veteran father of Pam (Teri Polo) (right), who has brought home her hapless beau, Greg Focker (Ben Stiller) (second from right), in the light comedy *Meet the Parents* (Universal Pictures, 2000). Blythe Danner (left) plays Dina, Jack's wife. (Photograph by Phil Caruso.)

setting up hidden video cameras. He fears the worst in all strangers, especially those who are interested in his daughter. This comedy is uncomfortably funny at times as it exploits the awkwardness of a domestic *folie à famille.*

The Comic Sidekick

The war veteran comic sidekick to the war veteran straight man is usually a figure of relief in a more serious movie. William Bendix performed that role as wisecracking veteran, appropriately named Buzz. He is the tough, brain-injured, racially biased sidekick to Alan Ladd in *Blue Dahlia,* released in 1946. He is quick to anger and quip and loyal to his wartime buddy. A similar comic character is Harvey, played by Reb Brown, in *Distant Thunder,* which was released in 1988. Harvey, in his drunken state, sings the song that mocks the comparison of patriotic romanticism and the bloody reality of combat. An even more vicious comic sidekick is the character Mouse (played by Don Cheadle) in *Devil in a Blue Dress*. Philbert Bono is a comic mystic in *Powwow Highway*, playing against the wired style of his partner, Sonny Red Bow.

These war veteran "fools," have an outrageous personality of a jester who mocks normality, and at the same time have a rough, serious virility. Such figures are also displayed by the earthy knight's squire, Jöns (Gunnar Björnstrand), in *The Seventh Seal*, and the fool Wamba in *Ivanhoe*, who speaks the truth in witty rhymes. An earthy variation of the theme is Stepin Fetchit's Jeff, the servant to the Confederate war veteran, Judge Priest, in *The Sun Shines Bright*. An unusual and gifted variation of this theme is in Bill Murray's Mr. Bloom, who plays the war veteran's unhappiness *against* the comic plot in *Rushmore*. (For an excellent discussion of the role of the fool, see Willeford, 1969.)

The War Veteran and Aging

The Grim Reaper is a character brilliantly portrayed by Bengt Ekerot in Bergman's *The Seventh Seal*. He stalks every veteran in various forms, usually subtly and invisibly, sometimes dogging, snarling and biting, as in *Akira Kurosawa's Dreams*, from the day he leaves the battlefield. Of course we are all subject to pay Death his due, but the veteran of combat and multiple traumas, knows Death intimately, and one could say, prematurely. Death's cold whisper is beside one when bullets fly. Stress-related diseases follow from multiple exposure to psychological traumas, not the least of which are diabetes, spastic colon, and esophageal cancer from gastrointestinal reflux. Habits that form from coping with symptoms of long-term survival (e.g., over-work, risky business, substance abuse, social isolation) can of themselves reduce one's chances of a long life. Only a percentage of the genetically well-endowed war veterans continue to senescence. Four good films capture the problem of the aging war veteran, with deteriorating physical health.

The Presidio, 1988

Filmed on location on the choicest piece of real estate in San Francisco, *The Presidio* is a murder mystery that features an army lieutenant colonel provost marshal, Alan Caldwell, a Vietnam War airborne veteran, and his buddy, a recently retired Medal of Honor winner, Ross McClure, played by Jack Warden, who received the highest wartime medal for, among other things, saving the provost's (then infantry lieutenant's) life. The plot deals with a diamond smuggling scheme that had its genesis in Vietnam

War era black market. Sean Connery plays the crusty provost marshal who investigates the murder of a female MP, Patty Jean, who was shot during a break-in at the officer's club. A jurisdictional dispute arises when a young Seattle police detective, Jay Austin, played by Mark Harmon, participates in the investigation. The detective was once an MP who was disciplined by the provost and quit the army. The suspect in the murder, a colonel, was also in the Vietnam War and involved in getting the police detective disciplined as an MP. Primary in the plot is the love relationship between Donna, the provost's spunky daughter played by Meg Ryan, and the police detective. She wants to defy her father's iron rule, but ends up loving the guy.

The Presidio was directed and photographed by Peter Hyams. The sets are rich in San Francisco's best fog-bound scenery. The retired top sergeant McClure is drawn into the murder investigation tainted by his association with the Vietnam War era black market. He declares that his Medal of Honor was easier to win than to wear, and is associated with the guilt of his involvement with the smuggling ring. Death redeems him, however.

The Vietnam War takes on many symbols. The black market and the CIA's involvement in smuggling during that era are metaphors that carry the sense of contamination, like Agent Orange, as if the war revealed the dark side of the U.S. collective psyche. In this film, written by Larry Ferguson, the man behind the diamond smuggling, Peal (Mark Blum), was a CIA "province advisor" during the Vietnam War, and a man totally unredeemed. When Peal is finally killed, Jay Austin, the police detective, acknowledges the Vietnam War connection and announces, "the war's been over a long time."

Alan's relationship with his daughter is the source of his redemption. She is able to transcend the rule-bound standards that govern his career. Alan accounts for his Scottish accent by explaining that he immigrated to the U.S. as a child, and has felt a strong sense of love and duty toward the country. The film seems to be saying that rules and hierarchy set up a structure that allowed the shadow to emerge, and prevented its elimination. The provost's daughter's love for the police detective, who rebelled against army authority in the name of righteousness, leads her father finally to allow his feelings to surface.

An important sidebar to the story is the complicating fact that Donna's mother, Alan's late wife, committed suicide when Donna was two. She blames her father's cold style, developed after the Vietnam War, for her mother's death, and the cold eyes of Sean Connery's Alan back her up.

The film ends with Alan at the funeral of his friend, McClure. He tells

Vietnam War veteran, now Presidio provost marshal, Army Lieut. Col. Alan Caldwell (Sean Connery) aims his revolver at the assailants in *The Presidio* (Paramount Pictures, 1988). (Photograph by Ralph Nelson, Jr.)

his daughter that he's "going to make things right." He salutes his rescuer in his coffin, saying, "it was his luck to be a hero in a war nobody liked."

Gods and Monsters, 1998

Gods and Monsters is a war veteran story about a man who served in the "Great War" on the British side. The young officer, James Whale, learned the movie directors' trade while a prisoner of war, putting on stage productions for his fellow prisoners and their German guards. James Whale immigrated to the United States after some stage work in England following the war. He had a successful career as a movie director in Hollywood, working for several studios. His biggest successes were monster movies, *Frankenstein*, and *Bride of Frankenstein*, although he made a comfortable retirement nest egg with movies like *Hell's Angels* (a World War I flying movie), *Waterloo Bridge*, *The Invisible Man*, *The Man in the Iron Mask*, and *Show Boat* (Curtis, 1998).

His major failure was the World War I follow-up to Erich Maria Remarque's best seller *All Quiet on the Western Front*. *The Road Back* was Remarque's sequel about the German soldier's return and readjustment after the war. Unfortunately Whale made the film during the 1930s period of the Great Depression when European sales determined the financial success of a film, and Hitler's Germany was on the rise. Whale's version of *The Road Back* was intercepted before release and not only re-edited, but also partly re-shot by other directors. It was a disaster when released and no copy has survived to video.

Gods and Monsters, released in 1998, is directed by Bill Condon from his adaptation of the novel *Father of Frankenstein*, by Christopher Bram, which is a fictional depiction of the last days of James Whale. The story begins with Whale after he has had a stroke and has lost some of his ability to inhibit memory. He is sitting in the poolside studio of his Hollywood home pretending to paint, while he watches the gardener, a young ex-marine named Clay Boon, played with bashful bravado by Brendan Fraser.

Ian McKellen gives a masterful performance as the elegant James Whale in his last days. Whale, in fact, was a man who maintained a frankly homosexual public life. Whale, in the story, persuades Clay to pose for him while he pretends to sketch, an ability his stroke has deprived him of.

His attachment to the gardener takes on the odd twist of fantasy, turning the hunk into a Frankenstein monster, who will kill him. It seems that the stroke has also cost Whale the ability to inhibit wartime traumatic memories. One memory in particular concerns the death of a young officer, new to the trenches, whom Whale had taken a fancy to. The young officer was killed and lay hung up in the wire for days, visible from the trenches, before Whale's company was relieved.

James Whale died of drowning in his own pool. The question raised in the book and the movie is the possibility that he committed suicide. The movie does a cute twist, flashing forward as the credits are about to roll to Brendan Fraser's Boon with his own child stomping though a puddle pretending to be a monster.

The tale of Dr. Frankenstein's monster was first penned by Mary Shelley as a gothic novel written during a summer idyll contest among friends to see who could write the best ghost story. Others in the contest of note were poets Percy Shelley (Mary's husband) and Lord Byron (Mellor, 1989). Not coincidentally, the summer weather was unusually bleak and stormy, influenced by a volcanic eruption on the other side of the world the year previously. Days turned dark and cold, lightning flashed and thunderclouds roiled on the Swiss landscape. Mary Shelley was a survivor of the childhood traumatic loss of her mother, who died in childbirth, and then of her nursemaid and nanny, who deserted her abruptly as a toddler. The monster created by Dr. Frankenstein is the loneliest creature on earth. He has no mate. His creator rejects him in horror. He is rejected by all civilization, save a blind man and a little girl. He yearns like a clumsy voyeur for a life of intimacy he cannot have. Frankenstein's monster is an archetypal symbol, the survivor of technological malpractice, created from traumatized psyches of his author and his film director.

Whale, who as a young man did all he honorably could to avoid being drafted into the British army, who was the survivor of the trenches as an infantry junior officer, who was captured on a patrol, who was held as a POW in Germany, directed the movie *Frankenstein* quickly, with tongue in cheek, and brought it in on budget for his studio. The creature *he* created *became* Frankenstein, and *his* creature's rubber masks walk around every Halloween trick-or-treating, an icon oddity of rejection.

Dementia on war veterans occasionally presents the problem of disinhibition of war-related memories. This is when granddad patrols the nursing home in a dissociated state, attacks the Asian-American nurse who has come with his morning medication, or agonizes over a bad decision he made in a crisis 60 years previously.

Lawn Dogs, 1999

Lawn Dogs is an odd, offbeat film that deals with the posttraumatic aspects of major medical surgery on a child and the bonding between outcasts. Misha Barton plays ten-year-old Devon, who has just moved with her family into a gated community. *Lawn Dogs* was filmed in Kentucky. The hired gardeners are seen in the introduction riding their machines clipping lawns. Devon's ambitious parents, who want her to fit in, are played unsympathetically by Christopher McDonald and Kathleen Quinlan. Devon has a sense of spooky maturity, with a taste for the macabre. She has had major heart surgeries. When sent out by her parents to sell scout cookies, Devon strays away from the community, reciting in voice-over a fairy tale of a girl running from a witch.

Sam Rockwell plays Trent, a creature of nature, one of the community's lawn dogs. He's a bit of a trickster. He stops his pickup truck in the middle of a rural bridge, takes off his clothes and jumps in the river as the traffic is stopped on both sides and on-lookers are aghast. Devon, wandering away from the gated community, enters a clearing where Trent has his travel trailer. Her imagination is titillated by what she sees — a kind of an unplanned community of trash made meaningful. Doghouse, but no dog. Devon peers into the entrance of the empty doghouse as though it were a cave. The fantasy she narrates is of "Baba Yaga" chasing a girl.

At home at night, her father lectures her about being popular. "A popular girl is never bored or boring." He wants her to "keep the old Devon secret." That night she sneaks out of her second floor window, casts off her nightgown and howls until she is answered by coyotes.

Devon finally connects with Trent, who tries to run her off. She tells him about her heart surgery and he tells her how he was shot in the gut. They hit it off, as Devon is further alienated from her parents and community and Trent, a young adult, is taunted and debased by age-peers of the gated crowd.

Devon has a macabre fascination. When Trent cuts his finger, she sucks the blood. She tells him, as he jerks his finger away, how she is not afraid of blood, because "every time they open me up I lost a bathtub full." When Devon plays checkers with her doll, she dismembers it for losing. Director John Duigan plays with macabre details, mocking the conventional people in the gated community and finally, it seems, mocking authority, in general, and government.

When Trent's commercial lawn mower is sabotaged, he goes to visit his father, taking Devon with him. Trent's father (played by Tom Aldredge) is dying of lung disease. Trent has been sending his parents money and he informs them that he can't afford to help them for a while. His wizened father takes out a collection of American flags that he brought back from Korea. He tells them how the men he was with slept with flags, and when they died, he took them. The story conveys the uncomfortable feeling that it was no more appropriate to take their flags than to take their jewelry. Trent refuses to accept the flag collection. Instead he grows angry and exasperated with his father and walks out shouting, "When are you going to die? I don't want them. Send them to whatever bastard sends you your pension."

Trent's father gives his own soft flag to Devon after rubbing it against his cheek. When they are driving away, Trent explains to Devon that the "Korean War didn't fuck up my old man." He explains that his father got sick from bacteria from cans of cheese in their rations. The government

Trent (Sam Rockwell) holds the arm of Devon (Misha Barton) as they stand on top of Trent's pickup truck. Trent is a "Lawn Dog," a gardener, in *Lawn Dogs* (Strand Releasing, 1998).

denies it. His father had one lung removed and now the other is going. Trent cruelly mimics his dad struggling to breathe. Devon throws the flag out the window.

Lawn Dogs was written by Naomie Wallace and released in 1999. The plot twists our values. It depicts the son's ingratitude and frustration at the dying war veteran, and then, further twists in the finale when Devon's father becomes outraged at the mistaken idea that Trent has sexually molested her. (She confesses to her parents that he touched her scar and she touched his.) Her parents find this intimacy horrifying. Her father and the men of the gated community attack Trent, and the outraged but mistaken father righteously beats Trent repeatedly with a two-by-four, and then urges another to continue the beating. Devon shoots one of the attackers and threatens to shoot her dad, while urging Trent to get away.

Contributing to the oddity of *Lawn Dogs* is the territory, a kind of borderland between fantasy and traumatic reality. All the magic seems to come from the face of Misha Barton's Devon. She has earlier transformed a tree in front of Trent's trailer by hanging red ribbons from it, and in the final scene she has her father at gunpoint place her in the tree as the film fades and loses its color, turning chiaroscuro.

There is something ignoble about the war veteran in *Lawn Dogs*. He did his duty all right, but at the same time, he had the victim's ignominy of dying slowly from a wasting illness, suffering beyond the tolerance of even his own son. At the same time the son's immaturity is brought out. The strong implication is that the war veteran has been wasting for years, and Trent's working class "trash" status derives from his father's condition. The "Baba Yaga" that Devon envisions is an overbearing authority that is snobbish, persecutory, class-conscious, and corrupt.

Straight Story, 1999

In *Straight Story* Richard Farnsworth plays Alvin Straight in a reenactment of his ride across Iowa on a 1966 riding lawnmower. He is going to see his brother, Lyle, who's had a stroke. Alvin doesn't own a car and doesn't have a driver's license, but he can operate the lawn mower without a license. Sissy Spacek plays his daughter, who isn't entirely there. She paints birdhouses and gives them away. Sissy Spacek is an acting gem in the part.

About five weeks into his trip across Iowa, Alvin's mower breaks a drive chain and careens out of control down a hill, crashing into a field, coincidentally where a barn is burning as an exercise for the local fire brigade. He is aided by a local John Deere repairman. While telling his story, Alvin reveals that he "fought in the trenches" in World War II. While

In the scene above, the late Richard Farnsworth, in his last motion picture, plays the Second World War veteran Alvin Straight, in *The Straight Story* (Disney Enterprises, 1999). Seated beside Alvin in this scene is his daughter, Rose (Sissy Spacek). Alvin will shortly make a trip across the state on his riding lawn mower. *Below:* Alvin did not have a driver's license and so the only way he figured he could visit his brother, Lyle, before he died, was to drive for six weeks on his '66 John Deere. *The Straight Story* (Disney Enterprises, 1999).

his mower is being fixed, Alvin is invited out by another old-timer to have a beer. Alvin says that he doesn't drink liquor anymore, but will go anyway for a change of scenery. In the next scene they are sitting at the bar facing the camera. Alvin explains that he picked up a taste for liquor in France. "I was mean. I wasn't worth a stick of stove wood," he said, until a preacher straightened him out by telling him that he was drinking, because he "seen all them things here from over there." He goes on to say that he can see combat experience in a man right away. His friend says "yep" and gulps his beer, and then goes on to tell his story about how, during the Battle of the Bulge, his company mess tent was bombed by "a stray

Fokker that came out of the trees and dropped one on my buddies and banked away," just after he had left the tent.

Alvin reflects and replies, "One thing I can't shake loose: all my buddies faces I see are still young. Not just buddies, Germans, too. The more years I have, the more they've lost." Then he goes on to tell a story that we feel he's really telling for the first time. "I was a sniper. I'd look for officers, radiomen. We had a scout, name of Cox. Polish boy from Milwaukee. Recon. Little fella. We took fire. There was movement in the woods. I took my position and fired at the movement. We found Cox, head shot. He'd been working his way back. Everyone thought a German sniper had shot him. Everyone but me." (My paraphrase of the dialog.)

Straight Story features the incongruous combination of a G-rated Walt Disney Production being directed by David Lynch, director of such torrid movies as *Blue Velvet* and *Wild at Heart*. The above-mentioned veterans' scene is a fine example of the director's achievement of profound simplicity. Lynch managed to retain his odd twist, but with a subtle, comically quirky Midwestern humor. An odd pair of identical twins who repair Alvin's lawn mower have to be bargained with. When Alvin crashes his lawnmower, the ongoing barn fire-department exercise proceeds against a backdrop of midwestern plains and sky. And there is a darkly comical scene out of a Godard scrapbook, when the "Deerlady" drives by Alvin and hits a deer on the road. She gets out of her car as Alvin stops his rig. She screams and stalks around the dead deer frantically gesturing, "this is the fifteenth deer I've killed on this road, and I have to drive this road every day to get to work!" In the next scene we see the adaptable Alvin with deer antlers on his trailer and cooking a large piece of meet over his campfire.

Farnsworth's Alvin Straight is a lesson in adaptation, which in the end is the final contest that separates successful versus unsuccessful in the life of a war veteran. It was only after his death in October, 2000, that we learned of his pain and discomfort, which he carried so stoically during the filming, turning pain, with his acting skills, into heroic depth.

Film Noir and the Returning War Veteran

Noir was created by the conditions during the Great Depression and influenced the return of the Second World War veteran to the U.S. Foster Hirsch writes that "full-fledged *noir* dramas in the immediate postwar period [were presented] as a sign of contemporary disillusionment and malaise" (1981, p. 17).

The plots of 20 *film noir* films featured the war veteran as a contemporary figure (Selby, 1984), recently discharged and ubiquitous in uniform and civilian clothes. In these films the war veteran was as likely to be the protagonist as the villain or the victim. References to the war were everywhere with cynicism and danger in the streets. Fatalism is characteristic of the genre. *Crossfire, Cornered, The Blue Dahlia,* and *The Fallen Sparrow* are four U.S. *noir* films with war veterans featured prominently.

Technically the *noir* period lasted for only a few years after the second world war. Otherwise more recent films, like Roman Polanski's *Chinatown, Taxi Driver,* and *Red Rock West,* would easily fit the *noir* theme.

The Fallen Sparrow, 1943

"In a world at war, many sparrows must fall," is the opening quotation of *The Fallen Sparrow.* John Garfield plays Kit, a volunteer who fought in Spain during the Spanish civil war. Kit was captured, held prisoner and tortured by the Fascists. He was able to escape with the help of a friend and has been recuperating on a ranch in a Western state. He is released from treatment only to learn that his friend has died in a fall amid suspicious circumstances. Garfield plays Kit as a tough guy who has been significantly weakened by torture. He described to another friend how he faired in the prison, the torture routine that involved his torturer dragging one foot as he came to take him from his dark cell. He tells his friend, "I've licked it. I can talk about it," although it is obvious that he is disturbed by his own tale. Kit periodically hallucinates the sound of the foot dragging when he is under stress or in the dark.

Maureen O'Hara plays Toni Dunn, a high society beauty in ball gowns and sculpted hair, who is involved with refugees. She is a *noir* duplicitous woman who is finally revealed as allied with the Nazis. Kit learns that, while he is hunting for the killer of his friend, he is being hunted by others who still want what he knows, which is the location of the "Standard," the flag of his cause.

The Fallen Sparrow was released in 1943. It was directed by Richard Wallace from a screenplay by Warren Duff, based on a novel by Dorothy Hughes. The movie's plot keeps it in the arid pose of high New York City society and lacks soul, even when Garfield sweats with fear.

The fears generated in the war veteran by chance associations to the trauma are major, and often unconscious, sources of stress. Kit's cringing fear when he hears the dragging foot is evidence of classical conditioning: dragging foot = torture. The power of the association comes from the repetition of the torture as well as the pain. One of the chief benefits in psychotherapy for wartime trauma is the identification of those chance associations, so that the veteran can at least understand why the anxiety is occurring. When there are many traumas and many associations, a condition of complex trauma exists (Herman, 1997).

The Blue Dahlia, 1945

One of the great uncertainties for war veterans is how they will be received by their spouses or girlfriends when they return. In *The Blue Dahlia,* Alan Ladd plays Johnny Morrison, who returns home to find his wife, Helen, played by Doris Dowling, having a big party. It seems she's barely read his letters. Drunkenly, she reveals that she caused the death of their son, Dickie. Johnny takes a semiautomatic pistol out of his suitcase and ominously sticks it in his pocket. Before he leaves he turns, takes it out, but only throws it onto her couch.

When he first arrives, Johnny meets Eddie Harwood (Howard DaSilva), who owns a club called the Blue Dahlia and sends big blue dahlias to his friends. (We are told they are blue, the film is black and white and there's no other clue to the hue.) Harwood is sweet on Mrs. Morrison.

Johnny was a pilot who flew Liberators for the navy. Two of his crew return with him: Buzz, played by William Bendix, and George, played by Hugh Beaumont. George is an attorney and cautious, but Buzz is pugnacious, hates cops, and has shrapnel in his head, near his right ear. Music drives him crazy. He calls jazz "monkey music." He also has lapses in memory that seem to be associated with loud music.

The Blue Dahlia was released in 1945, directed by George Marshal and written by Raymond Chandler. Chandler's signature line comes when the house dick, Leo (Don Costello), refers to Johnny's wife: "Mrs. Morrison is poison. All women are poison sooner or later."

Johnny is a suspect in the murder of his wife. It was his gun that killed her and he was seen by the house dick arguing loudly with his wife. On the run, he is picked up by Joyce Harwood, played by Veronica Lake. She is a *noir* woman who always seems to be convincingly sincere, even when she is duplicitous. Joyce and Johnny hit it off, intuiting each other's problems. Mr. and Mrs. Harwood are separated at her behest. Johnny's accused of killing his wife and Joyce seems to sense his dilemma, or does she already know who he is?

Although under pursuit, Johnny is never seen lacking in confidence. He fights hard and in the end the killer is revealed to be the blackmailing house dick. Johnny's wartime buddies stick by him. People in military uniform are everywhere in the public scenes.

Cornered, 1945

Film noir is dominated by shadows, small spaces, like bleak hotel rooms and dark, impersonal offices. In *Cornered*, Dick Powell plays Laurence Gerard, a Canadian who volunteered to serve with the RAF, was shot down and captured, but escaped with the help of the French underground. He was briefly married to one of the underground cadre before she and her comrades were killed. Powell, first seen processing out of the service after a hospital stay, plays Gerard as a tough, terse man bent on revenge, pursuing the leader of the Nazi killers, Marcel Jarnac. The white scar on Gerard's left temple has the striking quality of the *Bride of Frankenstein*. As he says at one point, "I don't like talk, I'm in a hurry."

Cornered was directed by Edward Dmytryk and released in 1945. Screenplay was by John Paxton from a story adapted by John Wexley. Powell gives his character the right kind of reckless determination that reflects compulsion. He is clearly willing to suffer for his personal cause. He follows Jarnac's trail to Buenos Aires. The sets, however, could well be anywhere. People speak American English and say *senor*.

Dick Powell, speaking to Mme. Jarnac (Micheline Cheirel), plays Lawrence Gerard, a Canadian former POW searching for the Nazi who was responsible for his wife's death in *Cornered* (RKO, 1945).

Walter Slezak plays Senor Inza, a self-appointed guide who double-crosses everyone. Micheline Cheirel plays a vulnerably beautiful woman who poses under various names, a perfect *noir* character with mixed motivation. At one point she tries to lure Gerard away from his cause. "Don't go, I could make you forget," she says. He replies, "Not for long and not enough."

Cornered has a theme that repeats periodically in cinema, which reflects the fear that fascism is a virulent pest that cannot be totally eliminated, and, like Dracula, will arise again to cause evil. The word Jewish is never mentioned in the film, but Gerard finds himself allied with a group that is actively hunting down Nazis who fled Germany. Part of the tight suspense of the film is the ambiguity of the villain, Jarnac, who is almost faceless, and his pursuers, who seem like shape-changers themselves.

Crossfire, 1947

Dark shadows of men fighting is the first scene after the credits in *Crossfire*. Released in 1947 and directed by Edward Dmytryk, *Crossfire* is a murder mystery with Robert Young as the calm, tough, pipe smoking police detective Captain Finley. The murder victim, it turns out, was a medically discharged veteran of the invasion of Okinawa. He is killed by another war veteran, named Montgomery, played by Robert Ryan, in an act of racial hatred. Montgomery reports, posing as a bystander, that another war veteran was in the murdered man's apartment and left drunk or sick. Montgomery is unable to conceal his contempt for the murder victim for being a civilian of Jewish descent. Robert Mitchum plays yet another veteran, Sergeant Keeley, a tough combat veteran who is dragged away from his poker game by the news of the murder. Montgomery blames Mitchel, played by George Cooper, who left the apartment sick and drunk, wandered and stumbled into a bar where he struck up a relationship with a working girl named Ginny, from Virginia. Ginny is played as a gem with a hard polish by Gloria Grahame. Mitchel finally tells Sgt. Keeley how the murdered man was trying to give him some readjustment advice.

Robert Mitchum gives his character a toughness of being that requires no violence to come out of him. Sgt. Keeley finds Mitchel, who was an aspiring artist before the war, and hides him in a movie theater. They talk, sorting out what happened as they sit beside the glowing movie projector in the theater balcony. Later Mitchel's wife goes to the theater to find him. He says he does not feel worthy of her love. "Guy like me starts hating myself after the war. I can't be an artist again."

Robert Young as the calm police captain gives us a preview of his later television father icon, when he delivers a monologue about the perils of racial hatred. He is trying to convince Leroy, the young hay-haired veteran from Tennessee, to help them trap Montgomery and prove he is the killer. Captain Finley tells the story of his grandfather, who was murdered because he was an Irish-Catholic immigrant. Leroy, played by William Phipps, conspires to lie and lure Montgomery to the scene of his murder. Cornered, Montgomery runs away, until the Captain calmly, albeit improbably, shoots him with his revolver from a second floor window. He comments wryly when he hears Montgomery is dead: "He was dead for a long time, but just didn't know it."

In the last scene we see Keeley address Leroy. "Well, how about a cup of coffee, soldier?" They walk off together up the dark, wet street.

An interesting character in *Crossfire* is the murdered man. When he is talking to Mitchel about the veteran's doubts, Samuels, played with enigmatic feeling by Sam Levene, speaks intimately as they sit at the bar in front of a bowl of peanuts. "We've been focusing on the win-the-war peanut. We don't know what to fight. We have a whole lot of hate with no one to hate. Maybe we'll stop hating and start liking." Given the time from conception to production, the fear of the war veterans' anger presented in *Crossfire* could well reflect the concern in the public mind as the war came to its conclusion.

The *film noir* sentiment is summed up by a line from Ginny's erstwhile dishonorably discharged ex-husband who said, "We made a lot of plans, but they all fell through."

Dead Reckoning, 1947

Duty is sometimes regarded as loyalty to the dead. In John Cromwell's 1947 film *Dead Reckoning*, Humphrey Bogart plays an army airborne captain, Rip Murdock, after World War II has ended, accompanying one of his men, Johnny Drake, on a train to Washington, D.C. Johnny is to receive the Congressional Medal of Honor. But Johnny disappears in Gulf City and Murdock finally finds him dead, murdered, and sets out to find the murderer. This is a classic *film noir* effort, also starring Lizabeth Scott as Jasmine, whom Rip calls Dusty. There is a disturbed erotic undertone of misogyny ("All women are the same with their faces washed." "Get back in my pocket." "Women should spend all their time just being beautiful." "Women are made to be loved." "I don't trust anybody, especially women"), cynicism ("Love never comes the way you want it." "It's a loose, sick world, Rip"), and toughness ("I'm the brass knucks in the teeth kind of guy"). This wry, crisp dialog is by the team of Oliver H.P. Garrett and Steve Fisher, from an adaptation by Allen Rivkin, from a story by Gerald Adams and Sidney Biddell.

Macao, 1952

Robert Mitchum plays Nick, a man of declining fortune who gets mistaken for a cop. Before he ever reaches Macao he gets his pocket picked by a wise dame, who greets him on the boat deck with a catchy phrase, "One side, Clyde." Jane Russell plays Julia Benton who is traveling between engagements, and is capable of picking any man's pocket. When she pick's Nick's pocket, she takes his money and throws his passport overboard. William Bendix plays the real cop who is posing as a salesman, Lawrence Trumble.

Macao is a thriller about tough guys and dames, set in a borderland city where cultures mix and blur, "the crossroads of the east," where anything goes and everything has a price. We are told in the opening that a New York cop has been murdered. The chief suspect is an owner of a Macao gambling casino, the "Two Week Reward."

Mitchum plays Nick Cochran as a guy who is looking for a break and becomes the victim of mistaken identity. *Macao* was directed by Joseph von Sternberg, with help from Nicholas Raye. It was released in 1952. Russell has a mobile face, expressive of enjoyment, but her singing lacks appeal. As she says, "I was never considered a brain." Mitchum is the vet who is "not partial to the law." We learn from the Macao police lieutenant Sabastian (Thomas Gomez) that Nick was a lieutenant for three years, four months, in the army signal corps, but there is no mention of his having been in combat.

Screenplay was by Bernard Schoenfeld and Stanley Rubin, from a story by Bob Williams. *Macao* lacks intimacy and suffers from flat direction, but it has style, nonetheless.

CHAPTER 5

The War Veteran in Action

A prominent subcategory of the war veteran action theme is the war veteran exploitation film, which develops, amplifies, and distorts inherent sentiments of war veterans. Sentiments that are common in war veterans, certainly not in all or even most, are the wish to return to combat, the sense of unfinished business, survivor guilt, wanting to go back and free POWs, compulsion to repeat traumatic experiences, and, most commonly, social alienation. Unfortunately for war veterans with PTSD, the compulsion to repeat, stimulated by the unfinished business of combat, leads the veteran to fight in various, repetitive ways, depending on his style; bar-fighting, jousting with institutions, especially the VA, disputes with neighbors and family, and entering into emergency-oriented employment by joining the ranks of police, fire departments and emergency medical units.

Any kind of fight, after combat, can take on extra meaning. It is not necessarily that the war veteran is more combative than the average Joe—in fact he may actually be *less* so—but it is rather that when he is angered and takes action, if only in his mind, *his* associations are to vivid combat memories replete with physiological responses. To say this does not belie the validity of each of the immediate situations, but rather states that what causes the emotion and the emotion itself triggers the recall.

Several authors have confused the cultural reaction to war veterans in movies and contend that the movies created rather than exploited the veteran's image, although it appears that even Homer did not create the war veteran character. Exploitation films tend to be thin on character development and thick on enlarging bravery to heroic and even super-human dimensions, just as the comic books for decades have been developing indomitable heroes, like Batman and the Incredible Hulk, from trauma survivors. Chief among such action films is the Vietnam War veterans' movie *First Blood*.

A subgroup of the vet exploitation genre is the war veteran vs. outlaw biker films, in which outlaw motorcycle clubs are portrayed as harassing figures of evil with references to perverse paganism and fetish Nazi and gothic Christian motifs. The veteran is the good guy, the straight john who skillfully defeats the Hollywood outlaw hoard.

The Hollywood Western of the middle of the 20th century featured Civil War veterans wandering the Western frontier of civilization. Dean (1997) gives a well-documented account of the problems that Civil War veterans had with intrusive thoughts and fears of repetition, when, with everybody armed, fear became a panicky flashback making it dangerous for all. The aging gunfighter who wants to quit, but the circumstances in his environment won't let him, became a Western theme mimicking the war veterans' situation.

For better or worse, the exploitation movie does not last long in most video archives. They tour the drive-ins and malls, spend some lucrative time on the shelves of video stores, and are gone, only to be remembered in survey books. Those that remain have some lasting popular appeal, which may reveal their archetypal punch.

The War Veteran Under Attack

It may not seem so to casual observers, but the combat veteran returns home with memories so active that he feels constantly under attack. One could describe this sense as paranoia, except that it is a mostly conditioned fear, conditioned over a long period of time. The fear may result in pathological paranoia if the veteran withdraws for long from social contact or has a history of disrupted development, and it may create paranoia in others, particularly those close to the veteran. In fact such fear may be immanently appropriate, given the veteran's circumstances. Movies often display this visually as a plot for an action film, as in *Mr. Majestyk*, acting out the emotions that exist as feeling states in many of the returning veterans, in which the war continues as salient memory. This is when a chance to fight becomes more meaningful than real.

Some veterans of combat try to avoid fighting. The war veterans in this category attempt to live peaceful lives, but the fighting continues after they are finished with combat. In some, *Mr. Majestyk, Ruckus, Billy Jack, The Born Losers*, the veteran is forced into fighting the oppressive forces when the local law enforcement agencies are slow to protect his rights, or, as in the case of *I Am a Fugitive from a Chain Gang, First Blood*, and *Conspiracy Theory*, the local cops become the antagonists.

I Am a Fugitive from a Chain Gang, 1932

Having been in particularly bad places in their wartime experiences, combat veterans have a rich resource of nightmares. *I Am a Fugitive from a Chain Gang* depicts a war veteran returning with the U.S. army's Sunset Division on a troopship after the armistice ending "*the* world war." Released in 1932, the film was directed by Mervyn LeRoy from a screenplay by Howard Green and Brown Holmes. Paul Muni plays army veteran, James Allen, who describes himself as a changed man. "The army changes a fellow — you think different," he tells his parents and girlfriend. He is offered his old factory job back, but feels like he wants to get away. He takes the job because his mother begs him, but he really wants to build bridges as a civil engineer. His factory job requires him to look out the window at a bridge under construction and the explosions set him "looking for the nearest dugout." He finds that he can't concentrate and feels restless. "I've changed," he tells his mother. "I'm different now. I've been through hell. I'm out of step."

Jim quits his factory position takes a series of menial jobs, taking him

Paul Muni plays James Allen in *I Am a Fugitive from a Chain Gang* (re-released by Dominant Pictures, 1932). Here he talks to his wife, Marie (Glenda Farrell), who will soon betray him.

about the country until he finds himself on the tramp in a Southern state, where he is arrested when his companion tries to rob a diner. His companion is shot and he is arrested with the money, although he had no criminal intention, and is sentenced to ten years hard labor on the chain gang. He is treated brutally along with the other prisoners. Blacks and whites are separated in barracks, but work together in the quarry breaking rocks. Jim manages to escape and travels to Chicago, where he finds a job as a laborer for $4 a day. Showing initiative and creativity, he receives a series of promotions until he becomes an executive making $14 a day. He meets Marie (Glenda Farrell) in his rooming house. She is an attractive, brassy, tough-talking blonde who blackmails Jim when she reads a letter from his brother identifying him as a chain gang fugitive. He is forced to marry her and she launches into a life of a profligate, while he studies civil engineering and becomes a respected citizen.

Eventually he fights with Marie and she makes good on her threat and turns him in to the police. He has been such a righteous citizen that the Chicago newspapers take up his cause to prevent his extradition to an unnamed Southern state. (Georgia is implied on the transitional map routes.)

Finally, Jim naively goes back voluntarily on the state official's promise that he only has to serve 90 days as a trustee. The nightmare quality comes when he returns to the decrepit prison conditions, with chains and wizened, wasted men in prison striped uniforms, an eerie omen of the coming Holocaust. The months of his prison life are presented with turning calendar pages and a voiceover work song chanting, "Raise 'em high," to the silhouettes of men slamming picks into rock. Jim rages after being repeatedly betrayed by the state prison board until he finally escapes with another prisoner. Jim gets away but his partner is eventually killed. There is a great chase scene with a dump truck of the 1920s vintage careening down a mountain quarry road, chased by an open car loaded with bouncing prison guards firing rifles.

Jim is last seen fading into dark shadow, doomed to his fate as a fugitive. As one headline bemoaned, a man "decorated for bravery in the world war," yes, and betrayed and cheated by the society of his homeland.

The Born Losers, 1967

It is fitting that *The Born Losers* was made by Otis Productions. Otis is a Greek word for *nobody*, which Odysseus shouts defiantly at the Cyclops Polyphemus. *The Born Losers* opens with a distant scene of a man bathing in a forest waterfall. A woman's voiceover tells us that he, Billy Jack, "had just returned from the war. One of those Green Beret men. Some say he had some Indian blood in him."

Tom Laughlin, the star of *Born Losers* (American International, 1974), plays Billy Jack, a Vietnam War veteran "said to be part Indian," who single-handedly confronts the Born to Lose outlaw motorcycle club members. Director T.C. Frank went on to direct several sequels in which Laughlin's Billy Jack returns to fight for justice.

The title of the film comes from the "Born to Lose" motorcycle club, whose patch symbol displays a tattoo-like cartoon figure of a naked babe on a cross, mimicking the crucifixion. This odd assortment of men and a few women are another of Hollywood's versions of what a crazy biker outlaw club would look like. They harass decent townspeople. They have names like Gangrene, Cueball, and Crabs, and they beat up and humiliate ordinary guys and rape girls without fear of retribution, because no one will dare testify against them.

War veteran Billy Jack is an out-of-work horse wrangler. Seems there aren't enough horses left. He is pure in the tradition of the popular cowboy stars of post war cinema. He even plays a guitar. Although he is gifted with courage and combat skills, and we are inspired by his confidence, he uses his talents sparingly, and only on the side of justice. Elizabeth James plays gamine Vicky, with expressive eyes and loose judgment. She is a bold college girl who rides a motorcycle while wearing a white bikini. When she is trapped by the outlaws, she remains perky.

The Born Losers was directed by T.C. Frank, who made the subsequent Billy Jack sequels, and was written by James Lloyd. In an odd bit of casting, one of the victims' mothers is played by Jane Russell in a gothic caricature of her aging screen image. (See *Macao* for the Jane Russell of style.)

The Born Losers has many racist slurs about Native Americans, elicited because Billy is "said to be part Indian." Released by American International, the film is in the B-movie tradition of tawdry melodrama targeting the young drive-in moviegoers of the age.

Satan's Sadists, 1969 and *Chrome and Hot Leather*, 1971

There are several B-movies about motorcycle outlaws who battle with war veterans. *Satan's Sadists* and *Chrome and Hot Leather* are illustrative. Both were made during the Vietnam War. Al Adamson, who has something of a cult following for his quirky camera work, directed *Satan's Sadists*, released in 1969, in which a Vietnam War veteran, Johnny, a handsome former Marine, is tormented by the motorcycle gang, and fights them one by one. Lee Frost directed and photographed *Chrome and Hot Leather* about four Vietnam War veterans, who are army rangers training recruits. They go after a motorcycle gang, the Wizards, after finding out that their harassment led to the deaths of one soldier's fiancée and her friend. Neither film commented on the war, and seemed to use the war veteran angle solely for the veterans' combat skills. In *Chrome and Hot Leather*, released in 1971, the sergeants all wear Combat Infantryman Badges and are training recruits to fight Southeast Asian guerrillas. The plots are basic sensationalism, quite dated, but a feast perhaps for motorcycle aficionados. It is sufficient to note that the bikers behave like outlaw psychopaths and the veterans represent the righteous who are pressed too far.

What these films don't show us is the attraction that motorcycle clubs have for disaffected, action-oriented men who are war veterans. Legend has it that the Hell's Angels MC was started by World War II bomber crews (Lavigne, 1993). The one-percenter theme, adopted by outlaw clubs, has the essential sense that the club member does not care if he dies, and will back up his brothers, no matter what. In fact, as Wolf (1991) documents with authority, outlaw motorcycle clubs are "outlaw" principally because they are not sanctioned by a national motorcycle club authority. However, so-called outlaw clubs are really quite detailed and formal in their club laws and customs and carry an identity among themselves as being persecuted for their independent lifestyle. They usually fight among peers, or with other tough guys, and to persecute weak citizens would be considered a sissy activity. The concept of the biker raid on a town comes from the media hype of a biker rally in Hollister, California, in 1947, that was immortalized by Marlon Brando in Stanley Kramer's *The Wild One*.

In these Hollywood B-films, however, including *The Born Losers*, the Vietnam War veterans are portrayed as decent, just, and righteous men who are harassed and attacked by dark forces of society represented by their shadow sharers, the outlaw bikers. Wolf notes, however (p. 58), that the Hell's Angels MC defended Vietnam War veterans when they were attacked, and Vietnam War veterans have established their own outlaw club on a national level.

Billy Jack, 1971

While Rambo achieves archetypal, if cartoon-like, status, *Billy Jack* merely strives to be archetypal. *Billy Jack* is a preachy, righteous, low budget production about a very romantic figure, a "half breed war hero who hated war and lived with a holy man." Released in 1971, directed by T.C. Frank, it is a fairly authentic depiction of hippie innocence and alternative culture enthusiasm. A "Freedom School" is created on an unnamed Indian reservation in what looks like New Mexico. As the school director, Delores, played with flat sincerity by Jean Roberts, explains, anybody can come and stay as long as they want, pretty much do what they want, so long as they are creative.

Billy Jack begins with a disturbing mustang roundup featuring sweating, tumbling horses driven by local men. As they are about to shoot the horses for their meat, a rider appears from the woods to the accompaniment of mysterious, reverent music. Billy, played with a nice convincing sense of quiet by Tom Laughlin, with all the steely bravado of a pulp Western hero, shoots the guns and cows the cowboys. We learn from bitterly voiced gossip among the bad guys that Billy shows up mysteriously just like that, wherever there is injustice brewing.

Billy is kind of a Buddhist holy man on horseback and a protector of "Freedom School." We learn nothing more about how he feels about the war, although it is clear from one fight in town against a circle of bad guys that Billy had Green Beret training, and he refers with ominous humor to "my violent temper — I try to control." At one point, counseling a Native American boy, Martin, played by Steve Rice, Billy advises adopting "mental toughness" in which mistakes can be made if one accepts one's imperfections.

This movie is on the same level of popular appeal as the "Rambo" films, *First Blood*, etc. Laughlin's portrayal of *Billy Jack* spawned its own sequels, *The Trial of Billy Jack*, and *Billy Jack Goes to Washington*. The war hero who hates war, but is grudgingly pulled back into it, practicing his well-honed skills of combat to fight injustice. The appeal is to the violated sense of justice that trauma survivors feel, and especially Vietnam War veterans feel, given the expense and outcome of the war.

Several of the songs sung in *Billy Jack* are sad, sentimental protest songs. "Tin Soldier," is the theme, sung by Jinx Dawson of the group Covin. One girl is drawn bashfully onto the stage of Freedom School to sing a song she'd just written about how she got the news her brother, Johnny, died. "I'll never forget that moment."

Members of the San Francisco improvisational theater group, the

Committee, perform several skits with enough skill to make their professionalism look smoothly amateurish.

Billy Jack is a spin-off star vehicle for Tom Laughlin and director T.C. Frank from a true biker exploitation film, *The Born Losers*.

Mr. Majestyk, 1974

Charles Bronson plays Vincent Majestyk, a hard-working melon farmer. His old yellow Ford pickup displays a "Majestyk Brand Mellons" on the door. He is first seen hiring farm laborers and meeting an attractive labor union organizer, Nancy Chavez, played by Linda Cristal. However, when he arrives at his melon crop, pickers are already at work, winos hired by a local sharpster, Bobby Kopas, well played as a weasel by Paul Koslo.

Majestyk drives off Kopas and his workers, after beating and humiliating him in front of his henchmen. The sheriff then comes out and arrests Mr. Majestyk. The cops are played as competent, but not very helpful.

Vietnam War veteran and ex-con Vincent Majestyk (Charles Bronson) stares out the window of his truck as he tries to make a living growing melons in Richard Fleischer's *Mr. Majestyk* (United Artists, 1974).

One deputy reads the rap sheet on Mr. Majestyk. Enlisted in the army after high school. Served as a Ranger in Vietnam, was captured and escaped. Received a Silver Star. Was married for four years, until his wife divorced him. Was sent to prison for nine months for assault. Bronson plays Mr. Majestyk as a working class hero who identifies with the values of the migrant workers. He drinks Coors beer and sprinkles salt on the foam.

The plot twists when he is incarcerated in the county jail and meets an infamous gangland hit man, Frank Randa, played by Al Lettieri with black, bushy brows and a convincing, dark passion for violence. When the prisoners are transported in the jail bus, they are intercepted by Frank's gangster friends. There is a shootout with the cops. Majestyk commandeers the bus, with the hitman handcuffed, and they escape to the bush.

Mr. Majestyk takes place in rural Colorado. It was directed by Richard Fleischer and written by Elmore Leonard. Majestyk bargains by phone with the sheriff to have the charges dropped in exchange for returning the hitman. As it turns out, however, everything goes wrong and Majestyk returns without the hitman, and when he's finally behind bars, the gangster's lawyer frees the gangster on bond, with the implication that a deal was made with some officials.

The gangsters then go after Vince Majestyk. They intimidate his workers and shoot up his valuable melon crop stored in a warehouse. The film, which was released in 1974, flirts with satire as Majestyk talks repeatedly about only wanting to harvest his melons, and when the gangsters with automatic rifles shoot up the crop, splattering red flesh from exploding fruit, it seems the melons take on the overdeveloped role of symbol, more than just the honest rewards of a poor man's labors.

Bronson plays the war veteran as a cool and fearless character, although there is a tongue-in-cheek tone, a man of few words, who can take a lot of pressure without cracking. He is short, however, like his fellow action figures, Sylvester Stallone, Clint Eastwood, and John Wayne, on emotional depth. When his foreman (Alejandro Ray) gets his legs crushed by the gangsters, he can only say, "I'm real sorry, man." As is the tradition of these action heroes, Mr. Majestyk keeps his emotions contained.

Ruckus, 1980

Dirk Benedict plays Vietnam War veteran Kyle Hansen, an inarticulate hobo who happens along the road, shuffling in a silent, dirty, derelict state. When he plods into a country drive-in restaurant, several of the good ol' boys recognize that he is wearing a fatigue jacket with an army

Special Forces patch. Kyle orders in a hoarse voice a hamburger — raw. What, after all, is the risk of *E. coli* bacteria after surviving in the Vietnam jungle?

Written and directed by Max Kleven, *Ruckus* was released in 1980. The richest and most powerful man in the rural Alabama county is Mr. Bellows (Ben Johnson), whose son is MIA from the same Special Forces outfit. Mr. Bellows asks Kyle, who is sitting with Odyssean humility on the curb eating his raw hamburger, if he knew Jack, Mr. Bellows's missing son. Kyle refuses to answer and shuffles off. Mr. Bellows sends several of the boys after him and Kyle receives them silently, but when they threaten to lock him up and begin to restrain him, he beats them all up and runs off. Whenever the boys get to chasing Kyle, banjos start to play. Kyle steals the police car and drives to Mr. Bellows's house where Jenny, who was married to Mr. Bellows's son only a week before he went off to Vietnam, lives with her father-in-law. Jenny, played with inadequate direction by Linda Blair, receives word that her husband is dead, just as Kyle arrives to explain to her personally that he didn't know her husband. He enters her house uninvited and confronts her with his filthy demeanor. She asks without startle or fear, "Can I help you?"

Jenny takes a liking to Kyle, but the boys keep chasing him, and Kyle keeps evading and humiliating them. *Ruckus* begins with a Willie Nelson song, "What Can You Do to Him Now?" While the boys are hunting for Kyle, he sits in Jenny's dining room and eats crudely off of her white tablecloth. Jenny's major emotion appears to be blunted bemusement. She asks, "They say you're dangerous—are you?" He replies ambiguously, "They're trying to lock me up. I can't handle that." She responds, "Those men are all hunters." "I can handle *that*," he says.

Jenny finally gets Kyle to clean up and put on some of her late husband's clothes. He emerges looking spiffy clean, reborn like Bart in *The Stunt Man*, with bleach blond streaks in his hair. Jenny is delighted, and declares, "I'm just going to have to get used to you all over again."

Kyle takes a dirt bike and breaks out of Mr. Bellows's barn like a daredevil stunt rider. He returns to Jenny after he again evades and humiliates the boys. She tells him he's the most exciting thing to hit this county since the hurricane of '68, and they go dirt bike riding in a romantic montage of natural habitat destruction.

The boys, Deputy Dave, Bubba, and the others, are finally completely humiliated, although it is important to note that no one is seriously hurt. One shouts in anguish the archaic fear of returning war veterans everywhere, "He's not human. The Commies got to him. He's going to destroy this country from within."

But, in the end, he wins the heart of Mr. Bellows, who gives him an island in the river that belonged to his late son Jack.

In its innocence as a B-class vet exploitation movie, *Ruckus* captures the repeating theme of the returning veteran under siege and establishes the Robin Hood traditional assertion that the common man is behind the war veteran, who served his country, win or lose. *Ruckus* preceded *First Blood* by two years, but the theme is similar up to the point that the veteran leaves his dirt bike behind. *Ruckus* cannot go beyond the chase and banjo picking and Kyle hasn't the charisma of Johnny Rambo. In the beginning, though, when Kyle is in his Thorazine shuffle, he captures the spirit of the ignominy of the returned veteran, a kind of redneck version Bearskin.

Kyle, when he is caught in a grain elevator and put into a cage, has an auditory hallucination that mixes the country boys talking with Vietnamese language, and finally merges with an echoic dog barking, eerily reminiscent of the former POW's experience in the tunnel episode of *Akira Kirosawa's Dreams*. One of the Willie Nelson songs sums up the plight of the unwelcomed war veteran in a nutshell, "Ain't life hell?"

Firefox, 1982

Clint Eastwood's *Firefox* is pure action, within which a war veteran, a former POW, U.S. Pilot Mitchel Gant, played by Eastwood, is called back into his country's service. Gant lives alone in a large remote house in Alaska. An army helicopter approaches as he is out jogging and causes him to panic. He has a flashback of events in Vietnam related to his capture and to napalm strikes, not dissimilar to the flashback scenes in *Sundays and Cybèle*. These scenes will appear for brief moments throughout the film, whenever he is under levels of very high stress. I use the superlative because the whole film is stressful, as a good action yarn should be. It seems that the Soviets have developed a super high tech jet plane that can fly so fast it can't be detected and can read the thoughts of the pilot to fire its weapons. The Air Force wanted Gant to steal and fly the plane out of the country. Gant's the only choice because he speaks Russian, his mother was Russian, and when in the Air Force he flew in the legendary Aggressor Squadron, which meant that he trained on Soviet aircraft.

Eastwood's Gant is smuggled into the country posing first as one man, then another. Along the way is his own *Rio Lobo* succession of helpful, dedicated natives who yearn for freedom, along with suspicious police and KGB. In addition, this movie has the high tech glitter and video game appeal of jet planes flying low through mountainous terrain and fighting in the air, like dogs with their ears pinned back.

Clint Eastwood (left) produced, directed and starred in *Firefox* (Warner Bros., 1982). His character, Mitchell Gant, a Vietnam War veteran pilot, is called back to the service of his country, fulfilling the unfinished business fantasy of many war veterans. Here he negotiates his way through Russia with the aid of a friendly underground helper, Pavel (Warren Clarke, right).

Firefox was based on a novel written by Graig Thomas and adapted to the screen by Alex Lasker and Wen Wellman. Released in 1982, *Firefox* is solidly in the action genre of heroism and camaraderie. Clint Eastwood picked up the John Wayne icon of grim determination and muted emotional expression. As a war veteran he grits his teeth and bears his posttraumatic symptoms while complying with the dream of so many former combatants, that his country asks him to serve again, even at his age.

First Blood, 1982

There really aren't many films that create a character or title of such archetypal proportions that the name, itself, enters the lexicon. *Lolita*, *Frankenstein*, and *Rambo* are the first to come to mind. (The commonality of *those* three characters is another book.)

First Blood features John Rambo, whom we first encounter walking a country road as the titles roll. He is wearing a fatigue jacket with a U.S. flag above the right pocket. He carries a sleeping bag hanging from his shoulder by a rope.

First Blood was filmed in Golden Ears Park in British Columbia. Directed by Ted Kotcheff and photographed by Andrew Laszlow, it was released in 1982 and developed an immediate popular audience.

Sylvester Stallone plays Rambo, a Vietnam War veteran of heroic dimensions. He was a Green Beret and recipient of the Congressional Medal of Honor, but we first meet him, like Ivanhoe, as the pilgrim. He appears in a vista approaching a beautiful Northwest bay, said to be in Oregon. He walks toward a house where an African-American woman in the yard is putting up laundry on a line. She regards him with suspicion. He asks about his friend Delmar, with whom he served in Nam. He shows her a picture. "Delmar's gone," she replies finally. "When will he be back?" asks John Rambo. "He died," she replies, of cancer. "He brought it back from Nam. All that orange stuff they passed around. Cut him down to nothin'."

We next see Rambo on the highway, headed toward a town, when he meets Sheriff Will, played by Brian Dennehy, who makes a series of prejudicial assumptions based on Rambo's appearance. He tries to escort the traveler through town, but Rambo insists on returning to get something to eat. The sheriff then arrests Rambo and has him booked in the town jail as a drifter. Rambo absorbs repeated abuse and calumny with a dark stoicism that seems itself ominous. He could well be Odysseus under the hood of a begger taking abuse at the door. The deputies strip Rambo and hose him down. We see scars over his buffed-out physique. When the deputies try to shave his face, he has a flashback of being held captive and tortured in Vietnam. He bulks, fights off all the deputies and flees the jail, taking with him his survival knife. The knife, which we are shown cuts paper effortlessly, becomes a kind of magical weapon with his survival items hidden within. It even gets special billing in the credits.

Rambo commandeers a motorcycle and is pursued to the edge of a mountain cliff by a band of sheriff's deputies and a dog handler leading three aggressive Dobermans. Trapped, he tries to climb down the steep cliff only to be shot at by a deputy leaning out of a helicopter. Rambo leaps into a river gorge as a helicopter attacks with one of the more abusive deputies shooting at him. The helicopter is so close that Rambo hits the windshield with a rock, causing the pilot to tip the ship and throw the deputy down to his death on the rocks.

The deputies withdraw and are joined by state police and National Guard troops. They are puzzling about maps when Colonel Sam Trautman appears in silhouette at the opening of the tent. The colonel, played stonily by Richard Crenna, commanded Rambo three years in Vietnam and tells the assembled just who they're up against. He is not just a former soldier, a war veteran, "he is expert in every aspect of guerrilla warfare. He is trained to ignore pain. He will eat things that would make a billy goat puke. His job was to kill and he was the best." The colonel tries to communicate by radio with Rambo, when the latter is trapped in an abandoned mineshaft after the soldiers blow up the opening with an anti-tank rocket. He calls Rambo by his code name, Raven. (He indeed grows darker as the film progresses.) "Talk to me, Johnny," he repeats over and over. Rambo mournfully reports that his one-time fellow survivor, Delmar, has died, "Killed in Nam and didn't know it. Cancer ate him down to the bone." At times Rambo sounds like an adolescent who is in over his head. "I wish I was in [Fort] Bragg now."

In *First Blood* we see the Vietnam War circumstances reversed as the veteran is being pursued with overwhelming technology, however ineptly utilized by the weekend warriors. His pursuers think Rambo has died in the cave blast, although he escapes by meandering through tunnels infested with rats. His mastery of inventiveness is expressed in the way he devises a torch and finds his way out. This all invites archetypal mythic associations to the hero who recovers in a cave, emerging as a stronger character for the next trial.

Colonel Trautman urges the sheriff to "leave the kid alone." Let him go, he says, and he will be picked up working in some Seattle car wash without a fight. Will, the sheriff, can't do that, for the issue has become a personal vendetta.

Rambo commandeers an army six-by truck and an M-60 machine gun. At night he crashes the truck into a gas station, explodes the gas, and starts a little holocaust as a series of secondary blasts occur in an adjoining used car lot. He shoots out the electrical boxes on the utility polls, firing the M-60 from a sling. He wears belts of machine gun ammo draped across his muscular chest, an image that became his advertising icon. By now his countenance has darkened with stains of dirt and blood. He shoots the Sheriff, who is on the roof of the police station, by shooting through the ceiling, reminiscent of the Branch Davidian shootout in Waco, Texas.

Rambo is finally confronted by his former CO and talked into surrendering. Stallone's veteran sobs that the war wasn't over for him. "Nothing is over. You just don't turn it off." He talks about the "maggots at the airports" spitting on Vietnam veterans. "Who are they to protest me, huh?" "You are the last of the elite," agrees the colonel. Rambo continues, mournfully, "There I was in charge of million dollar equipment, back here I can't even hold a job. Back here it's nothin'." He goes on to recall his dead friends and weeps as he tells the story of his friend, who is blown up in Vietnam while having his shoes shined.

First Blood was adapted for the screen by Michael Kozoll and William Sackheim, in collaboration with Stallone, from a novel by David Morrell. The film ends with Rambo being escorted in handcuffs from the wrecked police station by the colonel, to be taken back to Fort Bragg, setting the stage for sequels in which Rambo goes back to Vietnam and then on to Afghanistan for more heroic action. A romantic song, "The Long Road" accompanies the closing credits.

Sylvester Stallone was criticized for his limited acting range, although he has recently redeemed himself since with a good, if more paunchy, performance in *Copland*. In *First Blood* he appears bewildered, stony, and, when he has to emote, he seems adolescent. He is otherwise a quiet man of strength, a gentle giant of few words who appears to be something of a social isolate. As Rambo is pursued up the mountain, the deputies, grudgingly following his trail behind the dogs, call their leader's name in a manner that sounds like a chant extolling Rambo: "Will, Will, Will."

Rambo's ingenious heroic tactics achieve mythic size, like Hercules undergoing his divine trials. He sews up his own wounds, adapts leather rags into a smock and headband. He takes refuge, wounded and bleeding, in a cave, and there heroically emerges, reborn, in a manner of speaking. He seems to personify the dark fantasies of the maladapted man who feels victimized by the rabid technology and ponderous institutions of postmodern civilization. He is the war veteran whose face is blackened by the backfire.

Fred Turner in his 1996 *Echoes of Combat* suggests that the "Rambo films offer up Rambo's body as an emblem for the nation" (p. 89). He is referring to the scars and flashbacks to torture, as well as Rambo's beefed up physique. But I think the emblem is Rambo's sentiment and his simple (or simplistic) message that sincere patriotism, loyalty, and duty are not valued in his homeland, while at the same time a compulsion to kill remains quite strong among his countrymen. Lanning (1994, p 107) refers to certain similar action films as "Ramboesque." It is perhaps a tribute to the force that Stallone gives to the image of the innocent, inarticulate, down-to-earth man who through force of will strives to do right. That his will power is portrayed as Herculean is a tribute to the archetype.

The Desperate Hours, 1990

There are several films in which the war veteran status is merely mentioned. In *The Desperate Hours* Anthony Hopkins plays Timothy, a middle-aged man who is separated from his wife and family. The family house is invaded by an escaped convict and his two buddies. The invaders take Timothy and his family hostage. The convict, Michael Bosworth, played by Mickey Rourke, was aided in his escape by a sexy attorney. He has a rather brutal relationship with her. Michael is a psychopath. At one point he taunts Timothy, who he calls Timmy, holding up a picture frame of military medals, but without Combat Infantryman Badge. "Looks like you won the Vietnam War all by yourself, Timmy." Also on the table is a picture of a Vietnam War era soldier standing in battle gear.

Hopkins seems miscast as Timothy and it is a tribute to his acting talent that he makes the man convincing. We know nothing really of his combat experiences, but we see him in the situation in which his family is held hostage by a murderous trio. When a hapless real estate agent happens to knock at the door, he is brought in and shot dead. Hopkins' Timothy is indomitable. He fights as long and as hard as he has to.

Released in 1990, *The Desperate Hours* was directed by Michael Cimino from a novel by Joseph Hayes. Some parts of the drama work, but the supporting cast is weak. Mimi Rogers plays Timothy's wife, Nora. Kelly Lynch is Nancy, Michael's hot girlfriend. The film tries to create a torrid atmosphere, but it deflates in the end. When Timothy delivers the collapsed psychopath where he is gunned down in a spotlight, torrid dwindles to tawdry.

Usually, when the war veteran's status is mentioned, it is used as a plot device. In the comic *Meet the Parents*, the device is to use the veteran's paranoia and snooping experience. It also serves accidentally to display a rather common symptom in war veterans, of over-protectiveness. In *The Desperate Hours* we have the sense that because we know Timothy, a refined and prosperous man, had combat experience and was highly decorated, we believe he can overcome the odds and win. His war veteran status gives him depth, but we also, in the process, get to see him suffer again, and watch him enduring helplessness and ignominy.

Conspiracy Theory, 1997

Conspiracy Theory was released in 1997 and stars Mel Gibson as Jerry Fletcher, a Vietnam War veteran, and Julia Roberts as a federal attorney, Alice Sutton. He is working as a New York City taxi driver and is obsessed with conspiracy theories. He puts out a newsletter, mad paranoid that he is, and, as the plot would have it, one of his mad ideas happens to approximate a real government conspiracy. Seems a rogue government intelligence agency has murdered Alice's father. The plot is an excuse for nervous, rapid-fire action, fostering frenzied escapes by Jerry, making gibberish puns, as his worst delusional fears come true. The mixture of pun-ridden humor and non-stop action creates a heady feeling of exuberance.

The plot of *Conspiracy Theory* has the *Manchurian Candidate* and

Jacob's Ladder device that something was done to the veteran during the war that has altered his mind, the wholeness of which he gradually recovers as the plot develops. This device is a personification of the effects of psychological trauma. The conspiracy of rogue government agencies is a theme from the Vietnam War era that takes the U.S. tradition of wary suspicion of strong central government and cranks up the fear to paranoid intensity.

Directed by Richard Donner and written by Brian Helgeland, *Conspiracy Theory* addresses a psychological truth, which is the cynical reality of the war veteran, that "if it's all going to turn to shit, you have to be prepared." In the final scene, when Jerry is brought into the car of two good government agents, he discovers that one was earlier disguised as a legless Vietnam War veteran street newspaper vendor. Jerry confirms what he already knew, that nothing is real, everything is not as it seems.

Last Stand at Saber River, 1997

Last Stand at Saber River is a made-for-TV movie about a Civil War veteran who seems to be the last to learn that the war is over. Tom Selleck plays the veteran at war with the Kidston brothers, played for evil by the acting brothers Keith and David Carradine. The teleplay was written by Ronald Cohen, from a novel by Elmore Leonard. Fate seems to be the winner, and the prevailing force of tragedy follows the amplified hatreds of internecine fighting. Directed by Dick Lowry, the story is right for describing the returning combat veteran, who, because of posttraumatic stress symptoms, continues to live amid the fighting that persists in his mind.

Dean (1997) describes the symptoms of Union army veterans after the Civil War. He found that one of the more common symptoms was the belief that the enemy would return and the fighting start again. Intrusive thoughts, fear of repetition, plagued veterans, sometimes resulting in psychotic delusions. Films like *Last Stand at Saber River* are on one level descriptive of the disruption of the society caused by the war, while at another level describing the action in the war veterans' minds.

The War Veteran as Pursuer

The skill learned in combat can come in handy when the war veteran applies for a job in law enforcement, or is recruited to do the work of a reluctant pursuer of justice. *China Gate* depicts army veterans who continue to fight as mercenaries after the Korean War. The men who stayed in the army after the Civil War were from both armies, Northern and Southern, and they comprised the U.S. cavalry that fought for order in the West. The structure and camaraderie of the unit or agency, the task, and the action demanded day after day, keeps the adjustment to civilian life contained, but not completed. It is often only after the war veteran retires from his job, as we see in *She Wore a Yellow Ribbon*, that his ability to cope with combat memories and emotions is challenged.

Sometimes the war veteran is confronted with the task of pursuer as a result of circumstances that call upon him to take action, as in *Gordon's War*, *The Devil in a Blue Dress*, and the *noir* thriller *Cornered*. In *The Glory Boys* the war veteran is the daring agent, who is linked with the cop by wartime camaraderie. In *Electra Glide in Blue* the war veteran strives to maintain the righteous life.

Fort Apache, 1948

John Ford directed *Fort Apache*, released in 1948, after he himself had been wounded while doing his duty in wartime service. The screenplay by Frank Nugent concerns U.S. Army troops stationed in a Western frontier outpost, many of them Civil War veterans. Henry Fonda plays Colonel Thursday, who was a general by the end of the Civil War, and like others, has taken a demotion in order to stay in the army. He is surrounded by officers and NCOs who fought with him or know of him. John Wayne plays Captain York, who himself commanded a regiment during the war. A collection of John Ford repertory character actors make up the command.

For all the movie's romantic panache, Ford addresses the readjustment problems of war veterans who continue to fight and seem more caught up in duty as fate than in self-preservation. Shirley Temple plays the colonel's 19-year-old daughter with the awkward name, sounding like a stop on an itinerant's schedule, of Philadelphia Thursday. Temple still has her childish spunk that looks a little silly on a woman, as if she hadn't grown up, which may also be what Ford exploited in her image. Her role and manner are rather similar to Meg Ryan's as Donna, the daughter of the provost, in *The Presidio*.

Wayne's Capt. York represents a war veteran who has adapted to his new terrain, who has a sense of the Apaches as individuals and talks to their leader, Cochise. The colonel, on the other hand, is a man who is fighting to restore his honor and rank, essentially fighting to recapture what he achieved in the war, while bearing the judgment-clouding burden of his own racial prejudice.

John Ford, in his career, vacillated between racial stereotyping, with

comic mockery of minorities, and depicting real problems in the U.S. mixing of racial and ethnic groups. He claimed special insight as a son of an
Irish immigrant. "'Who better than an Irishman could understand the
Indians, while still being stirred by tales of the U.S. Calvary? We were on
both sides of the epic'" (McBride, 2001, p. 291).

Ford makes a joke of the trooper's thirst for alcohol. Victor McLaglen plays Sgt. Mulcahey, who, when asked to taste the contraband rotgut
whiskey being supplied to the Apaches by a government agent, replies, "It's
better than no whiskey at all, sir." Director Ford, son of an Irish-American tavern owner, was himself a binge alcoholic between movies for about
20 years (McBride, 2001, p 133).

Fort Apache addresses a romantic concept that many war veterans
keep with undiminished ambivalence, that courage, honor, and duty are
to be admired independently of judgment and without reference to the
damage the pursuit of those virtues may cause. This is best represented
in the colonel's treacherous intent to betray Captain York's promise to
Cochise, couched in the prolonged romantic scenes of the regiment's troop
movement leaving the fort, with women watching the men depart against
the background of the magnificent western sky of Monument Valley and
the men's chorus singing "The Girl I Left Behind Me." When the colonel
dies amid the needless slaughter of his men, his and the doomed troopers' courageous efforts are honored and remembered in Captain York's
closing soliloquy. McBride (2001, p. 457) put it nicely:

> The remarkable achievement of *Fort Apache* is that it enables us to see
> through the historical lie while understanding and sympathizing with men
> who are suicidally following the example of a leader, Colonel Thursday,
> aptly described by Sergeant-Major O'Rourke as "the madman."

And it is significant that these "suicidally" devoted troops were largely
composed of Civil War veterans on both sides of the fighting, who comprised a collective sense of survivors drawn to their fate.

She Wore a Yellow Ribbon, 1949

John Ford continued the stories of the U.S. Civil War veterans, both
Union and Confederate, who continue to serve in the military as frontier
troopers for the U.S. Cavalry in *She Wore a Yellow Ribbon*, released in 1949.
Veterans compose the senior command of the fort, along with the
sergeants. The scout is a Confederate veteran. The first sergeant, Sergeant
Quinncannon (Victor McLaglen), is a Union army veteran under the command of another war veteran, Captain Brittles (John Wayne), who is gimpy

with arthritis and approaching retirement, checking off his short-timer's calendar.

The historical checkpoint is Custer's Last Stand and an Indian uprising causing several Plains Indian tribes to unite in resistance to white settlement. The fort's commander, Major Allshard, played by with a tough edge by George O'Brien, has Captain Brittles go over the casualty list from the Battle of the Little Bighorn. The captain reels off several names, and later gives a soliloquy at his wife's grave, recalling one of the casualties, whom his wife also knew.

Captain Brittles is given an assignment he does not agree with, and with mock civility files a written protest to his commander. Brittles is to escort two women leaving the post, the major's wife (well played by Mildred Natwick) and a young woman, Miss Dandridge, played by Joanne Dru, who is the romantic interest of two competing young lieutenants. In escorting the women to a stage line, and taking safety precautions, the captain puts his forward patrol at risk of Indian attack. The overland stage way station is attacked by Kiowas. A sergeant is killed in the attack. The dead trooper's story comes out at his funeral. He was a Confederate army general, who went on to serve as a veteran cavalry sergeant. The captain remarks, "Rome Clay, late confederate brigadier general, known here as Trooper Smith."

The film was adapted from stories by James Bellah; the screenplay was by Frank Nugent and Laurence Stallings. Spectacular Technicolor photography in the Monument Valley is by Winton Hoch, who won an Academy Award for his work. Vista scenes of the troops riding with the vast Plains' sky active with stormy lightning are among the best in cinema. McBride quotes Peter Bagdonovich reporting that Hoch shot the scenes of the storm under protest written on the clapboard (p. 460).

There is a play on the phrases dog soldiers, referring to the cavalry, and the Southern Cheyenne warriors, who are referred to similarly as dog soldiers, giving recognition to their similar characters. Dogs follow the cavalry on their journey. The Native warriors (all Navaho) are dealt with sympathetically in this film. When confronting advancing warriors, the captain orders his riflemen to shoot over their heads. As in *Fort Apache*, Captain Brittles, on the day of his retirement, meets with the aged chief, Pony That Walks. They admit that neither can stop the Native warriors from clashing with the cavalry.

She Wore a Yellow Ribbon continues the tribute to the alcohol dependent Irish soldier and the role of whiskey as the all-purpose anesthetic and ceremonial beverage for the Cavalry. The Irishman and his whiskey plays to a reliable comic ethnic stereotype. McLaglen becomes the Irish version of Amos and Andy: "Reminds me of the old days, when whiskey was 50 cents a gallon." The University of Notre Dame logo of the Fightin' Irishman with the clay pipe could well have been taken from the bartender in this film. The war veterans refer to their whiskey as medicine. Ford, at the very end of his life and riddled with cancer, when he could not tolerate food, was drinking Guinness stout for nourishment (McBride, 2001).

Also excoriated are the drug dealers of yesteryear, the petty government clerks, here in form of the infamous Indian agent, who sells guns to the warriors. When Captain Brittles and his scout observe the Indians torturing the agent by rolling him across the fire, they merely watch, chewing tobacco to calm their stomachs.

It could be said that John Ford wore a yellow ribbon, for he was in love with the U.S. Calvary on the Western frontier. His films chronicle the post–Civil War period when war veterans continued to fight.

The film ducks an important issue for war veterans who stay in the service or enter civilian law enforcement or emergency careers. When they retire from uniform, as it were, they face a potential for renewed symptoms, especially the sense of survivor's guilt and intrusive thoughts of traumatic events. Captain Brittles at the last moment is promoted and appointed chief of scouts for the Cavalry and seems happy and relieved to continue riding with the troops.

China Gate, 1957

War veteran Sam Fuller wrote, produced, and directed *China Gate,* which takes place in Vietnam during the French war against the Vietminh. American mercenaries, played by Gene Barry as Johnny Brock, the dynamiter, and grease-gun-toting Nat King Cole, who does a credible job of acting as Goldie, are veterans of the Korean War. Goldie declares that he also fought with the U.S. army in World War II. Brock states that he was once a POW, but escaped before he was brainwashed.

The opening voiceover announces, "This motion picture is dedicated to France." It credits the French missionaries with teaching "the love of God and fellow man" to the Vietnamese, and credits the French colonialists for developing the country's "vast riches." The voiceover declares, "France became at the end of the war the barrier between Communism and the rape of Asia."

Angie Dickinson plays Lucky Legs, a sultry lady of mixed ancestry who runs Lucky's Bar and opium den. She also traffics in liquor to the Communist soldiers. Lucky had a child in a wartime marriage with Sergeant Brock, however, because Lucky had a Chinese mother, and although she,

Nat King Cole (right) plays Goldie in Sam Fuller's *China Gate* (20th Century–Fox, 1957). Gene Berry plays Johnny Brock. Johnny and Goldie are Korean War veterans who continue to fight in French Indochina.

herself, didn't have Chinese features, her child did, which Brock could not handle. He rejected Lucky and the child.

Nat King Cole sings "China Gate" at the beginning and at the end of the film. Vietnam, it seems, is the gate to China. Cole, as Goldie, declares that he started in Korea and didn't finish, "because there are still a lot of live Commies around."

The plot revolves around two themes: first, the reconciliation between Brock and Lucky, which is played out as she leads Brock, Goldie, and other mercenary war veterans to a tunnel complex that houses the Vietminh store of munitions that will potentially give them victory over the French. Along the way, one of their group, a Hungarian war veteran, experiences a nightmare in which he sees a Russian soldier that he killed with his bare hands. "I have the nightmare all the time." "I kill him over and over and over." Brock thinks that his nightmares will compromise their mission to sneak up on the tunnel complex, under Lucky's guidance, and blow it up. Brock suggests a rather radical treatment for the man's chronic nightmares. He proposes killing the suffering Hungarian, but others refuse, and Brock finally devises a longer managed care treatment regimen. "I'll pass this time, but the next time you have a nightmare it'll be your last."

Lucky traffics with the Chinese soldiers and seems to know them all. It seems that after Brock left her with child, she turned a desperate moral corner, dealing inebriates and erotic services. Dickinsen, as Lucky, plays a swaggering, wise dame who elicits sultry background music whenever she's around. Lucky, in one confrontation with Brock over his rejection of their child, says, "You're tough enough to handle explosives, but you're not tough enough to handle life."

China Gate was shot primarily on stage lots and has rather stagy set pieces of humor to relieve the tension. Director Fuller's blunt style featured gritty close-ups and violent action. The film idealizes the French and the Americans and demonizes the Communists. One Communist major, played as a Eurasian by Lee Van Cleef, explains to Lucky that the tunnel complex is using a Buddhist temple as a cover because the "stupid French and Americans won't bomb temples and churches." The major, it seems, also loves Lucky and wants to raise her son in Moscow. The boy is played as a symbol of Cold War confrontation. In the end, of course, Brock takes the boy to America, while Goldie sings amid the rubble, cleaning his grease gun as they walk away: "Bowl of rice, bitter tea, is this all the good earth has to offer me?" (Fuller, 2002, p. 351).

China Gate was released in 1957 and set in 1954. It makes a prediction that the Americans will soon be involved militarily in the war. American planes are already making airdrops of food and supplies to cut-off French garrisons. While it directly deals with prejudice against Asians, the film also makes stereotypical jokes, including having Lucky's five-year-old boy covetously fondling Sergeant Brock's wristwatch. The joke is carried to the final scene when the boy is wearing the watch as they walk off through the rubble on their way to America.

Typical of the time, there are no Asians playing the leading roles as Asians. Fuller makes his case that the Vietnamese benefited from the French colonial exploitation of their riches about as much as the Irish benefited from the British occupation. We see a small boy wandering the bombed-out town as the peasants run to pick up the airdropped boxes of relief supplies. The opening has the boy with a puppy under his coat running away from a hungry man. Says Lucky of her son, and she loves him, "His eyes are a cross he's got to carry."

A later bit of discontinuity has Goldie stepping on a metal pungie stake. We see it pass through his foot and boot and director Fuller dwells upon the agony of Goldie pulling his foot off the spike while muffling his own outcries. Then, however, after having it bandaged, he is back to trekking through the jungle without a limp.

Samuel Fuller served in the army during World War II with the First Infantry Division. He was awarded a Purple Heart, Bronze Star and Silver Star for combat action. As a war veteran, he made several combat action films, including *Steel Helmet*, *Fixed Bayonets*, and, after a period of semi-retirement, an autobiographical story, *The Big Red One*. *China Gate* seems to be a tribute to war veterans who didn't finish their work.

Electra Glide in Blue, 1973

An Electra Glide in blue is a motorcycle desired by a motorcycle cop named Zipper. He's an impulsive, lazy man who eventually goes crazy after stealing money from a murder victim's house and buying his object of desire. Robert Blake plays his partner John Wintergreen, a former Force Recon Marine, so he announces early in the film as he's giving another Vietnam War veteran a ticket. Later a hippie arrested for murder, abused and finally released, is also acknowledged to be a veteran busted for dope in Vietnam.

Released in 1973, *Electra Glide in Blue* is a B-movie with generally poor acting, scripting, and direction, but grade "A" scenery of the Southwest desert monuments. It was adapted by Robert Boris, from a story by Boris and Rupert Hitzig. It was directed by James William Guercio, with photography by Conrad Hall.

John Wintergreen is a straight-arrow cop. He works out and is remarkably potent, according to a local babe. He is called Big John because he is so short. He wants to be a detective, until he is taken as a protégé by a cigar-smoking, pompous but impotent detective investigating the murder of a recluse. John eventually goes back to being a motorcycle cop, disgusted with the corruption and stupidity he sees.

Zipper (played by Billy "Green" Bush) and John are taking target practice on the police range, shooting at a target of the motorcycle scene of Dennis Hopper giving the finger to the rednecks in *Easy Rider*—a gesture made just before he is shot. As it happens, in the final action scene of *Electra Glide in Blue*, John is shot by a hippie from the back of a van, ironically when he is riding after them to return the driver's license.

As a Vietnam War veteran, John Wintergreen has some interesting comments about loneliness. It "will kill you quicker than a .357 magnum." Perhaps referring to the film, John remarks to Zipper, "People do all kinds of things and most of it's bullshit." Robert Blake gives his character sad eyed sincerity, which serves to declare his loneliness rather than presenting it to us as a convincing lifestyle.

Gordon's War, 1973

This 1973 movie about an African-American returning from Vietnam to fight in the streets of Harlem is an example of a black exploitation action movie that is also a classical war veteran exploitation action movie. Paul Winfield plays Gordon, who is introduced at his wife's gravesite. She died of an overdose of heroin. Gordon in his captain's army class-A uniform wears a Combat Infantryman Badge above and jump wings beneath his ribbons. He wastes no time gathering his war veteran buddies, played by Carl Lee, David Downing and Tony King. They set up a command post and hunt down the drug dealers, working their way up to the big Harlem mover, Spanish Harry (Gilbert Lewis). "We've been in a war before. We'll do it just like in the Nam."

Gordon's War was directed by Ossie Davis and written by Howard Friedlander and Ed Spielman. The movie is all action, but with a flat ending, as if it stopped when it ran out of money. Action movies that have character development are rare gems, but this one is glass. The biggest criminals, seen sitting in a corporate type boardroom, are all white, while the rest of the cast is black, except for a white girl who gets shot in bed. Winfield seems one dimensional in his deadpan anger. The shots of Harlem, the fashions of the pimps and high rollers, and the photography by Victor Kemper are worth the look.

Gordon's War replays the theme of war veteran action films, conveying the idea that the police are ineffective and even overwhelmed. No token is given to collaboration with the criminal justice system. Gordon operates only with known war veteran loyalties.

The idea, however, that while being away at war, the veteran's home environment is changed for the worse, and, of course, hunting down criminals is a job, perhaps the only job, the combat veteran knows how to do. It is this same kind of righteous rage that Martin Scorsese plays to with his paradoxical vigilante Travis Bickle.

The Glory Boys, 1984

Anthony Perkins' Jimmy in The Glory Boys drinks an unidentified whiskey from a silver flask while going about his killing. The Glory Boys is a British made-for-TV movie about two governments protecting an Israeli nuclear scientist, David Sokarev, played smoothly and modestly by Rod Steiger, who has been targeted by Arab terrorists for assassination. The scientist is making a speech in London. A security official on the British side, named Jones, calls in a old air force buddy, Jimmy, who had once saved his life in a jungle during World War II.

As the movie develops, we learn that the terrorists are labeled Glory Boys, and later we get the impression that the security people are similarly labeled. It seems that the intent of the film is to show us the parallels of dedication and loyalty on both sides, which seem to be value-laden sentiments that transcend nationality and ideology. Of the two surviving terrorists, one is Palestinian, Famy, played by Gary Brown, while the other, Karen McCoy, played with electric intensity by Aaron Harris, is Irish.

The Glory Boys, based on a novel by Gerald Seymour, was directed by Michael Ferguson. As a drama, it is complex enough to show us parallels between the love of the professor, and the love of duty, compared to the love of the terrorist, Karen, by his girl friend, Nora, played with delightful expressiveness by Sallyanne Law.

Perkins, always a thin actor, manages to saunter through this action drama with a sense of cocky, ironic fatalism that works. We see how his alcoholism is a lubricant that slickens the fatal slide, but we don't see its ugly degeneracy at the bottom, when the war hero, who can't free himself when duty calls, finds himself with muddled mind.

Devil in a Blue Dress, 1995

Devil in a Blue Dress is based on a novel from the Easy Rowlins detective series, by Walter Mosley. Easy, for Ezekiel, is played by Denzel Washington. Nostalgia for post-war late '40s Los Angeles plays prominently as Easy returns from the war. Jennifer Beals plays Daphne Monet in the title role. Easy is a combat veteran and must return to a segregated town. He is hired by a rich white man, DeWitt Albright, played by Tom Sizemore, to find Daphne, who has disappeared into Darktown. Easy takes the job because he's broke and unemployed, having been laid off from his job. When things get

Ezekiel "Easy" Rawlins (Denzel Washington) is drawn reluctantly into the detective business when he is hired to find a woman who has disappeared into "Darktown" in the neo-*noir* thriller *Devil in a Blue Dress* (TriStar Pictures, 1995). (Photograph by Bruce W. Talamon.)

rough, Easy is assisted by his comic, vicious, psychopathic friend, Mouse, played with delightful amorality by Don Cheadle.

Devil in a Blue Dress was directed by Carl Franklin and has a satisfying sense of period authenticity, where cops and jazz aficionados were usually the only Caucasians to venture into the African-American sections of LA. Music for the film features T-Bone Walker's "West Side Baby," Amos Milburn's "Chicken Shack Boogie," and Pee Wee Clayton's "Blues after Hours."

Narmore (1998, p. 250) sums up Easy's character as a loner with a shady past. "Rawlins does not suffer from guilt or quasi-existential angst. He wants nothing more than a steady job, so that he can satisfy the American dream of having a home with a bit of lawn attached."

The War Veteran as Antihero

The war veteran can turn his survival skills to work in a variety of ways, not all of them honorable. He may be forced to make choices that he would prefer not to make, as does Shang in *Alamo Bay* and Michael, the luckless former marine in *Red Rock West*, or he may be one of those who finds living on the dark side is the choice that must be made, as does the expatriate in *Saint Jack*, and Frank, the dark war veteran brother in *Indian Runner*, and Travis, the alienated war veteran in *Taxi Driver*. In a dark corner of the dark side, are the psychotic and psychopathic war veterans represented in the low-budget sensationalism of *Tracks*, *Deathdream*, and *Motor Psycho*, and the high budget story of a down-going woman, *Looking for Mr. Goodbar*. *The Visitors* seems to take the position that the hero and antihero are but two tails of a normal curve, when most war veterans fall somewhere in-between.

It has been observed that the Roman legions, upon their retirement, were given plots of land on the borders of the Empire. There they could provide a line of defense against the enemy, and conveniently be occupied far from Rome. As noted above, the British film, *Mrs. Dalloway*, has politicians expressing the anxious sentiment that maybe war veterans should be sent to live in the outskirts of the former British Empire.

Howard Hawks' *Red River* presents a post–Civil War scene of Confederate veterans led by John Wayne's Dunson, who hardens with each killing. He is a war veteran who takes what he wants and kills to get his way.

What to do with the negative influences of prolonged combat? The fear produced in U.S. movies during World War II and the Vietnam War is fairly tangible in the imagined monsters who might return from the hellish regions of the war. The fact that war veterans return and abjure violence, even though it is now part of their personal symbol systems, is a tribute to the restraint and civilized foundation of the veterans. That moviemakers imagined what the war veteran would be like returning, caused the creators to produce a figure from the dark, the war veteran antihero. For the period during and just after the Vietnam War, U.S. press tended to label each illegal act by a Vietnam War veteran as related to the war by stating the association. Movies about war veteran antiheroes also become part of the historic legacy of a war.

Red River, 1948

John Wayne plays Matthew Dunson, a U.S. Civil War veteran, still wearing his cavalry pants in the opening scenes. His wagon is splitting from the wagon train and symbolically going its own way. He leaves his sweetheart, who he insists stay with the wagon train, although she'd willingly take her chances with him. Dunson is taking his wagon across the Red River into Texas. The wagon's driver is Pop Groot, played by Walter Brennan, who makes a great deal out of not having teeth. They quickly discover, however, that the wagon train they just left was attacked by Indians, and all but one were killed. They meet a boy who is the sole survivor. Dunson takes the boy and his cow with them. Together they reach Texas, and Dunson, with force of arms, takes the grazing land of his choice away from the Mexican owner, who, he asserts, took it away from someone else.

Red River was directed by Howard Hawks and released in 1948. Montgomery Clift plays Matt Garth, who is the sole survivor boy grown into a man. His cow and Dunson's bull have multiplied 14 years later into a herd of ten thousand cows, but there is no market in the post-war South for beef. To sell their cattle, they must drive them north. Dunson seems still more ruthless as he rounds up his neighbor's cattle in preparing for the drive. He rallies his cowboys and urges them to take up the dangers of a long drive with an appeal to their war veteran status, telling them essentially that they have nothing to lose: "Most of you men have come back to Texas from the war. You came back to nothing. You found your homes gone, cattle scattered, and land stolen by carpet-baggers. There's no work because there's no market for beef in the South."

Dunson's ruthlessness hardens as he shoots down men who would desert his crew in the face of hardships. After he kills, he turns paranoid, avoids sleeping, and takes regular slugs from his bottle of whiskey. "Funny what the night does to a man," he says to Matt. "You're all right during the day," Matt observes. Dunson replies, "During the day you can see."

As a romance, *Red River* is uncomfortably dated, but as a war veteran action Western, it is an example of the relentless repetition of a willingness to dominate with lethal violence to achieve his ends. He would even kill Matt, who is like his own son, because his obsessive determined goal is thwarted. Matt takes the herd away from Dunson and the crew mutiny. They drive the herd to nearby Kansas, taking a detour to meet the newly established railroad. In the end, however, for the sake of Hollywood and its code, Dunson is won over by reason and the amorous pleading of Tess (Joanne Dru), and grudgingly adapts to the changes before him.

Motor Psycho, 1965

The most callused genius of the exploitation film is Russ Meyer, who co-wrote, produced, directed, and photographed *Motor Psycho*, which was released into the world like a virus in 1965. It is of interest because it was made about a Vietnam War veteran at the very beginning of the war. Brahmin, an army veteran, and two of his pals are riding motorcycles, dirt bikes really, without any packs or other accouterments, as if they were on a day ride. They encounter, in a series, hapless couples in the California desert. Brahmin and his friends, Slick and Dante, rape and murder whomever they meet. They finally encounter a veterinarian who knocks Brahmin off his motorcycle for harassing his buxom wife. (All the women in a Russ Meyer movie are so buxom they are stylized parodies.) The bikers find out where the veterinarian lives and rape and murder his wife, while he's away on call. The vet, when he discovers what they've done, pursues the murderers, and after still more murder, he trails them into the desert, where Brahmin becomes delusional, talking about Communists. He sings, "When the war is over we will all enlist again," to the tune of "When Johnny comes marching home." We know he's going mad when he speaks to his one surviving accomplice, Dante, after having just murdered Slick, saying "All right, my loyal Petroclus, let's get this chariot rolling." He must be referring to Homer, but in the psychotherapy business, we would have to term this a head-turning loose association. Shortly thereafter he is telling his accomplice, "We got orders to wait for the chopper." Poor Dante is too worried to criticize Brahmin for mixing his metaphors.

At one point, the marauders meet an elderly World War I veteran, who talks about his wound that he got in the battlefield in such a manipulative way, so as to solicit help changing his truck tire. He previously had a burlesque spat with his busty companion, whom he called a "Cajun wench." Brahmin and his friends taunt the old man, naming various other wars that he might have been in. Brahmin beats the old man and shoots him dead and then wounds his companion, leaving her for dead.

Meyer is a popular filmmaker who laces each of his works with busty women and burlesque jokes. It is important that he made this film *before* the military buildup. The characters he created developed into the stereotypes that we have come to associate with the Vietnam War. The character of Brahmin is a collective fantasy of a team of writers, directed by Meyer, imagining what kind of man would come back from Southeast Asian combat. The team of writers seems bent on creating a tawdry collection of sexual and violent scenes solely to sell drive-in movie tickets. They project their seamy fantasies onto the current news, and out comes their corporal effluvia, *Motor Psycho*, get it?

The Ballad of Andy Crocker, 1969

The Ballad of Andy Crocker is a curious movie from the war veteran perspective. Released in 1969, directed by George McCowan and written by Stuart Margolin, this Hollywood B-movie has a strongly dated sense of the 1960s during the height of the Vietnam War. Based on a sentimental song, the film has about that much depth. We see the vet first in ill-defined jungle combat that mimics documentary footage. Then we see Andy on a plane in class-A uniform heading home with his buddy, played by Marvin Gaye. A medal is mentioned and Andy pulls from his pocket a case, opens it, and we never see the unnamed medal, only Andy's loving appreciative face, as though he were gazing at his first child. He fantasizes a romantic reunion with his girl friend, played by Joey Heatherton, who he reveals he has not heard from since she announced she was going to date other men.

Lee Majors plays Andy, a straight guy who just wants to race motorcycles. He steals a motorcycle from a drug-jaded hippie at a Hollywood version of a hippie party. The girls with dark mascara and fluffy long hair, are all dressed in garish silky colors. Andy steals the motorcycle after he is rejected and asked to leave the party. He rides from LA to Texas in a succession of traveling scenes. Home at last, he is greeted warmly by his mother and father. When he goes to his old haunts, he discovers that his business partner, played with audacity by Jimmy Dean, has cheated him out of his motorcycle business and his girl friend has married and lives in Dallas.

There is much motorcycle riding in *The Ballad of Andy Crocker*, and the theme is one of injustices heaped upon this returning Vietnam War veteran. The war itself is not criticized or much discussed. At one point Andy goes to the mother of his former girl friend to ask her to co-sign for a loan to save his business. An interesting character, the grandma, played with surety by Agnes Moorehead, is firing a shotgun on a skeet range as she asks: "How was the war, Andy? Think we'll win?" Andy replies, "maybe." She responds, "Lose today, can't tell from winning."

Andy finally beats his business partner with his fists and drives away, eluding the police. He is rejected by his father, who accuses him of being stupid. He drives off in the night, finally ditching his motorcycle after it runs out of fuel, and, after eluding the posse of highway patrol motorcycle cops, finds his way to Oakland, where his army friend lives, his fellow passenger on the "freedom bird." His friend's wife expresses reservations about putting Andy up until he gets a job, and Andy walks away in the rain. In the last scene we see him sitting huddled on the curb in the rain in front of the army recruiting office, waiting for it to open.

This renegade theme, riding the motorcycle till it runs out of gas, seen also in the higher budget, more convincing pursuit scenes in *First Blood*, is the modern equivalent of the movie western cowboy riding his horse till it drops. In reality the postwar adjustment was extremely difficult for the Vietnam combat veteran, not just because of the scapegoating prejudice in U.S. society, but also because of the high levels of stress (noise, pollution, etc) in an over-populated society that was not involved in the combat, but was involved in the national polarization of opinion. Veterans, who were arrested for crimes of mayhem, were imprisoned and prevented from ever readjusting.

The American Soldier, 1970

The American Soldier was written and directed by the unique German talent of Rainer Werner Fassbinder. Released in 1970, this film stars Karl Scheydt as Ricky, a Vietnam War veteran who hires out to the German underground as an assassin. He was raised in Germany and then went with his father to the U.S., where he served in the army in Vietnam. In Fassbinder's mock *noir* style we see Ricky carrying a bottle of Ballantine whisky, drinking from it as he shoots his prey. He is stone-faced and brooding. The screenplay is bare and sparse. The music, also co-written by Fassbinder, has a guitar epic western twang. Ricky is referred to by the crooked cops simply as the "Killer." After he kills one of his victims, he visits his mother. She asks, "Did you come through the war unhurt?" He answers obliquely, "It's OK."

Deathdream, 1972

Several steps below *Jacob's Ladder* in horror genre quality is a 1972 film called *Deathdream*. According to Devine (1995), this film was also released as *The Veteran, Dead of Night, Death of Night,* and *Nightwalk.* The mutability of the title seems to suit the plot. Directed by Bob Clark, *Deathdream* is a B-movie on the same premise as *Jacob's Ladder,* namely, that someone killed in Vietnam goes on appearing to live, refusing to die completely, and becoming quite disturbed in the process. In the beginning of *Deathdream,* the vet, Andy Brookes, played with wooden dedication by Richard Backus, is seen being shot in Vietnam in a poorly produced scene. We then see Andy hitchhiking, returning home, picked up by a trucker and oddly unresponsive. The garrulous trucker is found later with his throat slit, while Andy arrives home and is found lurking in the pantry in the wee hours of the morning. Spookily, the dog barks with suspicion. The arrival is doubly joyful because the family has just gotten a "sorry, Charlie" telegram announcing that Charlie's son is dead. (The army officer who delivers the telegram, actually says to Andy's father, "Sorry, Charlie.") John Marley plays the father, Charlie, who, we learn quickly from his conversation with the postman, is an infantry veteran of the World War II invasion of Okinawa.

Andy, the recently returned Vietnam War veteran, doesn't seem to want to do anything. He acts dead inside and only wants to rock in a chair in his bedroom. Whatever he says is an eerie, spooky double entendre. Mother, who is not the sharpest tool in the shed, is in anguish because her son won't talk and won't eat with them. Charlie explains that Andy has only been home two days. However, Andy alienates even his father when he strangles their little barking dog, Butch, in front of the neighborhood kids. The coroner finds Charlie that evening getting drunk at the tavern. He brings the doctor back to check out Andy. Andy follows the doc back to his office and kills him, saying, "I died for you, doc. Why shouldn't you return the favor?" A rhetorical question. The finale comes when Andy's naïve sister arranges a double date with Andy's pre–Vietnam girlfriend, Joanne, who is still smitten with Andy. Joanne is played by Jane Daley and gives the movie its few brief moments of charm. Unfortunately, Andy begins to rot and turn even more vicious, going on a tear at the drive-in movie. Charlie finally backs down from shooting his own son and accomplishes nothing by committing suicide, shooting himself, while his Vietnam War veteran son, now thoroughly rotten, eludes the police with the aid of his mad mother, and finally crawls to a pre-dug grave with his name scrawled on the stone, symbolically, by smearing away dirt.

It is the blatant symbolism from *Deathdream,* not the best from the gothic horror genre, that captures several important items in the popular bias of 1972. The Vietnam War veteran returns feeling and acting dead inside, with the near catatonic inertia punctuated by fits of brutal violence, with the veteran seeking revenge on his family, friends, and chance encounters. What he experienced in Vietnam will cause him to rot inside and contaminate those at home.

The Visitors, 1972

Elia Kazan directed *The Visitors* from a screenplay written by Chris Kazan, who co-produced the film with the director of photography and editor, Nicholas T. Proferes. The plot concerns a Vietnam War veteran, Bill (James Woods), living in a farmhouse with his girlfriend Martha (Patricia Joyce). They are raising their child, an infant. Martha knows very little of Bill's war experiences, except that he was involved in a military trial. Martha's father, Harry, owns the land and lives in a nearby cabin. Harry (Patrick McVey) is a writer and a World War II veteran of Guadalcanal. Two visitors arrive, who announce to Martha that they served with Bill in Vietnam. They are Sarge, (Steve Railsback), and Tony (Chico Martinez). They just got out of Leavenworth prison, having won release on appeal. Bill testified that they and others had raped a Vietnamese girl and killed her.

The circumstances, war veterans reuniting in the States, has all the ingredients of awkwardness, but Sarge and Tony present an extra menacing presence, while generating a paradoxical sense of sympathy. It doesn't seem that they have come for revenge but to visit, and the menacing tension builds. Tony tells Bill that he forgives him for testifying and there are no hard feelings. The paradox hits that Tony feels wronged, although it was *he* who did the crime.

Martha's father hits it off with the visiting veterans. Bill, it seems, is against violence and Harry thinks he's "half-queer." When a neighboring dog fights with Harry's dog and chews up the little dog's leg, Harry takes Sarge and Tony to shoot the neighbor's dog and drag it to his doorstep. They march back exhilarated, counting cadence and full of camaraderie.

The visitors are invited by Harry to stay for dinner. The old man gets drunk and tells a torture story at the dinner table before dozing off. He's been symbolically drinking Imperial whiskey. Martha remarks, "my mother couldn't stand him, neither could his other two wives."

There is a connection between the quiet, staring Sarge and Martha, who has already revealed her lack of responsiveness to her boyfriend. When she learns the story of the rape, she seems to draw even closer to Sarge. Bill remains passive and conflict-avoidant, until Martha and Sarge dance in sensuous embrace and he discovers them. Then Bill, in a rage, attacks Sarge. They fight and Sarge finally beats Bill unconscious. He then proceeds to rape Martha. Tony participates only in the sense of keeping Martha in the house as the fight ensues. Even though he develops a dislike for Bill, Tony remains non-violent, except for shooting the neighbor's dog.

Elia Kazan presents the ambiguity of a war veteran reunion. Released in 1972 when the war was still in progress, it is the story of a decent war veteran who is regarded as "half-queer," by his angry World War II veteran father of his girlfriend, who we see deteriorate with intoxication and nostalgia. It seems that the horrors of Guadalcanal were an undoing influence on him, too, although Martha seems to think he was always just an "asshole." Martha recounts her father's failures as a writer after an initial success, although, she said, he continued to turn out books.

Martha seems attracted to the hypnotic eyes of Sarge, even after he has admitted to the wartime atrocity. (It is difficult to see Steve Railsback without thinking of his mesmerizing portrayal of Charles Manson in *Helter Skelter*.) What sways Martha, it seems, is Sarge's passion when he tells how he went from being a high school honors student to participating so whole-heartedly in the catastrophic war. He describes how he was handing out candy to village kids when his friend's legs were blown off.

Tony and Sarge drive off leaving behind the battered Bill and Martha. Harry had long since staggered off in a drunken stupor, after begging his two new buddies to stay the night.

Elia Kazan by the time he made *The Visitors* had many successes in film and on Broadway, several of which were politically sensitive, e.g., *On the Waterfront, Gentlemen's Agreement*. In 1952 he testified before the House Un-American Activities Committee, admitting he was once a member of the Communist Party, and naming other members of his group. *The Visitors*, written by his son, has the feeling of a psychological working through for the director, couched in terms of a current politically sensitive drama of another era's controversy, with ambiguous, complex problems. In *The Visitors*, Bill finally resorts to violence, having reached the place where he could not avoid conflict. He gets badly beaten, his wife is raped anyway, but he made his stand. The ambiguity is profound, for there is a hint that his rage at Sarge dancing with Martha actually stimulated Sarge to rape her, although Sarge had provoked the scene to that point. Kazan also has sounds coming from Martha as she is raped that are disconcertingly ambiguous. When the veterans drive off, Bill is sitting in the darkened living room with Martha. "You were right," he says ambiguously.

Taxi Driver, 1976

In *Taxi Driver*, a socially maladapted, urban Marine veteran, Travis Bickle, played with extraordinary skill by Robert De Niro, is the implied war veteran. His interview with the taxi company dispatcher reveals he was recently a Marine and we can see on his jacket the Force Recon patch on his left arm. The patch is kept consistently out of focus, which makes the vague death's head seem spooky. Released in 1976, *Taxi Driver* was widely regarded as a tour de force for director Martin Scorsese. De Niro's Travis Bickle is a lonely, alienated young man in New York City. He cannot sleep anyway, he explains, and so he requests long shifts and would drive anywhere in the city with a sense of reckless disregard for his own safety. What he sees in the city as he drives, fits into his voiceover paranoid ramblings, recording a man on the verge of a psychotic break. Travis reveals that he was discharged from the Marines in 1973. We don't know what happened to him in the Marines, and he wouldn't tell us if we asked.

From the opening credits, watching the taxi drive through the steam from manhole covers and lonely urban jazz wailing, we have Travis' ranting voiceover as he cruises past the theater marquee that sets the tone with *Texas Chainsaw Massacre*: "All the animals come out at night. Some day a real rain will come and wash the scum off the street."

Travis, like a lonely dwarf from the mountains, asks the pretty, urbane Betsy for a date. She is working on a campaign to elect a Senator Palantine (played by Leonard Harris) as the next president. Betsy, played with charm by Cybill Shepherd, is tickled by Travis' direct, awkward charm. "I don't believe I've ever met anyone quite like you." She cannot help but smile when he flatters her. He wears a sports coat and tie when he introduces himself to her, but doesn't have any idea what would be a socially appropriate movie to take a classy young woman like Betsy to. He takes her to a Swedish porn film, cajoling her into entering, "Lots of couples come here." She bolts out of her seat, revolted and angry, and Travis is hurt by her abrupt departure.

It is not that Travis doesn't try to integrate and make it in society, it's that he's bothered by paranoid fantasies and eating a lot of pills, apparently speed. We watch him decompensate before our eyes, slowly and dramatically. When the senator gets into his cab with an aide, he asks Travis about what he thought was the one thing that bugged him the most about society. Travis starts shyly to respond, wandering quickly into his paranoid rant: "This city is like an open sewer. I get a headache it's so bad." And ends his thought with an eloquent request of the senator to "flush it right down the fuckin' toilet."

Martin Scorsese makes a cameo appearance as a cuckolded passenger in the taxi, who asks Travis to park and watch his wife standing in a lighted window trysting with a low-born man, and proceeds to describe graphically how he's going to shoot the couple. With the greatest of film ironies, the cuckold says to Travis, "You must think I'm pretty sick."

Travis goes to consult a fellow cabbie at a coffee shop, trying to get some direction. Wizard, played by Peter Boyle, says that he is called Wizard because he's been around. In a scene that could be used to train neophyte counselors, Travis tells Wizard that he wants "to go out and really do something." Wizard talks nonsense, although it seems that he's doing the best he can to be wise. Travis confesses, "I got some bad ideas in my head." Wizard, for all his wisdom, slaps Travis on the shoulder and responds to his fellow taxi driver's plea for guidance. "Go on, get laid, get drunk. You got no choice. We're all fucked. Don't worry so much."

Travis then buys guns from a freelance retailer, Easy Andy. He buys a .44 that "will put a round through an engine," a .38 snubnose service revolver, a Colt .25 semiautomatic, and a .380 Walther, "that replaced the army's P38 and is just for officers." What follows is a montage of scenes of Travis developing his deadly technique, drawing his weapon and speaking to the mirror, posing, working out. In the meantime he writes an all-purpose card to his parents, telling them that, due to the sensitive nature of his work, he cannot give them details, or even his return address, but not to worry, as he is going with a girl.

Periodically Travis encounters a young prostitute, Iris, on the streets. He tries to talk her into leaving her chosen work. Iris is played by Jodi Foster, stealing her scenes at age 12. Her pimp is Sport, played by Harvey Keitel, who refers to Travis as "Cowboy." Travis calls her "Sweet Iris" and urges her to leave. She retorts, however, "when I'm not stoned I got no place else to go." Keitel plays Sport with a smarmy intensity as he mesmerizes Iris to keep her working.

Travis intends to shoot Senator Palantine at a rally, but is driven away by an alert Secret Service agent. The senator's speech, though smoother, makes about as much sense as Wizard's. Travis has already alerted the security man by previously standing beside him and mocking him. Travis in his fatigue jacket and the giant Secret Service agent, played with mirrored sunglasses by Richard Higgs, are a study of contrasts.

Travis, now armed with an arsenal of cleverly concealed guns, rushes off to his alternative target. The denouement turns as violent and bloody as any scene could be turned, yet with a poetic slow motion choreographed horror in the tradition of Sam Peckinpah. In a most horrific gun fight, Travis shoots Sport, walks to the tenement where Iris is working, and shoots all the men who get in his way, creating a bloody path, while music by Bernard Herrmann drives unsparingly with a fated, mournful cadence that could be used to describe armies in pitched combat. (Herrmann died before the film was completed and Scorsese dedicated it to his memory.)

The scene shifts for relief to an ironic twist that makes the psychotic

Travis Bickle (Robert De Niro, right), a Vietnam War veteran, talks with a Secret Service agent, played by Richard Higgs in *Taxi Driver* (Columbia Pictures, 1976). This scene sums up in a visual statement the spirit of many returning war veterans vis-à-vis authority.

decompensation heroic. The camera pans to a close-up of newspaper clippings pinned to the wall of Travis' apartment: "Taxi driver battles gangsters." The clippings and a handwritten letter tell the story of how Iris has been returned to her family and Travis has been lauded for his sacrifice.

Taxi Driver was written by the conjurer of action/violence Paul Schrader and photographed superbly in urban dark and reflected light by Michael Chapman. Released in 1976, it has some of the feeling of the haunted, lonely urban male, somewhat demented, a kind of Lee Harvey Oswald ex–Marine. But for Travis' jacket with black jump wings and the constantly-out-of-focus patch on his shoulder that looks something like a death's head, we have no idea of Travis as a war veteran. The power of the film is in its paranoid intensity and the truth it conveys about the burbling cauldron of urban alienation and the innocents, like Travis and Iris, caught in the soup.

Scorsese himself acknowledges that he was trying to convey Travis as a war veteran.

It was crucial to Travis Bickle's character that he had experienced life and death around him every second he was in southeast Asia. That way it becomes more heightened when he comes back; the image of the street at night reflected in the dirty gutter becomes more threatening. I think that's something a guy going through a war, any war, would experience when he comes back to what is supposedly "civilization." He'd be more paranoid. I'll never forget a story my father told me about one of my uncles coming back from the Second World War and walking in the street. A car backfired and the guy just instinctively ran two blocks! So Travis Bickle was affected by Vietnam: it's held in him, and then it explodes. And although at the end of the film he seems to be in control again, we give the impression that any second the time bomb might go off again [Scorsese, 1989, p. 62].

Tracks, 1976

Henry Jaglom, who wrote and directed *Tracks*, an ensemble picture released in 1976, has something of a following for his independent comedies; however, this film isn't much of a comedy or a drama. The story concerns passengers on a train who talk, and talk, the cast obviously improvising their lines. Among the passengers is an army "super" sergeant with Combat Infantryman Badge, played by Dennis Hopper, who is escorting the body of his friend in a coffin back from Vietnam. "Black man in that coffin — a hero — he saved my life." He seems also to have served in the Korean War. "I lost 21 guys in Korea." The dialog is often stupid and Hopper seems to have no concept of what someone would think like, having just come from combat, although there probably weren't many E-9 sergeants in bush combat in Vietnam. He wears long sideburns and hair long enough to curl on the neck, hardly the style of one gung-ho enough to become an E-9, but consistent with the odd, out-of-context emotions that muddle the entire film. Also oddly inappropriate, the sound track consists of World War II popular songs.

Hopper's sergeant finally escorts the coffin to the station where no one meets him. He is alone at the graveyard and loses his cool, snaps, and has, as we say, a psychotic break. He jumps into the grave, opens the coffin and pulls out combat gear. He picks up an M-16 and shouts, "You motherfuckers, you wanna go to Nam!? I'll take you there!" In the background at this comically serious finale is the song, "There's a star spangled banner waving somewhere, a hero brave is what I want to be."

Tracks is another good example of a bad movie that exploits a real war veteran emotion as an anchor to the plot, but uses it for sensation instead of exploring its origins and meaning. In this case it is the emotion of grief and alienation caused by the death of a friend in combat and an uncaring public back home. The grave details of stateside military service

and the job of escorting the KIA's home, delivering the news, giving guidance and solace to grieving families, went on for over ten years during the
Vietnam War. Many young officers had that mournful detail during their
"break" between combat tours.

Looking for Mr. Goodbar, 1977

Richard Gere plays Tony, one of Teresa Dunn's several lovers. He is
a Vietnam War veteran and has scars on his body that he says got him out
of the war. He reveals he is a veteran when he is dancing about her apartment, naked but for a jock strap, with a fake knife that glows in the dark.
She asks if he's ever killed anybody. "In Vietnam," he says succinctly.

Tony is a tough street person, an impulsive psychopath who likes to
taunt Teresa. He is a precursor of Teresa's tragic death at the hands of
another, but this one perverted, lover. Teresa is played by Diane Keaton,
who is an Irish-American schoolteacher. She teaches deaf children. She
has a certain lust for life after a bout with death as a child. The opening
sequences of Looking for Mr. Goodbar are devoted to the Teresa as a young
girl being trussed up in a body cast after surgery for scoliosis. It is evident
that the procedure was a life-altering psychological trauma for the girl and
her scar is alluded to in comments by her various lovers. Teresa begins her
sexual adventures with her college writing teacher, and when he frustrates
her, she starts hanging out in swinging bars. She, with her sister, Kather-
ine, played by Tuesday Weld, are at odds with their father, played by
Richard Kiley, who insists that they be perfect models of Irish-American
girls. When Teresa meets a young social worker who went to Notre Dame,
her father is won over. Teresa, of course, can't stand the social worker
because he is so correct.

Released in 1977, Looking for Mr. Goodbar was directed with a strong
hand by Richard Brooks, who adapted a screenplay from a novel by Judith
Rossner. Gere's Tony is played in the style of James Dean and the young
Marlon Brando. He's a jazzy, confident, hyperactive bad boy. The bartender calls him "Drummer Man," because he taps spasmodically on the
bar. His attention seems to be flitting, though he is attentive when he
makes love to Teresa. When finished, however, he walks out of her apartment without goodbye, and no plan to return. When they fight, he retaliates by turning her into the police as a school teacher-profligate, yet
returns to her apartment unannounced on New Year's Eve, as if he had not
trashed her career. When she calls the cops and won't let him in, he calls
through the chained front door, "you are dead." But it is not Tony, the
veteran, who murders Teresa. Another street person pickup stabs her to
death.

Looking for Mr. Goodbar is more than a cautionary tale for those who would stray from the Catholic Church. It describes a treacherous path taken by a young woman who would attempt to break from the confines of a body cast that had held her trapped in childhood, and who waits for a man with a knife. The sequela of medical trauma is similarly played out in a more childish fashion in the morbid antics of Devon in *Lawn Dogs*.

Saint Jack, 1979

Saint Jack, like *The Sun Also Rises*, is a film about a war veteran living in exile. Jack Flowers (Ben Gazzara) is a Korean War veteran with a Purple Heart. He is making a living in Singapore by hustling and arranging. Something of a travel agent, tour promoter, and pimp, he helps people, it seems mainly men, have a good time. "Anything you want, anything at all." From the narrative we know that Jack was going to be a writer after the Korean War, but left the U.S. in 1959.

The movie was directed by Peter Bogdanovich and released in 1979. Bogdanovich also collaborated on the screenplay with Howard Sackler, and Paul Theroux, from a novel by Paul Theroux. Ben Gazzara plays Jack with a benign, melancholy dignity. It seems he is in competition with some rough local characters, who keep tailing him, giving the early part of the film a tinge of suspense. They finally try to intimidate Jack by forcibly tattooing his arms with vulgar Chinese slogans. Jack hires his own tattoo artist to turn the characters into flowers. When confronting the hoods, he seems to have no fear, yet remains passive and protective of the staff of his bordello.

Jack is approached by an agent of the U.S. military in Vietnam to arrange an R&R center. This he manages with ease, bringing in troops in civilian clothes by the busloads. His success is ended rather abruptly, however, when the war finishes with the 1975 U.S. pullout. The agent who hired Jack, Eddie Schuman (played by Bogdanovich), asks him to do a particularly tawdry deed. He is given the task of gathering compromising evidence on a visiting "outspoken" U.S. politician. Jack does the deed, but then throws the money away and quits, apparently to retire and return to the U.S. for his own betterment. Earlier we had seen him comment to Eddie at the height of his R&R success, "We're the ones who fatten 'em for the slaughter."

There are two nice touches in the film: one is a repeating visit by an English businessman, an auditor with a bad heart, William Leigh, played with bemused chagrin by Denholm Elliot; the other is a beautiful Ceylonese (Sri Lankan) woman, Monika, played by Monika Subramaniam, who becomes Jack's mistress for a while. Jack is friendly with just about every-

Ben Gazzara (left) is Jack Flowers, a Korean War veteran in *Saint Jack* (New World Pictures, 1970), who works in Singapore as a jack-of-all-trades. Here he is telling three GIs on R&R from Vietnam about the delights that await them in Singapore.

body and Bogdanovich gives the film a sense that it respects everyone across race and class.

At the height of his whorehouse R&R entertainment center, when a young man beats up a prostitute, the other women, prostitutes and house-keepers, gather round and aid her, much as they would in a factory, were she injured. Jack checks out the young assailant, no longer aggressive, and seems reassured that his friends are with him and he is calm. Marijuana is tolerated and seemingly abundant, but "scag" is banned, according to "saint" Jack. The men are boys from combat who seem to be enjoying themselves, although, they seem calmer than college boys on spring break.

Saint Jack was produced with support from *Playboy* magazine and takes an editorial position in favor of prostitution. The film gives the girls names and relatively unglamorous blue-collar personalities, and views their trade as an integral part of the tourist industry. They seem to enjoy their work as much as the "boys" from Vietnam enjoy them. The dark side of all this seems delicately sidestepped. As Jack says, "People make love for crazy reasons, why shouldn't money be one of them?" And, in this sense, the title is as much an irony as *The Sun Also Rises*. Jack is no saint, but he is a respectful, non-violent nice guy. Theroux, in his novel, tackles the paradox of his "saintliness."

> It wasn't the money that drove me; I can't call it holy charity, but it was as close to a Christian act as that sort of friendly commerce could be, keeping those already astray happy and from harm, within caution's limits. I raided my humanity to console them with reminders of safety, while reminding myself of the dangers. I was dealing with the very innocent, blind men holding helpless sticks; their passions were guesses [1973, p. 122].

The tattoos in vulgar Chinese, transformed into flowers, symbolize his twist of logic, and in the end he is apparently saved when he quits the tawdry trade and says he is heading home.

Alamo Bay, 1985

Portraying the antihero in film is difficult to carry off without resorting to melodrama. Ed Harris plays Shang, a Vietnam War veteran who sports a Texas Confederate flag on his hat and a shirt with "Vietnam Vets of Texas" displayed on the back, in the tense drama *Alamo Bay.* The name "Shang" is an esoteric reference to Shanghai Pearce, one of the great Texas cattle drovers (Malle, 1993, p. 149). Released in 1985, the film is about Texas Gulf shrimping, dwindling beds, obscure Federal regulations, and the scapegoating prejudice against increasing numbers of Vietnamese émigrés moving into the shrinking industry. Louis Malle directs and the French slant is an interesting one. There is no sentimental panache painted over the topic of the Vietnam War veteran's readjustment. As the movie begins, a Vietnamese young man, Dinh, played by Ho Nguyen, is hitchhiking, waving a small American flag. He is picked up finally by a gracious gentleman driving a delivery van, who offers him a beer. The driver says, "you're from Vietnam. I had a good time over there, myself. Dynamite drugs."

The local employer of Vietnamese labor is Wally, played by Donald Moffat. He runs the processing shed that buys the shrimp and packs it for shipping. His daughter, Glory, played by Amy Madigan, is the real protagonist of this movie. She has had a love for Shang from when they were in high school. She still sleeps with him, even though Shang is married to a small-minded, rather hateful woman, who works in the supermarket.

Alamo Bay deals with the harassment of the Vietnamese population by hatred cultivated and directed by a proselytizing Klansman, who refers to the Vietnamese as "Indochinese," the way an old Southern politician would refer to African-Americans, with condescending mock courtesy, as Negroes. The film begins with the written statement that gives it a factual

Vietnam War veteran Shang (Ed Harris, center foreground) unites with Klans-
men to intimidate Vietnamese immigrant shrimp fishermen, in Louis Malle's
Alamo Bay (Tri-Star Pictures, 1985).

basis: "In the years following the Fall of Saigon, a million Vietnamese fled
their country, many of them hoping to find a new life in the USA. This
story is inspired by a series of incidents which took place on the Gulf Coast
of Texas between 1979 and 1981."

Alamo Bay was written by Alice Arlen and is a terrific vehicle for Amy
Madigan as Glory, but the movie's hot center is Ed Harris' angry Shang,
who seethes with virility and the frustrated passion of a man whose efforts
to get ahead are blocked by circumstances beyond his control. He could
well be a Washington salmon fisherman or Idaho logger. The traditional
way of living is dying and the government seems to be doing more regu-
lating than helping. Shang is unable to secure a loan and his boat, *American Dream Girl*, is repossessed. He takes his angry aggression out on the
nearest foreigner, Dinh, who we saw hitchhiking in the beginning of the
film. Dinh wants to own his own boat and wears a cowboy hat and cowboy boots. He has the nervous audacity and appeal of Jackie Chan, without the latter's adroit maneuvering.

An interesting slant, made subtly by Malle, is a Mexican worker, Luis,
played by Martino La Salle, who identifies with the struggles of the Viet-

namese. A poignant note is struck by the name of the bar frequented by the Texas fishermen, which excludes the Vietnamese, the Zanadew Lounge, suggesting a longed-for Texas Neverland of perfection that is beyond reality.

Few films really approach the racial prejudice that is associated with the Vietnam War. We have an easier time forgiving the veterans because we understand that their hatred of "gooks" is conditioned by a year or so of deadly fire. Yet the Mexican worker, Luis, seems to call attention to the racial and ethnic prejudice that is latent in the U.S. society, that lies at the very roots of Western Colonialism, dividing the world into ours and ours. *Bad Day at Black Rock, Snow Falling on Cedars, Ashes & Embers, Powwow Highway,* and *Dead Presidents* also tackle this problem, while John Ford's *The Sun Shines Bright* backdoors the problem with satiric stereotypes.

The Park Is Mine, 1986

B-movie tradition implies a certain tightness of the budget. *The Park Is Mine,* a story about the takeover of New York City's Central Park by a Vietnam War veteran, was filmed in Toronto. Tommy Lee Jones plays Mitch, a veteran whose buddy and fellow war veteran commits suicide, distressed about the onset of cancer. He leaves Mitch a letter and a key to his arsenal. Seems the cancer had interrupted his friend's plans to take over Central Park and make a statement.

The problem with *The Park Is Mine* is that it doesn't know what statement to make. Mitch, when he carries out his buddy's plan, is inarticulate when he gets on the phone or the short-wave radio. The movie was directed by Steven Hilliard Stern, with a screenplay by Lyle Gorch, from a book by Stephen Peters. The story portrays Mitch as a confused man who seems to become a folk hero, according to unconvincing TV interviews of bystanders. Mitch announces in his radio broadcast that he is a vet, and that his whole life has been directed by other people. "Couldn't hold a job. Couldn't put certain things behind me. My friend killed himself, a vet, good American." Compare this to the same thesis dramatized in *The Stunt Man.* Tommy Lee Jones' Mitch is no less articulate than Steve Railsback's Bart, although the thesis is brought home visually in *The Stunt Man* as the movie's theme.

The Park Is Mine lacks a credible premise — a war veteran, in some sort of outraged cry, sets off a pyrotechnic display, takes the city's park hostage, and intimidates the New York emergency forces until Veterans Day. The plot adds a blonde female television journalist, Valery, played by Helen Shaver. For no apparent reason Mitch has her take off her clothes and then gives her fatigues to wear. Mitch seems so totally absorbed with

larger events that he cannot focus on the sexual titillation of Valery's awkward disrobing.

The police hunt for the vet in the park takes on a video game feeling
with the redundant music of Tangerine Dream. When Valery asks Mitch
what he did in the Vietnam War, he replies that he was with the U.S. Army,
and he would "sneak into places and blow shit up and kill people." Later
he tells her, "I realize I am a total fuck up." When he finally gives himself
up at the appointed time on Veterans Day, Valery addresses him with
affection, "well if it isn't Lone Ranger."

Jones' portrayal of the loser vet is similar to that of the supposed veteran who takes over the Brooklyn bank in *Dog Day Afternoon*, only in a
less humorous and convincing drama. Something drives the veteran over
the edge, only he can't make his statement coherent enough to get it across.
He seems to be drawn by fate after his friend dies and compulsively brings
about the repetition of being pursued, dogged to death.

The Indian Runner, 1991

The Indian Runner was actor Sean Penn's first directorial effort. It was
released in 1991, written by Penn, and, according to the credits, inspired
by a Bruce Springsteen song, "Highway Partolman." The plot concerns
two brothers: Joe, played by David Morse, is the town's chief sheriff's
deputy who is a blond straight arrow, and Frank, played by Viggo
Mortensen, who is a dark-haired, sallow-cheeked man, who returns from
Vietnam and begins to lead an outlaw life. Their parents are played by
Sandy Dennis and Charles Bronson, each portraying a sad, muted character. Bronson, as the father, finally commits suicide after his wife dies of
cancer.

As the film opens, Joe is chasing a speeding car. The chase ends with
the man leaving his car and firing a pistol at Joe as he runs into the win-
try Midwest farm field. Joe reluctantly shoots him dead with his shotgun.
Then we see the dead man's parents raging at Joe in grief. Joe sits peni-
tently in his chair behind his desk. The dead man's father rants a hillbilly
chant with dark, mad fury as he is pushed out of Joe's office.

Then Frank returns from Vietnam in an army uniform and beret,
with an Air Cav patch, buck sergeant stripes, and a Combat Infantryman
Badge. When he meets his brother he says, "Town looks same-same."
Frank rides in Joe's police car, but jumps out, refusing to go visit their parents. Instead he hops onto a passing train with his duffel bag.

Joe, upright citizen that he is, has married a Mexican woman, Maria,
played by Valeria Golino, who smokes marijuana. It seems that Maria
reflects Joe's darker side that we see in his parents' darkness, and that is

represented entirely in the person of his brother. Maria, however, has her feet on the ground and is dealing with their toddler son.

Joe learns that Frank has been arrested, apparently for domestic violence, and goes to see him on the day of his brother's release from jail. In the crowded waiting room he sees Frank have his handcuffs removed and be greeted by his girl friend, Dorothy, played as a not-very-bright gamine by Patricia Arquette. Dorothy has a penchant for screaming when she is happy. Frank describes her as a hippie and a little squirrel. Joe follows Frank to a hotel, and when he sees Dorothy leave, he visits Frank. Frank appears shirtless, with tattoos on his chest, neck, back, arms, and legs, reflecting amateur prison artistry. Several of the tattoos reflect outlaw lifestyle — swastika on his hand, paired lightning bolts on the neck, skull with top hat on the back of his shoulder, spider's web surrounding his left nipple. Joe informs Frank that their mother has died, but Frank refuses the invitation to return home.

Charles Bronson as the father presents as a bitter, dark, brooding character. He tells Joe that he (Joe) is working for the same people who stole his farm. He calls Joe in the middle of the night, drinking whiskey, to tell him that some trivial thing in Joe's house needs repair. We next learn that he has shot himself with a shotgun, splattering gore about his living room.

In a montage of scenes, we see Frank on an outlaw rampage, stealing a car at a fey hippie wedding, then stealing money from a gas station, and later torching the car. Joe finally traces Frank to a hotel room to find him naked, stoned, and barely functioning.

Frank and Dorothy return to Frank's hometown to live in his dad's house. The brothers have a series of talks about the legendary Indian Runner, who is representative, Frank claims, of spirit and fire. Frank and Dorothy marry, but Frank continues to have episodic bursts of outlaw madness in which he engages in fights. In one bar scene, with the bartender, Caeser, played with bizarre wit by Dennis Hopper, seems to egg on Frank's rebelliousness in a discussion with his brother. Later Frank beats Caeser mercilessly with a chair in front of the horrified tavern customers.

Penn's direction tends to mute and turn away from dwelling in violence on camera. In one scene of domestic violence, Frank, taunting Dorothy in a sudden change of character, reaches into a bag of peas in the kitchen and tosses the peas at her for emphasis, one by one, as if they were blows, causing her to agonize tearfully. Finally he chews a handful of peas and spits them at her.

Sean Penn has a talent for filmmaking and a fascination for the dark

Viggo Mortensen (lying down) plays Frank, the Vietnam War veteran, in Sean Penn's *The Indian Runner* (Westmount Communications, 1991). He is conversing against the bar with David Morse, who plays his brother, Joe, a sheriff's deputy. (Photograph by Michael Tighe.)

side, later exemplified in his *Dead Man Walking*. In *Indian Runner* he makes an attempt to show us a positive theme, Dorothy's baby being born as Frank runs off, leaving Joe with his ongoing hopeful memory of Frank as a boy.

Indian Runner features original music by Jack Nitzsche, and a soundtrack full of first class blues, including the Band's "I Shall Be Released," and Janis Joplin with Big Brother and the Holding Company's "Summertime."

Penn manages to give us a very clear association to the Vietnam War veteran in this gritty drama about brothers. The Vietnam combat veteran is a dark, randy outlaw, while the brother who stayed home and became the town cop, is blond, steady, caring, optimistic, and fair. Joe loves his brother but cannot save him, although he gives it a good try. And Frank does try to give it a reasonable go as a workingman with family.

Although Frank drives away in the movie, disappearing into the night, we all know that he will die a rat's death, or end up in prison, or a drug rehab program, reading the Big Book in a halfway house. In spite of his best intentions, Penn cannot escape the message that the Franks of the U.S. went off to Vietnam, while the Joes stayed home and were righteous.

Red Rock West, 1993

Red Rock West has the feel of *film noir* from the opening credits. Directed by John Dahl and released in 1993, it is a Hitchcockian story of an honest drifter drawn into a deadly contest between wicked marriage partners. It is also a story of the struggle between two Marine veterans: Dennis Hopper, playing the vicious Lyle from Dallas, a killer who dresses in black and drives a black Buick V8, and the indefatigable drifter, Michael, played by Nicolas Cage, who was the ultimate victimized Marine, injured in the Lebanon Marine barracks bombing in which 241 other Marines were not so lucky. Hopper's Lyle shows Michael his tattoo and declares that he was Marine First Force Recon in Vietnam.

In the plot, Cage's Michael Williams is driving through Wyoming looking for an oil rigger job, but isn't hired because of his injured leg. Nearly broke (we see he has only five dollars in his wallet) he proudly refuses a loan from a friend, and turns away from an opportunity to steal bills from a cash drawer at a temporarily abandoned country gas station. Michael is directed to Red Rock West, and the eponymous tavern, where he might ask around to find work. When Michael arrives, the bartender, Wayne (J.T. Walsh), mistakes him for Lyle from Dallas, the man he hired to kill his wife. He gives Michael $5,000 with the promise of the same again when the job is done. Michael then visits Susanne, played with dark-browed, sultry allure by Lara Flynn Boyle. Several improbable twists have Michael accused of the murder of Susanne's lover, and nearly killed, himself, on the highway in several ways, as well as narrowly escaping death in interpersonal encounters, all the time trying to do the right thing. The movie has a nice satisfying twist at the end.

Red Rock West is a modern western with a good ol' sound track of western favorites, "A Thousand Miles from Nowhere," "Alone in San Antone," "Folsom Prison Blues," "Redneck Girl" (by the Kentucky Headhunters), and "Should've Been a Cowboy."

Hopper's Lyle from Dallas is reminiscent of Hopper's portrayal of the gas sniffing freak in David Lynch's *Blue Velvet*, and the smarmy bad toothed Vietnam veteran killer, played by Willem Dafoe, in *Wild At Heart*. He is the dreaded psychopath who learns his trade in combat and becomes a professional. Martin Scorsese's Travis Bickle in *Taxi Driver* was another maladjusted former Force Recon Marine. Together at the bar, Lyle orders a shot of "JB" and Mike orders a Bud. They click glasses, "*Semper Fi!*"

At first Mike turns down Lyle's offer to buy him a drink. Lyle scolds him. "Us Marines got to stick together. What the fuck's wrong with you?"

Also played for humor was the repetition of movement, in and out of Red Rock West, with the cue being the sign, Entering and leaving Red Rock West. John Huston did a similar trick in *Prizzi's Honor*, turning plot weakness into strength, when he had the comical sequence of scenes of the airplanes flying to signal movement from coast to coast.

Cage's Michael is the indefatigable Marine survivor. While Dahl plays the Marine connection for laughs, the heart of the picture is Michael's perseverant honesty. He's the scrappy 17-year-old boy who leaves his abusive home to join the Marine Corps, only to discover that abuse comes in an endless variety of forms and uniforms. But, however much abuse he endures, he does persevere and fights until he finally is the only survivor, penniless, rolling away on a freight train, tossing the loot into the wind, no, wait — he's kept some back for himself, a little primer for the old financial pump. *Semper Fi!*

The *film noir*'s dark touch comes with the eyebrows of Lara Flynn Boyle playing Susanne, the woman who will love a man or shoot him, whichever is convenient. She turns out to be the scheming, bank robbing accomplice of Wayne's. She has the look of a dark Persephone who would lead you down into hell and make the whole trip interesting.

The War Veteran Revenge Movies

It is worthwhile to pause and compare the war veteran revenge movies of the *noir* period with the revenge movies of later eras. *The Blue Dahlia* (1944) and *Cornered* (1946) have the veteran seeking revenge for the murder of his wife. Each pursues the killer with a vengeance illustrated by tough, gritty determination, and a willingness to fight and die for the cause. Similar themes are found in the Westerns depicting veterans of the Civil War, notably, John Ford's *The Searchers* (1956) and Howard Hawks' last movie, *Rio Lobo* (1970), which share the same ethos as the post–World War II films. The character of Alan Ladd in *The Blue Dahlia* differs from that of the other vengeful veterans. Ladd has a suave style that plays with Veronica Lake's. His toughness comes out as determination and when his violence is forced he is fearless. Dick Powell in *Cornered* is a character more in the line of John Wayne's Western film style. His mean style has a passion that has a self-destructive edge in which vengeance will be had at any cost and little value is placed on the life of the war veteran protagonist. Wayne's Ethan especially rings true, while Dick Powell's Laurence has an alacrity that is symbolized by his scar. Both veterans have the sense about them of having lost their souls.

The image of Ethan slaughtering the buffalo in a fit of rage has a similar feeling to another grizzly slaughter in yet another vengeful war veteran scene in *Rolling Thunder* (1977). There are multiple criminals in the 1977 film and the slaughter is facilitated by an arsenal of weapons. William Devine plays the war veteran, Charles Rayne, whose family is slaughtered and his hand ground off. He replaces the losses with weapons and goes after the murderers. The slaughter of the criminals is depicted in vivid, drawn-out scenes reminiscent of Odysseus' slaughter of the suitors, without the hawkeyed Athena.

Ethan's vengeance in *The Searchers* is directed at the Comanche Natives. Chord McNally's vengeance in *Rio Lobo* is against traitors who flee to the border town, where the victims include the mutilated Mexican-American woman, Maria. Laurence's vengeance in *Cornered* against the Nazi murderer takes him to Brazil. In *Rolling Thunder* the veteran's vengeance takes him to the border town, Nuevo Loredo. Border towns in these films seem to represent the symbolic edge of civilization.

The movies all end with the climax of murder; however, only in *The Odyssey* do we have the message that the war veteran's life is not going to end with peace and quiet. As is characteristic of vengeance in the combat veteran, it is never satisfied. Even with the deaths of the perpetrators, the anger associated with revenge has been kindled and will not be quiet.

War Veteran Capers

The war veteran has a number of romantic film qualities; in addition to his military training and combat experience is his PTSD sense of there being no future. Another factor that joins groups of outlaws together like the Robin Hood band is the bond of camaraderie, the spirit that duty-bound brothers fight to protect each other.

That men are driven to robbery for their survival is central to *Dead Presidents*. Their combat experience gives them the skills, the control over fear in action, a sense of having no future, a nonconforming anger at false authority, all presented with Hollywood panache in *Ocean's Eleven*, and with gritty individualism in *Who'll Stop the Rain* and *Absolute Power*. *Extreme Prejudice* addresses the *Ocean's Eleven* cliché of the old squad together again in a variation, the rogue squad of elite commandos.

The leading characters of *Ocean's Eleven* (Warner Bros., 1959) are all Korean War veterans from the same outfit. Sammy Davis, Jr., is in the center, seated. Standing around him, casual and hip, are, from left to right, Frank Sinatra, Dean Martin, Peter Lawford, and Joey Bishop.

Ocean's Eleven, 1960

Ocean's Eleven, released in 1960, was directed by Lewis Milestone. It is a '50s studio film about hip men who are brought together by their former army leader, Danny Ocean, played by Frank Sinatra, to rob a casino in Las Vegas. Of course what crime could be more acceptable to the general movie-loving public than a crime committed against a gambling casino? Indeed, Sinatra's band take on a kind of Damon Runyon prohibition gangster air.

The film exploits the skills and courage learned or developed in combat. It masks the outlawry in the Robin Hood spirit of stealing from the rich and unworthy. The film was the first of several films involving the flashy Rat Pack, which actually began a year earlier with Frank Sinatra, Dean Martin, and Sammy Davis, Jr. Also in strong supporting roles are Angie Dickinson, Richard Conte, Cesar Romero, Joey Bishop, and Henry Silva. *Ocean's Eleven* is probably best described as a pleasant vet exploitation in the spirit of Hermes the thief. Steven Soderbergh's 2001 remake, though a better film and technologically updated, drops the war veteran motif completely. It has all the men involved be professional criminals and their leader just out of prison. It in effect takes the crime out of the hands of the war veteran amateurs who apply their military training and gives it to the professionals, while managing to retain the cool panache.

Dog Day Afternoon, 1975

The only thing that makes the mundane 1975 comedy by Sidney Lumet, *Dog Day Afternoon* a war veteran film is one phrase, part of a threat which the Brooklyn bank robber, played by Al Pacino, makes to the tellers. "I'm a Vietnam veteran and don't mind killing people." There is no other mention made of this boast. The Pacino character seems like a ne'er-do-well hapless native Brooklynite; he is ostensibly trying to get money for a sex change operation for his friend. He shouts to the gathered crowd of onlookers and cops, "Attica, Attica!" And the crowd is roused to cheering frenzy. The beleaguered Vietnam War veteran is the cheerleader for rebellion. If he's not really a Vietnam veteran, we can see how reputations are started.

Who'll Stop the Rain?, 1978

Who'll Stop the Rain? is another *noir* Vietnam War veteran drama. A man who served as a Marine in Vietnam returns as a merchant seaman and conspires with a photojournalist friend to smuggle heroin, hidden deep in the innards of a piece of machinery. The smuggler, Ray Hicks, played with grim determination by Nick Nolte, steals the heroin when undercover police try to bust him delivering to his friend's wife in Berkeley, and then fights to elude the rogue cops trailing him.

The movie was directed by Karel Reisz, with a top-drawer screenplay by Judith Rascal and Robert Stone, from Stone's novel *Dog Soldiers.* Released in 1978, the film is probably the best dramatization of a song since *Singin' in the Rain.* It shows a Vietnam War photographer, Johnny

Nick Nolte is Ray Hicks, a Vietnam War veteran in *Who'll Stop the Rain?* (United Artists, 1978). His companion, Marge Converse (Tuesday Weld), watches him as he digs up his buried M-16. They are about to hit the road with their contraband.

Converse, played aptly by Michael Moriarty, who turns to heroin use following a friendly fire catastrophe. He then enlists in a smuggling effort ("two keys of scag — bad karma"), in a manner reminiscent of Christopher Walken's emotionally vacant character in *The Deer Hunter.*

Nolte's Ray Hicks follows fate to the end with the gritty perseverance of a Marine under fire, after he finally ends up with the heroin. He tells Converse's wife, Marge, played by Tuesday Weld, who escapes with him, "All my life I've been taking shit from inferior people — no more! When I left the Marines, I made myself a promise, never again am I going to be fucked around by morons." Nolte's Hicks virtually lights up the movie.

As all Jungian scholars and romantics know, rain is a common symbol of feeling expression, and the plaintive refrain from Creedence Clearwater Revival describes the agony of unhappy feelings in the wake of the fateful quest to sell the heroin. (The song "Who'll Stop the Rain?" was written by John C. Fogerty and seems to be the most frequently played song in war veteran films, appearing prominently as well in *The War* and *The Big Chill.*)

Hicks and Marge end up in a Hippie haven, a natural amphitheater in mountains of New Mexico. Hicks looks through binoculars as the rogue cops approach for the final gunfight. Tuesday Weld's Marge Converse asks, "Is anybody coming, Sister Anne?" a line from a fairy tale about a fated woman, Grimms' *Bluebeard.*

Nolte is everything one could ask of *Semper Fi,* as he marches down the railroad track mortally wounded, chanting marching limericks: "I'm going to take a three day pass, I'm going whip old Jodie's ass.... Your left, right, left."

Perhaps *film noir* could be described as the tale of fated, down-going individuals. In this case, it is a Vietnam War veteran on a destructive course.

Extreme Prejudice, 1987

Nick Nolte plays Jack, a Texas Ranger who does battle with a drug lord in *Extreme Prejudice.* Jack is straight and hard as nails. He grew up with the drug lord, Cash Bailey, played by Powers Boothe, who lives across the border in Mexico. They are both in love with the cabaret singer, Sarita, played by Maria Conchita Alonso. The wild card in this film, directed by Walter Hill and released in 1987, is that six commandos in civilian clothes are under orders (or believe they are) to kill Cash and get his accounting books. Several of the commandos are Vietnam War veterans, as is their supposed leader, Major Paul, played by Michael Ironside. Actually the major is a rogue and his men are set up to die in the firefight between them and the ragtag army surrounding Cash, while the major walks away with the cash. In the end all the main characters are shot dead, except for Jack and Sarita.

This cynical action movie, which has the sweaty intensity of a spaghetti western, was written by Deric Washburn and Harry Kleiner, from a story by John Milius and Fred Rexer. Rip Torn, as a semi-retired sheriff and friend of Jack's, appears, and dies, early. The film glories in shooting. The war veteran theme deals only with the concepts of repetition and camaraderie, bonding in violence, and the exploitation of combat skills. Hill uses tight editing to create a flow of action, interspersed with melodrama that has to be drawn out illogically to maintain the weave.

Dead Presidents, 1995

Dead Presidents, released in 1995, is a socially aware and realistic caper film. Set in the '90s, it is an excellent example of the triptych created by

the before, during, and after the war division, this time from an urban
African-American point of view. Boys, neighborhood friends from the
northeast Bronx, go to war in Vietnam. The movie was based on a story
by Allen and Albert Hughes, brothers who also directed and produced the
film. Their scenario was suggested to them by a story from Wallace Terry,
author of *Bloods*. The protagonist, Anthony Curtis, is played with haunting endearment by Larenz Tate. His father is a virtually silent Marine veteran of the Korean War. Anthony announces that he wants to go into the
Marines in 1968, so that he can experience something different. *Dead Presidents* does a startling cut from a lovemaking scene featuring Curtis and
his sweetheart, Juanita, played with impressive breadth of character by
Rose Jackson, to the centerpiece of its triptych, when we next see Curtis
during a bloody Marine Force Recon extraction.

In the central macabre Vietnam scenes of the recon unit, Curtis is with
his buddies from the Bronx, namely Cleon, played by Bokeem Woodbine,
and Skip, played by Chris Tucker. This is one of those improbables of the
Vietnam War that a number of members of a neighborhood group are
assigned together in combat. (The one exception is perhaps those few
National Guard Units that were sent over intact.) Cleon goes a bit off the
deep end and chops off the head of an enemy corpse to take for a souvenir.
The head becomes a source of deadpan debate among the team as it begins
to stink. Finally Cleon is forced to give it up, but warns them all ominously
that it will mean bad luck.

In the macabre makeup tradition set by *Apocalypse Now*, the faces of
the Force Recon Marines are painted in camouflage. Especially striking is
the bald Caucasian lieutenant, who has apparently gone mad after multiple tours, and is so green with face paint that he looks like a fierce
Dionysian vegetation god. These scenes presage the later white facemask
scenes of the robbery.

Anthony Curtis is in the thick of the bloody madness and we see him
return home almost oblivious. His parents are aghast that he eats with his
fingers. He maintains that he picked up no bad habits over there, except
for killing.

Anthony returns to the Bronx neighborhood and visits his mentor,
Kirby, played with a fine sense of humor by Keith David, as a Korean War
veteran who lost a leg in the war. In a fight with another man, Kirby's
prosthetic leg is pulled off, and in a comical rage he picks it up and beats
the man with it.

A contrast is established between the pre-war Anthony and the post-
war Anthony when he viciously beats a man with his pool cue for taunting him, a man with whom he traded taunts harmlessly before he did his

Four war veterans are about to rob an armored car in *Dead Presidents* (Hollywood Pictures, 1995). The two in center are in white facemask makeup. They are, left to right, Vietnam War veterans Cleon (Wokeem Woodbine), José (Freddy Rodrigues), Anthony (Larenz Tate), and Kirby (Keith David), a Korean War veteran. (Photograph by K.C. Bailey.)

26 months with Force Recon. Anthony now drinks too much and is unable to get a lucrative job. He ekes out a living working as a butcher's assistant. He is laid off when the shop closes, and ends up seeking a way to make some money. His girlfriend taunts him: "You ain't the same man I married before the war." "Marine man with no job!" Anthony proposes a plan to his friends to rob an armored car of old currency. They gather their accomplices (Jose, played by Freddy Rodrigues, Kirby, Skip, Cleon, and a revolutionary woman, Delilah). Their plan goes awry, however, and there is a fearsome shootout in which the armored car is blown to pieces, giving us the slow motion burning of money and the title: the pictures of presidents on the burning dollar bills.

Martin Sheen makes an uncredited appearance as a self-righteous judge sentencing Anthony to life in prison, stating that he, the judge, was a veteran of Guadalcanal and didn't want to hear any whining about Vietnam. At the finale, Anthony throws a chair at the judge, shouting, "Life! After all that I did for this country!"

Dead Presidents established a remarkable icon in the world of cinema, with its white facemask on the black robber. He is the desperate man who pops out of the garbage container blazing away with two semiautomatic pistols, the same person who wanted to join the Marines to experience something different.

Absolute Power, 1997

Absolute Power, released in 1997, is an effective crime-action drama that pits an aging Korean War veteran, Luther, played by Clint Eastwood (who also directed), whose anti-authoritarian life has led him to a career as a jewel thief, in and out of prison. He is now semi-retired, but witnesses, while on a burglary caper, a murder of a woman during an episode of rough sex with none other than the president of the United States. A Secret Service agent shoots and kills the woman when she gets the better of the president after he beats her. She is about to stab him when the agents intervene. Luther witnesses the shooting and cover-up when he hides inside a vault that is also a voyeur room with a two-way mirror.

Absolute Power is marked by excellent casting. Gene Hackman plays the sleazy president, who is convincing both as a drunken philanderer and charming national leader. Judy Davis plays the president's chief of staff with puckish humor as she leads the cover-up conspiracy. The murderous Secret Service agents, Burton (Scott Glenn), who is also a wounded war veteran, and Collins (Dennis Haysbert), are strong characters, as is the local homicide detective, Seth, underplayed gracefully by Ed Harris.

In eluding the police and the Secret Service, Luther involves his daughter, Kate (Laura Linney). She has been neglected by her father, who, in pursuing his chosen career, has never been close to her, although it is revealed that he has watched her from secret. She admits that she always sensed his presence. Her father even enters her apartment when she's not there. The metaphor works well to describe the emotional distance and the efforts to control in the relationship between war veteran father and offspring.

Luther, the police detective learns, was wounded in the Korean War and has "decorations up the kazoo." He is also a master of disguise and could easily elude capture, except that he chooses to *not* run when he sees the president on TV embracing his supposed friend and major campaign supporter, the grieving cuckolded widow (E.G. Marshall) of the murder victim. Luther mutters through his teeth as he watches from the airport bar, "you heartless whore, I'm not about to run from you."

Absolute Power is an extremely cynical movie, playing on the saying, "Absolute power corrupts absolutely." Screenplay is by William Goldman from a novel by David Baldacci. The story twists our loyalties, so that the thief becomes the nobleman, while the politician stoops to besmirch himself.

Eastwood not only directed and produced and starred convincingly as lead character, he composed the music. There is a remarkable sequence during his composition "Power Waltz" which has the president dancing with his chief of staff at a White House ball. As they dance before the public eye, they realize that the necklace she is wearing was the one the woman was murdered in. They keep smiling and twirling as they realize that it is a signal from Luther that he is going to expose their murderous conspiracy.

Luther has the qualities of a super-hero, in being a war survivor and a master of disguise, appearing, Hermes-like, and disappearing mysteriously. Yet he is also merciless when protecting his long-neglected daughter. She has been contaminated by his post-war life of crime and by the shadowy conspiracy that he has witnessed. The Secret Service agents try to kill her because she probably knows the ugly truth about the president.

One of Luther's problems with aging appears to be that he cannot let his habit go. He breaks into the wealthy man's house as though it were a compulsion. At one point, as he is leaving his daughter, Kate, she cautions him, "It's dangerous out there." Luther turns and, with his Clint Eastwood rugged, wry smile and gravelly voice, says, "It always is."

The War Record Revelation

There are various ways that the war record of a veteran is revealed. One of the most common dramatic methods is to use the opening scenes to depict the nature of his combat in the flashback. *Mrs. Dalloway*, *Deathdream* and *Jacob's Ladder* do this. Also a common method is the revelation of military history found in the police background check, where one cop tells another that the man they have or are looking for is a combat veteran, with "medals up the kazoo" (*Mr. Majestyk*, *Absolute Power*, *First Blood*). Sometimes the revelation debunks the veteran's claim, as in *The Man Who Wasn't There*. A more subtle method of revelation is the implied history by the war wound. The most subtle methods are a background shot of medals or framed pictures (*Ulee's Gold*, *Desparate Hours*). Other films suggest the veteran's background with a tattoo (*Devil in a Blue Dress*) or shoulder patch (*Taxi Driver*). And if the veteran declares his own war record as a threat or boast, we start to wonder (*Looking for Mister Goodbar*, *Dog Day Afternoon*).

CHAPTER 6

Looking Back

Triptych (Before, During, and After the War)

As in all traditional triptychs, of the three panels of pictures, the middle is the most emphasized. Only a few movies have captured all three sections with comprehensive skill; the story really is often the stuff of three movies at least. Others previously mentioned that achieve this comprehensive view are *Birdy, Dead Presidents, Snow Falling on Cedars,* and *Born on the Fourth of July. Deer Hunter* and *Forrest Gump* are reviewed here because of their unique contributions to the triptych theme.

Deer Hunter, 1978

Deer Hunter was a timely, comprehensive movie about the Vietnam era, coming out in 1978 and stunning the movie-going public with sterling performances by Meryl Streep, John Savage, Robert De Niro, Christopher Walken, and others. Directed in a brilliant sunburst of feeling by Michael Cimino (which he followed with a counterbalancing flop), this movie is about young Pennsylvania steelworkers, three of whom go off to Vietnam, and then return, more or less.

Deer Hunter tries to do justice to all three parts of the triptych. Cimino manages to orchestrate a vast panorama encompassing not only the U.S. Steel factory landscape (filmed in Cleveland, Ohio), but the mountain peaks of West Virginia, as well as the urban and jungle settings of "Vietnam" (locations were in Thailand). The Vietnam scenes were largely symbolic to set up the final gambling sequence.

The movie opens inside the factory with steel furnaces blasting. The work shift ends and the young men exit toting lunch boxes. We learn from their conversation that they are going to a wedding of one of them, then off deer hunting, and then three will go off to the army and Vietnam. They are Michael (Robert De Niro), sallow-eyed Stan (John Cazale), Stevie (John Savage), who is getting married, Nick (Christopher Walken), and Axel (Chuck Aspegren). They are later joined by John, the emotional bar owner, played by George Dzundza.

Director Michael Cimino seems very familiar and comfortable with these steel town scenes. The men party in the tavern and, when one of the burly women comes to drag away the groom, they go off drunkenly to dress in tuxes for the wedding. These scenes are layered with scenes of the women getting themselves ready. Angela Rutanya plays the tearful and sad bride, Angela. She is to be married and her newlywed husband will go off to the army. Bridesmaid Alice is played with passion by Meryl Streep. The wedding is Russian Orthodox and the party is a believable romping good time. At one point in the bar of the reception hall, Michael and the guys see a soldier with combat ribbons. Michael shouts, "Hey, Green Beret. Buy that man a drink. Here's to America, love it or leave it." The soldier turns and delivers a hard, angry glare.

Also in this sequence is a profoundly stated scene in which George is telling Nick that "you know I'd be going with you guys, if it wasn't for my knees." As they are standing facing the camera, in the bottom of the frame is a sad, red-faced older man wearing a war veterans' service organization hat.

The wedding sequence ends with Michael running in front of the wedding couple's bedecked car, stripping off his clothes, until he finally lays naked on a playground with a basket ball hoop pole between his legs, looking oddly Christ-like from the overhead camera shot. Nick comes and sits beside him. Michael says, "Hey Nick, think we'll ever come back from Nam?" Nick replies after a pause, "Yeah."

Cimino captures the male hunter ritual with religious chanting music. Nick wears a Russian bearskin hat with a symbolic red reflector in the center of his forehead. The hunting ends at the bar with a beer-spurting bacchanal that suddenly segues to Vietnam.

Vietnam, the center of this triptych, is intent on establishing the war's brutality. Michael, Nick, and Stevie are army Rangers (they are wearing "Screaming Eagle" patches of the 101st Airborne) captured in a firefight. They are kept in a bamboo cage submerged in brown river water. They are all wounded and beaten. Stevie is the most severely injured. Each man is taken out of the cage and forced to engage in a game of roulette with a pistol. The sense is that this game is an ultimate gamblers' fetish. The prisoners are slapped and taunted and threatened until they comply. Stevie shoots himself but manages to deflect the shot, taking out part of his scalp

Michael (Robert De Niro) (right) helps his wounded friend Stevie (John Savage) (left) out of the river in Michael Cimino's *Deer Hunter* (Universal City Studios, 1978).

and knocking himself silly. Michael and Nick finally engage in a roulette contest, and, through Mike's scheme, manage to put three bullets in the chambers, enough to surprise and kill the guards. They escape floating along the river until they are picked up by a Huey helicopter. We see the helicopters coming with other LRRPs suspended from ropes and skids.

One helicopter turns and descends to their rescue, but never quite gets them all aboard as they are bobbing on a rickety suspension bridge. Steve falls off the skid and Michael jumps into the river to help, while Nick stays in the slick. Michael finally carries Steve to the "safety" of a refugee evacuation that is taking place on a highway. We next see Nick agonizing in a hospital, then in a Vietnamese bar. Later we learn he has gone AWOL after discovering a gambling den in which the deadly roulette game is played with toxic intensity.

Michael returns home, but is seen as alienated from his friends. He avoids his homecoming party and squats alone, backed against the wall in a dark motel room, in one of the truest of homecoming icons. He is now an E-6 with an impressive Ranger uniform, but paradoxically with a close-cropped beard and longish hair.

Michael's friends want to go hunting with him, "just like old times." Mike says to Linda, "I feel a lot of distance, I feel far away." After Vietnam, nothing for Mike will ever be just like old times. Michael and Linda do finally make love, with a sweet feeling of fate pulling them toward each other. At the wedding party, prior to leaving for Vietnam, Nick had vaguely proposed to Alice. They are both mourning the loss of Nick, who is AWOL in Vietnam. Linda says to Mike, "Did you ever think it would turn out like this?" Mike says succinctly, "No."

Michael finally visits Stevie in a VA hospital (filmed at the Cleveland VAMC). On a hospital ward older veteran volunteers with court jester hats are entertaining the patients with a game of bingo. Stevie, along with the other men, appears sad and disinterested. He sits in a motorized wheelchair in pajamas, a triple amputee. The veteran service volunteers struggle to keep things cheerful; "those boys who can't help themselves, somebody help them please."

In the most grossly unrealistic Hollywood convenience scene, we see Michael arrive to visit Steve. He drives up and parks at the curb in front of the main entrance of the hospital!

Michael with pitiful irony says to Steve when he meets him, "We made it. You look good."

Michael learns that Nick has been sending Steve cash, meaning he's still alive. As Saigon is falling we see Michael arrive back in Vietnam in Ranger uniform, landing on the embassy roof as civilians are mobbing the U.S. embassy trying to escape. Michael travels through the chaos until he finds the gambling den where Nick is performing as a contestant, his head wrapped in a blood red band. Bribing his way in, Michael tries to dissuade Nick. Nick's arms are scarred with needle tracks and his face is pasty. Michael in desperation engages Nick in the roulette contest, buying himself in to replace the other contestant. The referee (played by Po Pao Pee) is the epitome of macabre humor in a macabre scene. He is an elderly Chinese man wearing glasses in which one lens is blackened. Michael actually pulls the trigger on himself, after Nick does, while begging Nick to come home. Nick finally shoots himself, and the final scene of the film is his funeral, followed by a sad gathering at George's bar, where his assembled friends mournfully sing "God Bless America."

The suddenness of the Vietnam transitions are jarring. This device was also used with shocking success in *Jacob's Ladder*, and *Dead Presidents*. (The sudden transition was performed in reverse, Vietnam to France, in *Sundays and Cybèle*.) The quick transition speaks to the quickness with which the boys went to Vietnam and the dazed veterans returned to the United States.

Cimino sandwiches the Vietnam scenes with scenes of the tavern parties and the deer hunt. The post–Vietnam deer hunt, in which Michael, the best hunter, cannot kill, seemed to symbolize the movie. However, the symbolism that truly dominates the movie is of the suicide gamble, with the referee inserting a bullet into the chamber of a .38 police special, spinning the chamber, handing it to a contestant, who points it at his head and, wincing, pulls the trigger.

The fated gambling is a topic noted by W.G. Niederland, an early PTSD treatment pioneer, who collaborated with Henry Krystal (1967) on the psychiatric interviewing of Holocaust survivors. Niederland, in a letter to a psychiatric journal (1984), described compulsive gambling as a facet of the "survivor syndrome" (a term he coined). Gambling taps fate. It is after all, in the end, *chance* that determines who lives and who dies. It is true that the Grim Reaper gets us all, but it is *chance* that cuts down the troops when shrapnel and bullets fly. Ask someone who was in a mortar or rocket barrage. He or she will confirm that goodness, wisdom, morality, character, justice, all other virtues and values are irrelevant when the first shell hits. Only *chance* prevails. And *chance* then becomes a haunting gauge of one's future survivability. *Chance* becomes the association that elicits the adrenaline that fires up the thrilling hyper-alertness.

The roulette game (Russian for the purposes of the film) is also the compelling call back. No one is ever free of combat so long as memories influence the war veteran's behavior. Danger, threat, and thrill become influences that, like psychotropic chemicals, is capable of bringing on euphoria or harm, momentary peace or eternal death.

Forrest Gump, 1994

The war veteran movie with broad biographical scope is the 1994 triptych film *Forrest Gump*. In the tradition of the country fool, *Forrest Gump* attempts to review the happenings of the period from Forrest's childhood, through his chance encounters with fame and the famous, the turbulent decade of the sixties, drugs, protest, and Vietnam. He is swift of foot, unthinking, optimistic, cognitively challenged, and lucky. Forrest was most influenced by those he held dear, his Momma (Sally Field), his life-long love, Jenny, played as a child by Hanna Hall and as an adult by Robin Wright, his army friend, the shrimp-obsessed Bubba Blue, played by Mykelti Williamson, and Lieutenant Dan Taylor, played by Gary Sinise.

Directed by Robert Zemeckis, with a screenplay by Eric Roth, from a novel by Winston Groom, this film was a technological marker in cinema history. *Forrest Gump* takes us through most of what is important for the Vietnam generation by having Forrest bumbling into the middle of famous newsreel footage, a technique displayed most prominently by Woody Allen in *Zelig*. The news events are publicized meetings of various presidents, prominent assassinations, the fall of Richard Nixon. Forrest picks up the notebook and follows a girl into the school surrounded by National Guard troops during the Alabama school desegregation confrontation with Governor George Wallace. Elvis learns his bump and grind from Forrest as a child (played by Michael Conner Humphrys) dancing in his braces.

Forrest Gump is also a film about child sexual abuse and the long-range posttraumatic effects when the child, Forrest, crippled in braces, is befriended on the school bus with the pretty Jenny. He witnesses her hiding from her drunken dad and incest is suggested. Forrest runs off with her through the corn stalk rows. Forrest will grow up with Jenny, but she will not settle with him until later when she is ill, after she has gone through tawdry show business, hippie drugs, anti-war activism, and cocaine-snorting high living. Jenny presents herself as a girl with PTSD on a self-destructive course.

Forrest sustains his own "Criterion A" traumatic events in the destruction of his platoon, the death of his friend Bubba, and the traumatic amputations of his beloved Lieutenant Dan. The scene of sudden ambush in Vietnam is said by combat veterans to be the most realistic and hair-raising of all the simulations of the real combat seen on film.

Instead of Forrest having PTSD, we see Lt. Dan acting it out with the abandon seen in John Heard's Alex Cutter in *Cutter's Way* and Tom Cruise's wheelchair-ridden Ron in *Born on the Fourth of July*, with his bottle-smashing bouts of drinking, wheelchair crashing, hoisting himself on the shrimp boat mast screaming into the hurricane winds. Forrest, the film explains, has denied Lt. Dan his heritage, his right to die in combat as granted him by family tradition.

Forrest is our Everyman, that populist fellow who watches events like assassinations, wars, and political outrages with the unthinking aplomb of someone with no historical comprehension of the profound significance of what he is witnessing. Forrest is the naïve victim, who as a child has to wear braces, even though "his legs are just fine," said the doctor, "but his back is crooked as a politician." In another generation, Forrest would have been one of the troops in the Nevada trenches witnessing the A-bomb test explosions, or in the living room watching the TV courtroom entertainment of the OJ trial.

Director Zemeckis makes much of the whimsy theme with the bookend symbol of the floating feather. He lets us know that collective events pick us up and carry us with little willful choice of our own. Usually, before we can orient ourselves to what is happening, the event has passed and we have stumbled along with Forrest through the trees.

When he wasn't stumbling, Forrest ran. His compulsion to run paid off in keeping him from bullies as a child, from napalm and the North Vietnamese Army in Vietnam, and from grief after he loses Jenny. He is taken for a football star and given a university scholarship, he is awarded the Congressional Medal of Honor for heroism in Vietnam, and taken as a guru and national sensation for his (literally) cross-country running marathons. He doesn't know what he is doing, and when he gets tired he stops and goes home to Greenbow, Alabama.

The War and
the War Veteran

Reviewing the variety of movies so far discussed, all of them, in some fashion, about war veterans, I cannot say that the symptoms of post-war alienation or the influence of the war itself are made up by manipulative political or media forces. I suggest that those characteristics are inherent in the process of depicting a survivor of combat. A very brief scene from *Lawrence of Arabia* describes the war veteran from an era distinct from the Vietnam War period.

Lawrence of Arabia, 1962

When David Lean gave us *Lawrence of Arabia* in 1962, he began the film with T.E. Lawrence as an enlisted man, *after* the war, mounting his motorcycle and driving at increasing speed along country roads. He suddenly swerves to avoid hitting pedestrians and the audience is taken quickly from funeral reminiscences to the Arabian Desert. The heart of the film then takes us through to the end of the war, Lawrence's several traumas, glossing over his rape while held captive by the Turks. The film leaves us with Lawrence, still an officer, withdrawing from the negotiations that will lead to betrayal of his Arab cause. We do not see Lawrence after the war is over, as a war veteran, enlisting back in the army under an assumed name. We do not see him discovered, kicked out and again re-enlisting, this time in the air force as an enlisted man, abjuring promotions, friendly but avoiding intimacy, contracting with a motorcycle manufacturer for delivery of the fastest models that were produced. The story of Lawrence as a war veteran, self-effacing, avoiding advancement, and driving at dangerous speeds, would make an excellent sequel to Lean's magnificent film biography of the bright-eyed warrior. The British made-for-TV movie *A Dangerous Man* shows Lawrence after the war but still an officer at the negotiations, but does not follow him after his discharge. One of the elements we would have as viewers would be the knowledge of the traumas that Lawrence endured, including executing a wayward fighter *after* he had rescued him from dying in the desert — and Lawrence's confession that he *liked* the killing, which reveals the addictive nature of his hyperarousal.

Cinema tries to do visually what the body of a survivor does in a variety of ways, recalling the traumatizing experiences of combat. Neurobiologist Antonio Damasio (2000) described the feeling state created in the core of the brain by receptors that are devoted to the monitoring of body functioning; and, of course, memory is also part of the body's functioning (van der Kolk, 1994). The job of these receptors is to provide a feeling state that influences the survivor, largely unconsciously, like the thirst resulting from a lowered pH level, or the craving for a particular food. We know that a vivid dream can activate body memory and so can a vivid film. Combat veterans have reported *smelling* the churned up dirt and cordite in a relatively realistic film like *Platoon*, just as a junky can smell the heroin cooking by watching a film portrayal. Anniversaries of traumatic experiences can produce physical pain and dour mood states, and stimulate feelings of helplessness and hopelessness, without the survivor's conscious recollection of the significance of the date. The feeling states of a war veteran can evoke vivid memories and radical mood changes.

Not very many films, in all those reviewed herein, render the clear message that the combat veteran's life after the war is connected viscerally to what happened during the war. The war's impact, when it is related in film, is usually shown visually in the form of the flashback, which is a cinematic device for conveying vivid memory, and a term adopted by the mental health community to convey the essence of a dissociative state caused by intrusive memory. The audience may see the veteran in a state of grief or panic at the war memory visually displayed, which gives the viewer a privileged position in the drama. The post-war *noir* films of the 1940s convey the war veterans' sense of pervasive danger of the streets, the sense of danger being another visceral experience of combat memory. The *noir* films also convey the sense of betrayal, particularly from the feminine. The sense of betrayal is developed in the war veteran, as a result of the effort produced, the sentiments of loyalty and duty, and the sacrifices endured in combat. Life goes on at home as well, however, and even under the best conditions, participation in combat is tough to follow. The bonding of combat teams, the sense of the risks involved, are rarely duplicated when the war veteran returns, except perhaps in situations where home was part of the war zone.

In Country managed to show the imagined action take place surreally in the veteran as he is enduring a thunderstorm. In *Jacknife*, we, the audience, see Ed Harris' drunken war veteran's hallucinated image in the form of a realistic, bloody-but-smiling guy leaning on the bar with a Boston *Red Sox* ball cap. In *The Visitors*, we see fade in and out, a Vietnamese girl amid bamboo as Sarge lies exhausted on the hood of his car after raping Martha. In *Ashes and Embers* the veteran acts out his trauma in psychodrama fashion in a hallway, and in *Desert Bloom*, when Jack, the veteran of the Battle of the Bulge, crawling in the hallway in the throes of a flashback. We see Thomas Rath's flashback come upon with him as he sits on the commuter train. In Kurosawa's "The Tunnel," in *Akira Kurosawa Dreams*, we, the audience, see the marching white-faced forms of the commander's annihilated platoon. And in *Manchurian Candidate*, we see in the various veterans' dreams the surreal nightmares on stage. In *The Presidio, Conspiracy Theory, Who'll Stop the Rain?* and *Lethal Weapon*, the contaminating influence of the war is presented as a shadowy continuation of government drug smuggling, when institutions and reputations are compromised.

The traumatic event can be a life-changing event, especially when repeated, that permanently alters the course of the survivor, even to death. Most of the dramas under review, however, merely give us the war veteran without depth psychology built in. He may be wounded and the society to which he returns is awkward in receiving him (*Born on the Fourth of July*). His family may see him coping existentially, but few films seem to be able to truly integrate his struggle with the specific kinds of combat action. Those that do specify the event are prone to present a surreal twist that gives it symbolic impact. In *The Fallen Sparrow*, the image and sound of the dragging foot are drawn out to a surreal level. *Jacob's Ladder* did this by adding the horrific element of clandestine psychedelic experimentation. *The Manchurian Candidate* similarly incorporated a trick hypnosis into the POW indoctrination, where the torture is specifically applied in order to hypnotically cause the repeating of the act of murder on cue. In *Black Sunday* a resentful POW is converted by terrorists. We see John Rambo panic and bolt in *First Blood*, when the police attempt to restrain him for a shave. This action, we are told visually, relates directly to the kind of torture administered during his Vietnam imprisonment. In *Ruckus*, the war veteran, Kyle, screams and leaps into action out of a catatonic state when the good ol' boys start to manhandle him. In *Deer Hunter* we see the game of Russian roulette played out as a compulsive need to repeat the trauma of torture. In *Sundays and Cybèle* we see the Indochina war veteran mesmerized by the image of a girl the age of the girl he saw killed in Indochina. Similarly, in *Mrs. Dalloway*, the war veteran, Septimus, is so haunted by his friend's death that he sees the figure coming toward him in the park, and James Whale in *Gods and Monsters* is driven to suicide by his inability to repress the memory of his friend's battlefield death. In *Jacknife* the veterans are tied together like convicts, in alienation over the death of their mutual friend.

Drives and Stressors

The movies that require the war veteran's guilt or loyalty to drive the plot give the viewer convincing motivation for action dramas that move the veteran to fight to the death. While the drive may be compulsive, it has a moral grasp on justice, injustice being the common trigger, or at least a comprehensible connection to traumatic war experiences. The *Lethal Weapon* veterans' drive is to cover their buddies' backs. In *The Presidio*, the war veteran, McClure, is driven by guilt and duty to sacrifice his life to prevent more larceny. The drives in *Key Largo* and *First Blood* are for the veteran to look up his dead buddy's family, which sets the stage for convincing dramas that portray the "greater truth" of the war veterans' social alienation. In *Fort Apache*, the drive in Colonel Thursday is to achieve a military victory that will restore his lost wartime status. Korean War veteran Goldie was in *China Gate* to kill more Commies. In *The Visitors*, the war veterans are drawn without rationale to visit their war veteran betrayer. The war veteran reverts to his hard-won knowledge of weaponry and survival tactics and society is the better for it — and sometimes not.

The drive in *I Am a Fugitive from a Chain Gang* is one of restlessness, the inability to settle down after having had a taste of another, more demanding life. The drive of the veteran in *Indian Runner* is similar, in which the returning veteran acts like a drop of water on a hot skillet, unable to settle down.

Key Largo, *Rolling Thunder*, *Ulee's Gold*, and various motorcycle films, portray the stressors of the society as bad guys, outlaws who impose upon the war veteran. Only in *Ulee's Gold* do we see the complex variety of stressors, work, family, community, coming together to challenge the veteran's post-war adjustment. In *First Blood* and *Ruckus*, the local law enforcement authorities, seen as perverse, become the pursuers of the veteran. *Alamo Bay* portrays those stressors in a more complex fashion as the dwindling of resources and the impact of post-war immigration. In *Lethal Weapon*, *The Presidio*, *Who'll Stop the Rain?* and *Conspiracy Theory* the criminals are generated within the government as a result of the war. Post-Second World War films such as *The Best Years of Our Lives, The Man in the Gray Flannel Suit,* and *Some Came Running* portray the war veteran under pressure to compete in the expanding business world. *Heroes for Sale* portrays the war veteran from World War I as victimized by the financial disaster of the Great Depression. *The Seventh Seal* depicts the war veteran's drive to stay alive as a daily contest with Death in the Middle Ages. In *The Sun Shines Bright* the stressor is represented by the politician who urges the citizens to forget the war veterans and move on in the name of progress.

Guilt and the avoidance of guilt becomes the drive that keeps Captain Brittles in the Army on the dangerous Western frontier in *She Wore a Yellow Ribbon.* To leave the Cavalry requires facing the guilt of potential deaths caused by his absence, and implies the weight of the deaths from previous combat.

Photographing Fairies provides a plot twist in presenting the life-changing trauma taking place *before* the war. The man, who lost his wife when he lost his grip, goes into the war numb with traumatic grief and only comes alive when he becomes enchanted with the possibility of a psychopomp function of fairies who transit to a spiritual afterlife. Enchantment, here, comes from posttraumatic fascination and compulsion.

Impotence

The thorny subject of impotence reoccurs throughout war veteran cinema. There is a sense of nature achieving balance when a combat veteran expends such enormous amounts of energy on the battlefield and then returns home unable, or unwilling to procreate, or uninterested in doing so. In several films the war veteran is rendered literally impotent by the action of the war, because of wounds (*The Sun Also Rises*), spinal cord injury (*The Men, Born on the Fourth of July*). More symbolically, the veteran becomes impotent through psychic numbing, being cut off from body feedback (*Sundays and Cybèle*), or from traumatic causes, as T.E. Lawrence attests in *A Dangerous Man.* He may become impotent from contamination by memories of combat (*In Country, Distant Thunder*). In *Hatful of Rain* the veteran's post-war narcotics addiction leads to disinterest in sex.

The antithesis of this theme is exploited in the comic scene in *Electra Glide in Blue*, when John Wintergreen has three orgasmic sessions of lovemaking in one morning before going off to work. The most wrenching and soulful of the impotent war veterans is Joe in *Johnny Got His Gun*, who not only cannot procreate, he cannot even communicate with any effectiveness. However, the movie directly states with a dark and I think mean bit of humor, that Joe's sexual organ is apparently the only member he has left.

Regrettably, for veterans treated for PTSD or depression, impotence can be a side effect of medication and the price paid for quelling unwanted symptoms. Often, the medicinal side effect is not so much one of physical impotence, as loss of sexual interest. Peace is always bought at a high price.

Many of the early action movies involving Vietnam War veterans, movies made while the war was still going, emphasize the war veteran's potency when he is forced (usually reluctantly) to prevail over forces of anarchy and chaos (*Motor Psycho, Satan's Sadists, Chrome and Hot Leather*). These films are also noted for constraining the veteran's potency within the realm of what is now called political correctness, while located in an environment of political and police ineffectiveness.

Potency can also be a metaphor for effectiveness. It seems true of almost all recent war movies that the wars end inconclusively. Evil is not really defeated, but changes shape or geography and returns to haunt the war veteran. *Cornered* is one example of the ongoing cancer of Nazi fascism. The Korean and Vietnam wars were especially fraught with indecisive conclusions in which the war ended in political compromise, never having been even officially declared over. The current so-called War on Terrorism, appears designed to play out with indecisiveness. The war veteran returns to the U.S. from these wars somewhat like the medieval crusader or the European colonial soldier from foreign duty, returning to a society that did not participate in the war or perhaps even understand its purpose, but rather views the war veteran as someone compromised or contaminated by a brutal but *foreign* experience. The feeling of impotence follows when one expends the whole of one's being and fails in one's goal, and may even be blamed for the failure.

Loneliness

Cohen (2001) in her study contrasting post–World War I treatment of British and German disabled veterans, found the British veteran felt well cared for by the public.

"Ex-servicemen were angry at the state, that is indisputable — they despised generals in plush chairs behind the lines, Whitehall bureaucrats, profiteers — but their attitudes toward the general public were benign when not sympathetic. It was true that the war had resulted in an indefinable cleft of experience separating soldiers from those who had stayed at home..." (p. 47).

The result of that "undefinable cleft" is loneliness, the most pervasive war veteran theme, and related to the concept of impotence. Being repeatedly traumatized places a bell jar around the survivor, which is invisible, yet separates the veteran, in any sort of feeling way, from his fellow man, like the supposedly decorticated veteran in *Johnny Got His Gun*. We see in almost all the serious war veteran films the veteran preoccupied with the war just passed, still living by its tradition, like Christmas lights in January, while about him life, for what it's worth, goes on. This image is best portrayed by the war veteran in *Desert Bloom*, on his porch on guard against an unknown enemy as his family parties inside his house. The films which show the aging veteran, such as *The Straight Story*, *The Presidio*, *Gods and Monsters*, and *Absolute Power*, show him alone or self-contained in emotional isolation. *She Wore a Yellow Ribbon* has the war veteran visiting his wife's grave to talk about combat losses as he contemplates retirement. Lord Stockbridge in *Gosford Park* is isolated in a world of vague sounds amidst a crowded household.

Suppressed memories are the secrets of traumatic history that separate the initiated from the naïve and the hip from the innocent. Things that cannot or will not be described are the stories from which innocents should be protected. They will learn soon enough. In *Electra Glide in Blue* the Force Recon Vietnam War veteran talks vaguely about the deadly effects of loneliness, a theme played frighteningly in *Taxi Driver*. In *Spitfire Grill* and *Distant Thunder*, the loneliness imposed by interpersonal trauma is compounded by self-imposed exile as the war veteran avoids the stressors of modern life, having all he can handle coming from his memory. In *Desert Bloom*, the World War II veteran has his locked room where he can be alone in contact with the war. As Pierre states to the fortune teller in *Sundays and Cybèle*, "I'm more interested in the past than the future."

The social alienation of Vietnam War veterans has been the subject of some controversy. *Taxi Driver* (1976) has been cited as shaping public opinion with the implication that the establishment or government is somehow out to show the Vietnam War veteran as a disturbed creature (Lembcke, 1998; Lanning 1994). *I Am a Fugitive from a Chain Gang* (1933) has a theme that shows the veteran unable to settle down to a dull job, during a time when any job was becoming prized. Remarque's novel *The Road Back* presents its protagonist as similarly abandoning a secure job. The war veterans depicted in *Taxi Driver* and *I Am a Fugitive* are similar in that they try to break out of their social restrictions, but are discouraged in their efforts to change. Travis Bickle (Robert De Niro) is socially naïve and awkward, and quick to paranoid anger when rejected. In *I Am a Fugitive*, James Allen (Paul Muni) is also naïve and victimized by a woman, albeit a much more evil character than the sunny innocent who is Cybill Shepherd's Betsy in *Taxi Driver*. Both films present the environment as overwhelming and working against the war veteran, who hasn't the skills to cope.

The Crusader Knight Antonious Block in *Seventh Seal* confesses, "Through my indifference to my fellow men, I have isolated myself from their company." In his 2001 speech to the West Point Class of '61 reunion, Hoy (2002) seems to speak of a similar sentiment:

> Vietnam, which fate gave this class for its mission, turned out to be unsatisfying, demeaning in ways we rarely mention, and in the aftermath, hauntingly traumatic for many. We were sent by the nation to *endure* the bloody business of a civil war not our own, but almost nothing in our background, nothing in our training and education, had prepared us for the loneliness of that endurance. No one, during those formative years at West Point or elsewhere, had hinted that such loneliness could last a lifetime — ripping the very soul out of a man's service.

David Halberstam brilliantly caught the war veteran's isolation in his description of the line waiting for an afternoon Times Square showing of Oliver Stone's *Platoon*.

> They looked like they were blue-collar workers, construction men, and outdoor men for the electric company, and they had come right from work without changing. Nor was this in any sense a social occasion, for they had not brought dates or wives or buddies. There was a certain apartness or aloneness to the men in that line, one that would match the aloneness showing on the screen. It was a very quiet group; there was no joking, no instant camaraderie of men with common experiences establishing their connections [Halberstam, p. 110].

In the end, evidence of the psychological traumas of war veterans is seen in the severing of their attachments to others. Future attachments can be mimicked by the talented, but never really restored. Bill Murray captured this concept, of the war veteran's loneliness while participating in a materially successful way, most poetically as Mr. Bloom in *Rushmore*, while his similarly lost character in *Razor's Edge* was lacking in humor. John Heard's Alex Cutter depicted the passionate veteran creating a perimeter around himself by clear-cutting away all life with outrageous action in *Cutter's Way*. The ill-conceived satire of a disabled veteran, Eddie, in the macabre *Blackenstein*, fails to integrate into society after his limbs are restored. His crude attempts at socializing spell death to his victims. Jon Voight gave us the emotion-numbing insulation of the war veteran's alcoholism in *Desert Bloom*. Max von Sydow's Crusader Knight, Antonious Block, in *The Seventh Seal*, and John Wayne as Ethan in *The Searchers*, both render a loneliness that maintained itself like a magnet of repelling negative force. Ethan Hawke's Ishmael, in *Snow Falling on Cedars*, stares down from the balcony at the woman he desires but cannot have. In the end it is the loneliness of the war veteran separate from his world that defines his fate. The vigorously copulating Officer Wintergreen in *Electra Glide in Blue* said it most simply: "The loneliness is the worst of it."

The counterweight to the war veteran's loneliness is the role of friendship. As was pointed out earlier, friendships for war veterans often involve other war veterans (*The Blue Dahlia, The Deer Hunter, The Presidio, Jacknife, Gardens of Stone, In Country, Jacob's Ladder, Birdy, The Best Years of Our Lives*), or working partners, such as the war veteran and his servant (*Seventh Seal, The Sun Shines Bright, Gods and Monsters*), or partners in action (*Cutter's Way, The Big Lebowski, Lethal Weapon, Dead Presidents, Ocean's Eleven, Some Came Running*), or comrades in exile (*O.C. & Stiggs, Distant Thunder*). The odd friendship in *Sundays and Cybèle* is qualified because it seems to be based on the Fench-Indochina War veteran's compulsive fascination with the girl, because she resembled one who died as the result of his combat action.

There is an interesting study of the strain on pre-war friendships when the war veteran returns in films such as *Birdy* and *The Deer Hunter*. What were friendships that were spontaneous and free become obligatory and painful after the war. *Born on the Fourth of July* and *Dead Presidents* give us a sense of the stress that sunders pre-war friendships when the war veteran returns with incapacitating wounds or irrevocably changed character.

Family

Odysseus, when he finally returns home in Homer's *Odyssey*, trusts no one, not even his wife. He tests her and finally she tests him, to see if he is truly who he says he is. Wives, children, and parents generally have a rough time in movies about war veterans. In *Deathdream* the mother is stupid and hysterical, and in *Born on the Fourth of July* she is destructively ambitious and intolerant. The great bitch mother of war veteran movies, of course, is the queen of diamonds herself (Angela Lansbury), in *The Manchurian Candidate*. Her opposite is Mamaw, who exhibits good-mother devotion to her son's memory in *In Country*. Dads, usually also war veterans, are seen generally as ineffectual or uninvolved in those same movies.

Lanning (1994, p. 75) complains of women being missing in Vietnam War veteran films, but they seem actually to be quite prominent figures in war veteran films generally. In *The Blue Dahlia* it is Johnny Morrison's two-timing wife, whose untimely murder fixes the veteran with the crime. Wives are also played as long-suffering and loyal, as in *A Hatful of Rain* and *The War*. In *Ulee's Gold* and *Absolute Power* the wives are long dead.

In *Jacob's Ladder*, Elizabeth Peña's Jezebel is first seen as a hip, sexy, empathic, and caring wife, until she too turns into a hellish visitor. The brassy blond wife of the veteran in *Heroes for Sale* is a calculating psychopath. The most complicated war veteran's wife is JoBeth Williams' Lilly in *Desert Bloom*. She is cliché-ridden, but ever cheery, and doggedly supportive, although the price she pays is to helplessly watch her husband browbeat her daughter and neck with her sexy sister. In the end, she supports them all, as they look out at the atomic cloud glowing at dawn.

Betsy Rath, in *The Man in the Gray Flannel Suit*, is perhaps the ideal wife (from the veteran's point of view), when she says,

> Tonight while I was driving alone, I realized for the first time what you went through in the war, and what different worlds we've been living in ever since. I'm sorry I acted like a child. I want you to be able to talk to me about the war. It might help us to understand each other. Did you really kill seventeen men? [Wilson, p. 299].

And then there is the bitch wife, Marie, of *The Best Years of Our Lives*, whose harsh nag "Snap out of it!" has to be the ringing wish for all war veterans and their exasperated wives.

Several films give us a sense of the influence of the war veteran on his children. In *The Man in the Gray Flannel Suit*, Tom's children are preoccupied with death as the family catches chicken pox. In *Desert Bloom* the adolescent stepdaughter lives a precarious life coping with the war veteran's protean moods. In *Absolute Power*, Kate, the adult daughter of Luther, gets pushed over a cliff in her car because she is her father's daughter. Martha in *The Visitors* is caught in the middle between her war veteran boyfriend and her war veteran father as the baggage of war catches up with both men. Martha is compromised when her father invites the visiting war veterans to stay and continue the reminiscence of wartime. Meg Ryan plays Donna in *The Presidio*, a Vietnam War veteran's daughter whose mother committed suicide, because, she charges, of her father's post-war coldness. Donna's motivation in relationships is to rebel against her father's values. In *Fort Apache*, the war veteran's plucky daughter, played by Shirley Temple, accompanies her father to the remote outpost as he follows his military calling. The rule is, of course, that plucky young ladies stir the interest of lieutenants. The Korean War veteran, Brock, in *China Gate*, rejects his Eurasian child, only to bring him back to America in the end. From a post-war perspective, the ending presents a profound symbol of the heavy Southeast Asian immigration that followed the Vietnam War.

In *The War*, the boy dons his father's medal to fight his own turf battle, after his father has repeatedly preached non-violence. Perhaps the most soulful of all is Sam's attempt in *In Country* to find out about her dead father from her war veteran uncle, at the same time she tries to care for her uncle, who seems not to care for himself. And it is Sam's and Emmett's mutual love for the *M*A*S*H* TV series that gives us a sense of the interaction between war veteran, his offspring, and the culture that surrounds them.

> A leaf moved, a color flashed. Someone whistled a tune, "Suicide Is Painless." This was a joke, after all, for it was only Emmett, in an old green T-shirt and green fatigues. He was empty-handed. His running shoes were wet with dew and his hair was uncombed. She stood up, feeling like a jack-in-the-box. In Vietnam, this scene would never have happened. It would always be the enemy behind a bush [Mason, p. 218].

Addictions

In the fourth book of Homer's *Odyssey*, Odysseus' son, Telemachus, visits his father's war veteran friend, "the red-haired warlord," King Menelaus of Sparta, in search of news of his father. Sadness follows their talk of the Trojan War and speculation about Odysseus' whereabouts. Helen, Menelaus' recaptured wife, offers them an Egyptian drug, *nepenthe*, that would make them forget their grief.

> No one who drank it deeply, mulled in wine,
> could let a tear roll down his cheeks that day,
> not even if his mother should die, his father die,
> not even if right before his eyes some enemy brought down
> a brother or darling son with a sharp bronze blade.
> [Homer, book 4, paragraphs 247–250, Fagles, trans.].

The addictions of war veterans relate to the groupings of symptoms of posttraumatic stress disorder: hyperarousal, repetition, and avoidance. Those addictions could be broadly classed as alcoholism, drug (particularly opiate) abuse and dependency, the pursuit of excitement, compulsive work, and gambling. All of these are activities that place the war veteran in an altered state of consciousness. Addictions facilitate avoidance and manage hyperarousal. Repetitions may be experienced symbolically through the responses to compulsion and impulse.

As *The Deer Hunter* makes clear, gambling tests the fortunes, while the pursuit of excitement seeks the altered state of belonging, the feeling of participation. Both gambling and the pursuit of excitement act to cause adrenaline to flow in order for the veteran to achieve a sense of normalcy. Thus, when excitement is aroused by an external cause, concentration is enhanced and a homeostasis is felt in the war veteran for whom hyperarousal is a symptom. These pursuits place the war veteran in a here-and-now sense of immediacy, where the past and future are excluded. Mel Gibson's former sniper in *Lethal Weapon* has a gun in his mouth in suicidal anguish, but is drawn out of his memories by the constant emergencies generated by his work.

Compulsive work usually gets rewarded materially, but usually also serves to isolate the veteran from his family to the extent that there is little or no intimacy. This protects the family of the war veteran from the veteran himself who feels that he is contaminated. It also protects him from the complicated emotions of empathy and caring. *Ulee's Gold* suggests this is happening with Ulee's grudgingly independent labor. *Rushmore* portrays Bill Murray as an alcoholic war veteran who has achieved business success, but who lives isolated from his family within his own house. In the war veteran Westerns, compulsive work looks like cattle drives (*Red River*) or the devotion to military duty (*Fort Apache, She Wore a Yellow Ribbon*).

Movies that feature alcohol abuse and dependency in the war veteran are numerous: *American Soldier, Fort Apache, Rushmore, Cutter's Way, The Glory Boys, She Wore a Yellow Ribbon, Jacknife, Desert Bloom, Distant Thunder, The Sun Shines Bright*. Alcoholism was referred to as "the army disease" after the Civil War. John Ford, in his post-war film *The Sun Shines Bright*, portrayed the alcoholic veteran as the drunken rifleman with a coonskin cap, symbolically played by his own brother, and a character reminiscent of one in Henry Miller's comically soulful story "The Alcoholic Veteran with the Washboard Cranium" (Miller, 1960). In all wars, alcohol has the medicinal ability to bring a person down off the acute post-combat jitters. Men who flew or who regularly went out into enemy territory and returned to rear or safe areas found that alcohol was "medicinal," as Judge Priest observed in *The Sun Shines Bright*. Many war veterans found that alcohol, if quaffed in sufficient quantity, prevented nightmares, sometimes for years. It also provided the comfortable coat within which to hide oneself and one's emotions. We get a sense of the cultural style immediately after World War II by the casual and frequent use of alcohol in *The Best Years of Our Lives* and *The Blue Dahlia*. Note that alcohol manages to make the interesting transition from being "medicinal" to being the "disease," just as do many of the other habit problems related to participation in combat.

Movies that feature the drug abuse in war veterans, like *A Hatful of Rain, Taxi Driver, The Big Chill,* and *Heroes for Sale,* treat the subject seriously. As mentioned earlier, medicine can play a complicating role in treating war veterans, with painkillers, tranquilizers, anti-depressants, and sleeping potions, until the veteran becomes addicted or dependent. The drug (as opposed to medicinal) effects create the invisible mask, allowing the veteran to live in exile in the midst of his own land.

Methods that allow one to cope with the disorders caused by combat are often effective until the coping method itself becomes a habit problem, which attests to the chronic nature of the underlying post-traumatic symptoms. Clinicians find that substance abuse and dependency are common co-morbid disorders associated with PTSD.

The War Veteran in Film and His Culture

Lanning (1994) expressed the conviction that the large number of films he reviewed that depicted the Vietnam War veteran in dark ways were going to influence the viewing public for years to come. He decried the myth-making of Hollywood.

> Even if there were to be a miraculous change in movie production, the damage has already been done. For the first time in American history, the movie industry has focused on the problems rather than the successes of a war's veterans both during the conflict itself and in the years that have followed. The negative image has been projected and the stereotype delivered to audiences around the world. New movies, along with the hundreds already on the video store shelves and those in storage awaiting late-night airing on television, will continue to perpetuate Hollywood's version of Vietnam at the movies [p. 157].

Actually only a fraction of the many films Lanning reviewed are still available, even in large collections. There is certainly a contrast that can be drawn between the war veteran depicted in movies influenced by the mid-century U.S. Hays Commission Code and movies of the Vietnam War period that have tended to depict the veteran as disturbed by the war experience. The Hays Code was enforced vigorously during the Second World War and after, to the extent that a war veteran could not be depicted in a negative or compromising way. See the comparison on page 38 of the code-ridden movie about paraplegic war veterans, *The Men*, with the post-code *Born on the Fourth of July*. Exceptions would be the historical drama, such as John Ford's *The Sun Shines Bright*, which depicts drunken veterans of the U.S. Civil War as comical, and *A Hatful of Rain*, which depicts a bitter, drug-addicted Korean veteran as miserable. Naremore (1998, 113–117) presents a detailed examination of how the code forced changes in two war veteran movies, *The Blue Dahlia* and *Crossfire*. The brain-injured veteran Buzz, in *The Blue Dahlia*, could not be depicted in film as the killer, as was Raymond Chandler's original idea.

After World War II, American filmmakers were as bound to the studio system as to the Hays Code. Eight films reviewed that involve war veterans give a dark look at the world immediately after the war: *The Fallen Sparrow* (1943), *Cornered* (1945), *Blue Dahlia* and *The Best Years of Our Lives* (1946), *Crossfire* and *Dead Reckoning* (1947), *Fort Apache, Key Largo*, and *Red River* (1948). Obsessional revenge is depicted most prominently in all but Wyler's *Best Years* and Houston's *Key Largo*. Betrayal, murder, and revenge are themes that repeat. *Best Years* is the lightest of the lot, and yet it is devoted to the war veteran's problems upon his return to home and job. Hawks' *Red River* and Ford's *Fort Apache* have the same obsessional drive to achieve at any cost, only a variation of the revenge obsessions of the *noir* films. A dark mood prevailed between wars and movie directors of the time, even those who had sterling war records, were on guard against the fervid zeal of anti–Communists holding congressional hearings about subversive influence in Hollywood (McBride, 2001).

Lanning's reviews are an invaluable down-to-earth collection, offering a study of the impact of a war in the maturing years of a video-conscious culture. It is clear, however, that the wars of a nation are by definition disturbing and that veterans have come to symbolize that disturbance. Films dramatize the disturbance, with the war veteran serving as a symbolic conscience or catalyst initiating action. A survey of exploitation films made *during* the Vietnam War (*Motor Psycho, Born Losers, Chrome and Hot Leather, Ruckus, Satan's Sadists*), depict in the broadest sense the archetypal fear of the shadow let loose on the land, as if the same forces that created the war created the films. Compare these films to *The Fallen Sparrow*, made during World War II, about a veteran of the Spanish Civil War who obsesses about the rise of the Fascist shadow.

The movies of the United States are particularly attracted to violent action, as though the nation's citizens were continuing to fight its own civil war, although the U.S. has no corner on violence when compared to international entertainment media. The nation's war in Vietnam brought into focus again that the federal government's solution to some of its problems is through the concept of the "just war." And ultimately the "people" of the government come down to being its agents of action, i.e., the war veterans, who symbolize the wars in which they fought. U.S. Indian wars and enslavement of Africans, the catastrophic U.S. Civil War that killed 2 percent of the population, the immigrants fleeing pogroms and starvation, collectively provide the shadowy action heritage that cinema brought to popular focus.

In comparison, the Second World War killed .3 percent of the U.S. population, whereas the Vietnam War killed .02 percent of the U.S. population in combat action, though many more died soon after. The KIA percentage of any war is perhaps the center of the concentric ripples that affect the culture of the returning veteran. Those post-war readjustment ripples continue in the sense that each KIA has a family, each wounded veteran returns to his family and affects them, together with other loved ones, coworkers, friends, and associates, with the unsettling readjustments which combat exhibits. More subtle ripples form in larger rings when the tax losses, lost wages, disability pensions, problems generated by offspring, and the veterans' stress-related health problems come to be tallied.

At this writing, the Vietnam War veteran has been given the unwanted role of the cultural dark force that Lanning described as "awaiting late night airing." C.G. Jung (1957) observed the phenomenon of western European interwar society projecting its collective shadow with the rise of Nazi Germany. United States society, through the eyes of its cinema, has projected its own collective shadow onto the Vietnam War veteran, so that he is seen as both suffering from the actions of its citizens and causing suffering. *Taxi Driver* is an excellent example of such projection. In contrast, the British society, after the First World War, portrayed its veteran as wounded and staggering (e.g., *Mrs. Dalloway, Fairytale: A True Story*), while, in the U.S., the First World War veteran was portrayed as helplessly caught in a miasma of economic collapse (*Heroes for Sale*). Post–World War I U.S. *noir* films depicted the veteran as omnipresent and diverse, struggling with everyone else in a dark world, but with an angry edge (*Cornered, The Blue Dahlia, Macao*).

"Projection," like "flashback," is a cinematic term shared with mental health professionals. Interpersonally, projection in mental health circles refers to the imagining that someone else is thinking or feeling or doing something based on the thoughts or feelings of the observer. Thus, the bulk of the action films about Vietnam War veterans made during and immediately after the Vietnam War were created by individuals who were *imagining* how someone would behave returning from the war. Films like *Motor Psycho* and *Satan's Sadists* were not well-researched creations based on how past war veterans behaved, but films that were quickly produced to exploit contemporary sentiments about U.S. culture.

It seems that while violence and action are the transient subjects of popular cinema (and more intense the closer to the war with which they are associated), the soul of war veteran cinema I see is played out in the struggles with relationships, of changed philosophies, values, and beliefs, in efforts to achieve and succeed. The films that survive on the shelves of the video stores are probably the ones that say the most to the contemporary audience. Cartoon-like as he is, Rambo in *First Blood* will be available for a long time, because his image plays to the spirit of the archetype, guaranteeing its long-term appeal. So, too, will *Taxi Driver* and *The Seventh Seal*, although the quality of the art may be, in the latter cases, what sustains interest.

What is apparent, however we understand the role of movies in reflecting or shaping opinion, is that how war veterans are remembered will be passed on culturally, and movies will play a major role in the legacy.

The War Veteran Archetype

Jonathan Shay's *Achilles in Vietnam* (1994), as the title suggests, examined the Vietnam War from the perspective of Homer's *Illiad*. Shay's work has had a significant impact on the U.S. military, particularly suggesting ways to prevent psychological casualties. His inevitable sequel, *Odysseus in America*, is currently in press and addresses the war survivor's lot, again from Homers' perspective.

Movies like *Ulee's Gold* and *The Spitfire Grill* allude to the archetypal war veteran hero by directly referring to Homer's *Odyssey*. In *Ulee's Gold*, besides his name, Ulee for Ulysses, Ulee is seen talking to his granddaughter, Penny, about his squad in Vietnam all of whom were killed in action. They talk in front of the bulletin board with his First Air Cav patch and Combat Infantryman Badge. Penny is fondling a toy replica of the Trojan horse. In *Spitfire Grill*, Shelby is seen reading a worn and tattered copy of the *Odyssey*.

Walker (1991, p. 151) writes in the conclusion of his book, referring to the hero archetype as defined by Joseph Campbell, who was, in turn, describing Carl Jung's concept:

> The heroic image of the Vietvet [Vietnam War veteran] that emerges is one that varies from, but does not break from, archetypes that appear to be timeless. The hero archetype has been modified over time to suit audiences, but the image of the ... hero is clearly and strongly present in the system of ... films [about Vietnam War veterans].

Can a war veteran archetype be discerned that spans from the oral tradition of ancient Greece to the cinematic tradition of the 20th century? The word *archetype* is used here in the Jungian sense, (Jung, 1927, para. 53, and 1958, para. 565) defining a propensity to act and the symbolic psychic work that goes with it, based on hypothesized genetic inheritance, producing behaviors that, given the right conditions, play out in an unconscious fashion that is consistent throughout the species *because* of the way the being is built. (Odysseus is also archetypal in the biological evolutionary sense, being the *first* war veteran on record.) Jung's theory highlights the pattern that leads us to appreciate the motif that is repeated so consistently over the course of recorded history.

Usually the psychological concept of archetype is applied to very basic human functioning, such as the archetype of the hero, mentioned by Walker. To attempt to apply the concept to the specific reactions of a war veteran is a stretch, but justified if one remembers that the war veteran has been around at least as long as humans have gathered collectively in tribes or communities, and that when one struggles with death in that prolonged way of combat, the very basic animal chord is struck. The study of PTSD symptoms gives us some ideas for how physiologically the war veteran is influenced and how the problems of grief and anger play a role. This is different and more specific than the so-called hero archetype, which addresses the divine nature of the being.

Jung, in his writings, refers repeatedly to the term "patterns of behavior," when discussing archetypes. By this theory, the combat veteran acts consistently over time, regardless of war, within the restrictions of his culture. He acts that way because of the way humans are built, the way nervous systems function, and the overall commonality of conditions in combat. If the culture is constantly at war, he may be honored, which has its paradoxical implications. If the war was unpopular for whatever reason, he may be defamed or split into good and evil. If the war was distant, his war veteran status may be ignored, yet his behavior will still be archetypal.

Jung (1958, para 353) first formulated his thinking regarding archetypes while working with schizophrenics. He wrote:

Archetypes come from the same universal character as the mythological motifs which typify human fantasy in general. These motifs are not *invented* so much as *discovered*; they are typical forms that appear spontaneously all over the world, independently of tradition, in mythos, fairy-tales, fantasies, dreams, visions, and the delusional systems of the insane. On closer investigation they prove to be typical attitudes, modes of action — thought-processes and impulses which must be regarded as constituting the instinctive behavior typical of the human species. The term I chose for this, namely "archetype," therefore coincides with the biological concept of the "pattern of behaviour." In no sense is it a question of inherited ideas, but of inherited, instinctive impulses and forms that can be observed in all living creatures.

Thus the archetype is more realistically *released* in the form of feelings and behaviors, when the conditions are right, rather than *conditioned*, as, for instance, the startle response.

The Odyssey presents its war veteran protagonist with some basic qualities that may be useful, if abstracted, in examining the depictions of war veterans that follow throughout history. The qualities of Odysseus in *The Odyssey*, when abstracted, seem to consist of the following:

1. Wandering before the return home.
2. Fighting and struggling repeatedly.
3. Experiencing ignominy, despair, and humiliation.
4. Visiting the dead for guidance.
5. Prevailing with divine assistance to restore honor and name.
6. Harboring hidden strength and power.

Such elements should also be found in other classic war veteran tales, such as *Ivanhoe*, and *Bearskin*, as indeed they are, although not *all* are present in every case. To name and list the components of an archetype is to artificially rend it apart, when in fact all the components are uniquely formed, *living* in the individual and as intertwined as a Celtic knot. As a living symbol in film, any part of an archetype may be taken to represent the whole as a synecdoche, which, although poetic, confounds scientific efforts to describe it with precision.

The wandering soldier reaches home, late returning from the war. Odysseus was ten years traveling home. The concept of *nostos*, "returning home," could be taken symbolically as a period of readjustment of some personality dimensions or the fated lure of unfinished business that keeps the veteran from truly returning home in his mind and settling down. The war veteran may be exiled even while at home with emotional isolation, feelings of alienation, and may seem to friends and family members that he is not the same man, as if returning in disguise. The term "welcome home" has a load of conflicting meaning for the war veteran years after the physical return.

The war veteran returns still fighting, battling forces within and without. He continues the fight in his mind, in his memory, fearing a renewal of conflict. His battles are composed of restoring his legitimacy, authority, name, and meaning. His return marks the third phase of the triptych described in the text above. The middle phase that consists of war, importantly, was different for his family, friends, and society at home. They continued in a more or less natural course, while he, the war veteran, has been through a series of traumatic events. He has radically changed, as if refracted as light through a prism of war, while those to whom he returns have changed little.

Part of the humiliation of surviving combat is the shame of surviving when others have died. The war veteran must come to terms with the dead, who continue to live in his memory. He copes with ghosts and the Sirens' lure of nostalgia for battlefield camaraderie and abandoned ideals, such as loyalty and duty. Part of the humiliation is the dramatic deminution of his value and importance, from life-or-death expression of his competence, to civilian insignificance. Hidden also, among the losses is his youth, which, again, is disproportionately changed. Combat ages its participants in a manner that has not parallel in civilian life.

Divine guidance, Athena's and Hermes' role, for the mundane, modern war veteran refers more to psychic connections, which might be conceived as a benefit of combat. Connections in the form of some assistance from the spirit, or soul, may refer to the possession of secrets or powers gleaned from combat experience; that is, the psychic ability to understand, to *know* in a primitive manner, along with such learned skills as insight and timing. Exploitation films such as *First Blood, Ruckus, Billy Jack*, capitalize on this connection between spiritual powers and wartime learning, with grace of style also implied.

Divine guidance is, of course, also applied to literal faith in a religion or god as a divine being. Religious faith in the divine is an integral part of combat for many veterans, and a centerpiece of their healing process. However, there are also many war veterans whose faith in religious beliefs was damaged by the experience of combat and its aftermath.

I am inclined to take the term "divine guidance," such as Athena gave, however, in a psychological sense, as Otto (1954) suggested, to imply a special knowledge acquired as a product of psychic development. Divine here has the sense that the knowledge is just beyond conscious control. Veterans of prolonged combat describe developing a profound sense of knowing, of prescience, that I believe is the result of primitive brain activation. This neural activation is the product of the repetition of routine life-or-death emergencies activating coping skills that rely on senses highlighted and refined by adrenalin activation and intuition, leading to the reliance on irrational knowing, i.e., knowing without factual data gathering.

The hidden strength is a motif that has been taken over by cartoonists and pulp producers. The weary war veteran in disguise as a weak, aged, humble man, who has to be drawn out to fight. Spencer Tracy, as John J. McReedy, the one-armed war veteran, fighting beefy Ernest Borgnine as Coley Trimble in *Bad Day at Black Rock*, captures that archetypal characteristic. Director John Huston captured the hidden strength in the weary form of Humphrey Bogart's Frank McCloud in *Key Largo*. James Caan's Sergeant Hazard portrays a war veteran at the end of his career in *Gardens of Stone*, who is desperate to convey his knowledge of combat. The archetypal power of this motif is a lure in many a relationship in which the humble appearance is thought of as hiding a transcendent light.

The ironic twist of the concept of hidden strength suggests that when strength is manifest in the war veteran, there is a hidden weakness. The iron men of U.S. cinema have been actors who embodied tough characters who harbored inner weakness implied in the war veteran status. Portrayals by John Wayne in *The Searchers* and *Red River* and Clint Eastwood in *Firefox* and *Absolute Power* exemplify this. Mel Gibson gives a memorable portrayal in *Lethal Weapon* of the Vietnam veteran cop who proceeds from excruciating emotional pain, represented by the gun in the mouth, to a man of remarkable feats of courage.

It follows, then, that, for sharers of the archetype, certain similarities exist that transcend cultural differences. The war veteran in Odysseus is also in Travis Bickle, the 20th century New York City taxi driver, who struggles to find a place in society, *and* in Antonious Block, the Medieval Crusader Knight of *The Seventh Seal*, who must engage in a contest with Death. Wilfred of Ivanhoe, the 12th century English war veteran who has to restore his name when he returns from the battlefields of Palestine, is similar to Frank McCloud, returning from the Second World War under a dark cloud of guilt. The common threads of ignominy and isolating memory weave through fated or driven quests to achieve some return of honor, regardless of the war's outcome.

Integral to the war veterans' isolation is loss of faith; faith in themselves, in society, and even, as previously noted, in religious tradition. Dave Hirsh, in *Some Came Running*, refusing to write has the similar feel of Tom Rath's refusal to sacrifice family in order to achieve material wealth in *The Man in the Gray Flannel Suit,* or Ulee's refusal to resort to violence or trust the police, even at the cost of his own welfare. John J. McReedy, in *Bad Day at Black Rock,* expresses his contempt for society in a manner that conveys that the town's civilians don't measure up.

The archetype is a motif that transcends culture, gender, race, ethnicity, and age, but is common to the human species. It is so basic in human development that when an archetype is activated it gives the person a strong sense of fate. The cinematic portrayals of the wandering samurai warrior and the gun fighter on the U.S. Western frontier have the allure of the war veteran's fate as a perpetual outsider, unable to integrate into society. The fate of the Knight in *The Seventh Seal* is as clearly inevitable, given the circumstances, as the fate of the butcher's assistant, Anthony, in *Dead Presidents,* both obstructed by the environment and dogged by death to the end. James Allen in *I Am a Fugitive from a Chain Gang* is finally crushed by the dark forces and driven into the underworld. Shang's reaction to the invasion of Vietnamese shrimp fishermen is pulled out of his war veteran's being by his culture. Colonel Thursday's fate, in *Fort Apache,* is to die trying to recapture his glory. The veterans who died with him were bound to their fate by the power of tradition. These veterans are together like Odysseus clinging to the wreckage of his boat on the stormy sea, declaring that he would be better off to have died on the battlefield.

We see the war veteran experiencing a daunting inhibition to affiliate with others, isolated from society by a disguise or mask, sometimes set off by a companion fool, as in *Ivanhoe, Ryan's Daughter, Devil in a Blue Dress, Powwow Highway,* and *Distant Thunder.* When Anthony and his friends, in *Dead Presidents,* go to their death in white face, they are in mime acting out their fate. It is a mask to die in for the man for whom Death is a permanent, if premature, visitor. The trudging march to meet fate depicted by John Wayne's Captain Brittles in *She Wore a Yellow Ribbon* has the same dauntless compulsion as Nick Nolte's Ray Hicks marching to his death on the railroad tracks, calling his own cadence, "your left, your left," in *Who'll Stop the Rain?*

The war veteran archetype depicts loneliness, sadness, world-weariness, and a worldly wariness of one who has lost faith and identity, but who cannot necessarily free himself from fated battles and forces that continue to demand his allegiance and effort long after the last shot was fired.

The cartoon version of the archetype is an action figure, a caricature stripped of complexity, like a veteran in a flashback (*Billy Jack, Ruckus, First Blood*). One fights *with* him, as with a toy, popular battles of repetition, but otherwise he is on the shelf awaiting call. Cartoon figures will always accompany wars. They are symptomatic of the emotional ripple that the war creates. Rather quickly, however, the tawdry movie images fade and merge with the cultural flotsam. What we are left with is that which is true of all wars: the archetypal war veteran. It is a tribute to the power of Sylvester Stallone's portrayal in *First Blood* that his image continues to command attention.

Greater plot development leads to the individuation of the archetype, in which the archetype of the war veteran is imbedded in the complex plot (*Ivanhoe, Key Largo, The Man in the Gray Flannel Suit, The Stunt Man*), becoming either a central or secondary character. Two movies with Clint Eastwood as the central character, *Firefox* and *Absolute Power*, have the sense of the war veteran archetype with attempts to humanize his story, while putting him into action.

Although the archetype may be dormant, just like the symptoms of PTSD, the long-term adjustment of the war veteran can be compromised by stressful events, and the dormant archetype is then activated (*Ulee's Gold, Gods and Monsters, The Presidio*). When this happens, the feeling in the war veteran is one of being fated, so that what is happening seems inevitable and must be played out. The retired top sergeant's fated death in *The Presidio* is an excellent example. What is important about the archetype is its pull on the person in the fated role. One survivor may be attracted to another and sense that powerful lure (*Taxi Driver, The Spitfire Grill*). Once one falls into an archetypal constellation, there is a sense of compulsion to follow the collective age-old pattern with a strong sense of rightness, as if one had entered a river with a strong current. One's sense of individuality is then in danger of being lost. Films such as *The Legend of Bagger Vance, Distant Thunder, Jacknife*, and *In Country*, present the war veteran being pulled *out* of the archetypal flow, whereas the war veterans in *The War, Taxi Driver*, and *The Seventh Seal* succumb to the compulsive pull, which works for the species, though not necessarily for the individual's, well-being.

Mythology and folklore work on a psychic level as symbol. Before the story of Odysseus' wanderings reached print, it had been passed orally for centuries. The war veteran's story of travel amid the islands of myth, populated by ogres and demigoddesses, losing everything, *is* the soldier's lot when discharged. Bearskin, in the Grimms' fairy tale, bargains with the devil because he has no alternative. His ignominy is endured because it is the only way he can survive. That, in the end, he is transformed into a wealthy and handsome man, is the best of all outcomes, generated it seems, finally, as a by-product of his generosity, when, as the ugly, disgusting Bearskin, he gives shelter to a weary, old man who rewards him with one of his daughters. The youngest daughter takes him dutifully and, in return, he returns, re-energized, refined, and triumphant. He is Jacknife, clean-shaven, offering a box of chocolates to Martha on prom night. He is the Disinherited Knight who has returned to claim his due.

Afterword

A number of movies about war veterans have emerged since this book was written that deserve mention. Three of them are worth noting for their unique contributions to the study of the war veteran in film. *The Majestic*, *L.I.E.*, and *Little Lips*. In addition, the autobiography of war veteran filmmaker, Samuel Fuller, *A Third Face: My Tale of Writing, Fighting, and Filmmaking*, has just been published and requires a comment in the context of our theme.

The Majestic, 2001

A twist on the dramatic return of the war veteran is the story of the veteran who returns late from the war and is mistaken for another. *The Majestic* is a 2001 film by Frank Darabont that features Jim Carrey in a credible non-comic role. The script was written by Michael Sloane and gives the plot, set in 1951, a little wrinkle: the veteran who returns has no memory.

Carrey plays Peter Appleton, a writer of Hollywood B-movies. He has hopes for his latest script, "Ashes to Ashes." The film opens as the credits roll on Peter, sitting passively, listening to movie executives talking off camera disassemble and rearrange his plot. In a bit of high camp, the voices are credited to real Hollywood directors, Rob and Carl Reiner, Sydney Pollak, and Paul Mazursky. After his script is made comically unrecognizable, Peter finds out from the studio lawyer that he has become the subject of the House Un-American Activities Committee investigation into the Communist infiltration of Hollywood. Seems he attended a meeting in his college days that was a Communist front. Peter protests that he was simply hot for a girl and followed her to the meeting. Nevertheless, he is told, he must testify and give names or go to jail for contempt of Congress.

Hapless, Peter gets soused at a bar and goes driving along the California coast, in a drunken romantic inspiration that he will drive until he runs out of gas. Actually he drives until he runs out of road and crashes into a river. The scene of the crash and its aftermath is very well done. Peter bangs his head on a cement pillar and is finally washed ashore at the river's mouth, spewed out, sodden and battered, like Odysseus himself.

Peter awakens with a dog lapping his face. He is escorted by the dog-walker into town and fed a meal at the local café. (These scenes were filmed in the truly majestic Northern California coastal towns of Fort Bragg and Mendicino.) He remembers nothing, but seems to be familiar to everybody. Finally, the elderly Harry Trimble (Martin Landau) recognizes Peter as his long lost son, Luke. Luke has been missing in action since the Normandy Invasion.

Since Peter can't remember his identity, he can do nothing but go along with the discovery. He is greeted warmly by the townspeople and treated by the local doctor (David Ogden Stiers). The doctor's daughter was Luke's former betrothed, Adele, played by Laurie Holden.

It seems that the fictional town lost 62 KIA in World War II, and lost 17 at Normandy. They were declared a "War Memorial Town" and given a monument, which was never dedicated, but remained in the basement of city hall. Peter, now Luke, becomes a source of renewal for the town in grief, and is readily accepted as the Medal of Honor–winning war hero, although certain quirks start to show. Adele notes that he now can dance, though Luke never could. His old piano teacher sits him down at the town celebration and tries to revive his memory to play classical music, but this Luke spontaneously plays boogie-woogie and jazz.

Luke's father is the owner of the defunct Majestic Theater and Peter helps his "dad" refurbish it to play up-to-date films. The projectionist is a World War I combat veteran, Emmett (Gerry Black), who lives in the theater's basement. Finally, of course, a film is played that Peter wrote, and his memory starts to return as he sees his movie in a poster displaying coming attractions.

All this time the Feds are tracking him down and finally bust him in a melodramatic confrontation in the middle of Main Street. *The Majestic* finally succumbs to its Hollywood roots, a kind of regression toward the predictable. But for a while, it's a good war veteran drama. One wounded combat vet with a prosthesis arm never accepts Peter as Luke and confronts him in the street at night. "This town's had enough heartbreak. I hope I'm wrong. I haven't had to kill anybody since the war." Peter, as Luke, retorts that the vet's "come home more crippled that you thought." The vet slugs him.

When Peter recalls his history, he remembers that he had avoided combat and served out the war running a PX at Fort Dix, because he did not want to get killed. "You stand up for a cause and you get mowed down."

When he finally stands before the HUAC, with flashbulbs popping, he states his history: "I've never been a man of great conviction. I never saw the percentage in it. Fact is, I lacked courage."

Nice musical scores from the 40s jazz band era and Nat King Cole singing "I Remember You."

Appearances can be tricky, as Peter observes. We see that his familiar appearance, which fed the town's mistake, was just what was needed to lift them all out of their avoidance of collective grief. Through Peter they were able to properly dedicate the memorial to the dead warriors.

The script has crisp dialog, and if the ending gets sappy, it is at least a study of Hollywood's self-examination of its own cowering before the HUAC. The best line comes when Peter, as Luke, meets beautiful Adele for the first time. She asks, "Do you remember me?" Peter replies with his tongue wagging, "No, but I'll sure try." As one Hollywood exec says, "Don't split hairs kid — it's all a game."

L.I.E., 2002

Brian Cox plays an interesting and complex character in Michael Cuesta's 2002 independent film, *L.I.E.* He plays Big John, a bachelor in his fifties, who lives in an elegantly finished town house on Long Island. He is having a birthday party and singing a sentimental, charming Scottish song while holding his elderly mother. At the same time a gang of young thieves raid his basement, where they discover his war memorabilia: a "Vietnam Conflict" map and USMC insignia. The raiding boys also find a box of matching semiautomatic pistols marked with a Communist red star.

Big John drives a classic orange muscle car. He has a collegial rapport with the local police and we learn in the course of the dialog that he has done work with the U.S. State Department.

Big John is easygoing, but when he discovers that his basement was raided, he has an idea who is responsible. He tracks down 15-year-old Howie Blitzer (Paul Franklin Dano), gives the boy a ride in his car, and confronts him.

Young Howie is highly vulnerable. His mother has died in a freeway accident. In the opening scene, Howie peers down from a freeway overpass suggestive of suicidal intent. Later he does a tightrope walk on the overpass railing and we share a visual image of his mother coming to kiss him. He hangs out with a pierced and tattooed outcast, Gary, played by Billy Kay, and other boys who comprise an ad hoc burglary group. His father is a buff construction contractor who likes to romp in his dead wife's bed with gymnastic babes, while wearing his hard hat. His father is Marty Blitzer (Bruce Altman), played as a narcissistic clown who is eventually arrested by the FBI and thrown in jail for fraud.

As a former marine who is an upstanding citizen and has a perverse love for boys, Brian Cox is absolutely convincing. He plays the *Marine Corps Hymn* for a doorbell chime and has it on his car's tape deck, which he quickly switches to Mozart when his ebullient mood fades. We have the feeling that his history is not bogus and that he had a good record of government service. His gestures are warm and sincere, even when they are manipulative. The tension in the film comes when he chooses *not* to exploit Howie sexually, when Howie is at his most vulnerable, after his father has been arrested. Big John rescues Howie when the boy is arrested with his friends for the burglaries. The other parents come to the police station to pick up their sons, but nobody comes for Howie, until Big John happens by the precinct waiting room while schmoozing with his friends.

In case you were wondering how Big John juggles the words, "We are proud to claim the title of the United States Marines," with his pedophilic behavior, when his petulant young housemate scolds him for grooming Howie, "You should be ashamed of yourself." Big John replies, "I am. I always am."

Big John is still tightly associated with his elderly mother. She seems to call him on a regular basis, intruding on his activities. Yet he takes her in stride, and even with a certain amount of loving humor.

Howie is a boy battered by several forces and spends most of the film with black eyes and bruised face. His black eyes suggest exotic, macabre stage makeup. The film captures him in the throes of an identity flux as his home life crumbles. He finds his mother's lipstick in the bathroom and applies it to his lips. His friend Gary sells his sexual wares to passers-by and makes several implied sexual overtures to Howie, who yet remains passive and uninitiated.

Big John suggests that he and Howie are much alike. It seems that they both flirt with death. In one drawn out perverse scene, Big John shaves Howie's adolescent smooth face with a straight edged razor. In another scene, suggesting that he is on a fatal course, Big John sings to himself in his orange muscle car, "Oh, Danny boy, the pipes, the pipes are calling.... You must go, and I must die...."

Big John takes Howie to visit his father in the prison. Then Big John drives himself over to the area near the freeway where boys hang out to be picked up. He is surprised there and his perversion comes to a poetic end.

L.I.E. was written by Stephen M. Ryder, Michael Cuesta, and Gerald Cuesta. Its saving grace lies in its uncompromising look at the miasma of growing up amid abandonment, without condescension or rage. Fine original music is by Pierre Földes. A poignant tribute is paid to movie director Alan Pekula, who died the previous year in a mishap on a Long Island freeway.

Big John apparently pays boys to engage him in sex. But when it comes to exploiting Howie's vulnerability, he restrains himself, and we think of him as clinging to the vestiges of morality, yet the final scenes of the movie strongly suggest that Big John is drawn by a compulsive habit that only his death can curtail. The "L.I.E." is that life is going to be kind and simple. Big John, dominated by a kindly mother who will not die, treats with kindness a motherless child on his way to die.

Little Lips, 1999

In *Little Lips*, the World War *One* German veteran returns home wounded and emotionally moribund. He discovers a pubescent girl on his estate, an orphan of the war in the care of his servants. The girl awakens sexual feelings in the veteran and, when she moves on to have a tryst with a gypsy boy, the veteran commits suicide, as if he cannot stand another loss.

The film, *Little Lips* (1999, also known as *Historea de Eva* and *Piccole Labbra*), is a product of international commingling and betrays a certain struggle with identity as the multiple titles suggest. The director is Sandro Mancori. Production took place in Madrid, Rome, Barcelona and Vienna. The story concerns a German army officer who is wounded on the battlefield in the First World War. He first appears on a train in uniform. Pierre Clemente plays the veteran with meticulous mustache and slick black hair. We hear his wistful voiceover "after five years in a disastrous war, I return to civilian life. I left the doctors and the hospital. Left my crutches for a cane." He refers to his agony. His servant, Franz, meets him at the train and drives him home. He is greeted as "Heir Bore" and later called Paul. He is obviously a landed gentry and owner of the country estate.

Little Lips is dubbed in English. The dialog is somewhat stilted, but fitting. The drama, as it unfolds, is stilted, too. The story concerns Paul's struggle to readjust to civilian life. He holds his head painfully and imagines the battlefield. The camera takes note of the significance as he puts his semi-automatic service pistol into a drawer as he unpacks. The holster looks stiff and sturdy, meant not for quick draw, but for durability.

The camera captures the eye of a girl peering into Paul's room and he becomes increasingly aware of her elusive presence. The servants note that he isn't the same man who went off to war. They seem sad for him, tolerant and sympathetic. Paul has nightmares, not of combat traumas, but of an obscene, taunting, whorish woman. This is apparently explained by what we learn later, from a flashback sequence, when he recalls the surgeon's words that he will never be a man again.

Paul hears noises in the attic and investigates. He sees evidence that someone has been prowling and picks up a picture of a woman, apparently his former lover. Paul yearns such that he takes out his gun when he returns to his room and points it at his head in a flirtation with suicide.

His servants note that he has a poor appetite. Franz worries that if they call the doctor, "he'll kill us."

At last Paul catches the girl, played by Katya Berger, although she runs away quickly. First we see her spying on the servants making love. She is a curious voyeur, a wise, dark-browed pubescent girl with expressive eyes: a child beauty reminiscent of screen images of young Elizabeth Taylor and Brook Shields. Paul queries the servants in the morning and learns that she is Eva, their niece, an orphan whose father died in the war. She is now their ward living on the estate as their kin.

Paul's agitation grows. We see him drinking brandy, smoking, and playing solitaire, restlessly scattering the cards with exasperation. Then, when out walking in the woods, he happens upon Eva bathing in a creek. The camera peeks around her scant attire, and the scene, as are later scenes that gaze at her, is nervously edited to avoid the censorship barriers in distribution. A brief confrontation occurs when he steps on a twig as he stealthily approaches. He lingers, gazing, and then backs respectfully away only after she becomes aware of his presence.

He is obviously disturbed by his encounter with Eva. We see him in the next scene passionately playing the church organ. The priest approaches, sits beside him, and mentions that he seems almost positive. "The war made you change," says the priest. "No," insists Paul. "I'm the same."

The next time we see Paul walking in the woods, he hears hunters shooting. He panics, runs stiff-legged, and falls. The servants nurse him in a feverish state and refer to "that horrible massacre."

Paul is next seen standing on the brink of a steep precipice about to jump. Eva approaches, dressed as a peasant girl, a Teutonic muse in long dress and braided concentric curls on each side of her head. She walks up behind him, places her hand in his and draws him back.

Another example of the nervous editing to avoid censorship produces an anomalous scene. Eva is sleeping in bed. Her shoulders are bare, suggesting her nudity underneath the quilt. Vaguely, in the darkness, a hand gropes for her under the covers. The scene, which has the potential of being salacious, seems to be awkwardly suggesting that Paul sneaked into her bedroom, but it is never clear and ends up being a film editor's non-sequitar.

Paul shaves his stern, military mustache. Clearly he's feeling better. He muses while writing in his journal about his enchantment with the girl who is "capable of arousing instincts without having them herself."

Finally, Paul corners Eva in the attic playing dress-up. He invites her to put on a frilly dress and there follows a series of pastoral scenes in romantic soft focus, after photographer-filmmaker, David Hamilton. They walk together in a country field. She gambols in her gauzy white dress. He photographs her with a large period camera on a tripod as she rocks back and forth on a tree-born rope swing.

In the scene that follows, symbolically, Paul and Eva play checkers. She moves into a position in which he jumps her four successive times.

On Eva's 12th birthday, he takes her to the park. She's wearing a virginal white dress, gloves and stockings. As they sit in an open-air restaurant, having brandy and ice cream respectively, gypsy minstrels stroll by, one playing a violin, the other, a teenaged boy, is playing a mouth harp. Paul scolds Eva for returning the boy's staring gaze. As they walk back, she puts a flower in his buttonhole, which he later keeps in a vase.

In a following scene, a brief conflict develops when he bars her from seeing a horse apparently being mated. He tells her she's too young. She indignantly insists that he is a man and she is a woman, and symbolically lights his cigarillo.

In voiceover, Paul muses about the girl's ambiguity. He alludes to his struggle between sensual and pure love. Eva guides Paul through the woods to an abandoned cabin. They are caught in the rain and get soaked before they arrive. They build a fire and she takes off her clothes and we next see her with a towel wrapped around her middle. He tells her of the story he's writing, "their story," and of the despair he felt after the war.

Paul takes Eva with him on a carriage ride to town to do business. He leaves her in the carriage and, when he returns, she's gone off to watch a gypsy circus perform. A strong man with chains was the violinist from the park scene. The boy is juggling, standing on his head. When he is finished in the office, Paul searches for Eva and finally comes upon her watching the gypsy boy do seductively hypnotic magic tricks. Paul calls to her in a stern manner to come away.

Paul visits a city where he attends a party, and is introduced around as a writer whom they've all read. He meets his former girlfriend there. She is now a journalist and they dine together. He tells her of his preference for the country. Returning on the train, a blind man is led into Paul's compartment. He has a flashback of his own wounding and recalls the surgeon's words, that they've saved his life, but he may not appreciate the miracle of life because he'll never be a man again.

When he returns to his estate, he looks for Eva to give her a gift. When he can't find her, he searches the woods and discovers her in their refuge from the storm embracing her gypsy boyfriend. She sees the war veteran looking in through a window. Paul drops the gift, returns to his bedroom, takes out his service pistol, and shoots himself in the head, symbolically bleeding on the last page of his book. "Ende."

There are several movies mentioned earlier that parallel the theme of the war veteran made impotent by the war, though not necessarily in the clinical sense. *Little Lips* had the handicap of poor editing that awkwardly skirted the issue of voyeurism and child exploitation, while trying its best to wring out the promotional benefits of a sensational story. This approach is distinct from the head-on, dignified approach of the much better *L.I.E.* The idea that the veteran begins to feel alive in the presence of a prepubescent girl is seen also in *Sundays and Cybèle*, released in France in 1959, in which the wounded veteran is a flyer from the French-Indochina War. The girl, Cybèle, is younger and more childlike than Eva in *Little Lips*, and the French film, while dreamily romantic, tender, and sweet, manages not to be erotic. When the war veteran is killed by police, who think the veteran is a pedophile who has abducted the girl, the relationship between the veteran and the girl seems to be tragically misunderstood. The veteran is in the process of being reborn, as if the child were a guiding Hermes.

In the important U.S. film, *Taxi Driver*, directed by Martin Scorsese, Robert De Niro plays Travis Bickle, a young Vietnam War veteran living an urban marginal existence. He is so alienated and estranged that he cannot date a normal woman his age. Instead, he becomes concerned about the well being of a 12-year-old street prostitute, played by Jodi Foster. She has run away from her midwest home and he liberates her by shooting everyone involved in her exploitation. He, like the French-Indochina War veteran in *Sundays and Cybèle*, is not interested in the girl sexually and finds her exploitation by other men to be reprehensible.

Importantly, in all of these movies, the girl is abandoned, either through deaths of the parents, as in the case of Eva, and Cybèle's father's abandonment after her mother's death, or a run-away, as Iris in *Taxi Driver*. These are all events of traumatic potential. In each case the girl connects with the war veteran in a soulful, spiritual way. The more sophisticated films sidestep the issue of a sexual relationship by placing the subject of carnality as a collective misunderstanding. *Little Lips* trips over its own ineptitude, wishing to exploit the sensational aspect of a man-girl relationship. With *Little Lips*, the collective others are conveniently not concerned about the relationship. The girl's guardians, the veteran's servants, seem, if anything, happy that the veteran has come alive. The opprobrium seems to rest in the veteran's scruples. It seems he is sexually attracted to Eva, but knows the limits. He dies because his relationship with the girl is tainted by her more natural attraction to the playful gypsy boy and he cannot sustain his romantic relationship with her.

I am reminded of James Whale's *Frankenstein*, in which the rejected and lonely creature happens upon a little girl by the lake. She is playfully not judgmental and for the first time the creature connects with an accepting human being, while at the same time presenting her with danger.

Samuel Fuller: War Veteran and Filmmaker

Samuel Fuller was a copyboy and crime reporter on Manhattan dailies during the heyday of journalism in the 1920s. He went on the road during the Great Depression and wrote freelance stories and took pictures of his impressions of labor riots, strikes, and Hooverville life. In 1941, after Pearl Harbor, at age 29, Fuller joined the army and volunteered for the infantry. He even resisted attempts to recruit him for public relations and the benefit of a commission. Fuller served with the Big Red One (First Infantry Division) as an enlisted man and fought in North Africa, Sicily, was among the first waves landing in Normandy, and went through the Battle of the Bulge and the invasion of Germany. Fuller kept a diary of his army life and even took home movies of the liberation of a concentration camp. His remark about the infantry was stated with his usual candor and earthiness: "For Chrissakes, the infantry! Guys who joined the infantry, I discovered, came back from the war one of three ways: dead, wounded, or crazy" (Fuller, p. 110). He mentions receiving at least one Purple Heart and a Silver Star.

After his discharge, Samuel Fuller went on to write novels and screenplays, and to direct his own films, as well as act in others. In all, he published 11 books. Because he insisted on only directing films over which he had complete control, including the screenplay, Fuller rejected many film offers. He once rejected an opportunity to make a big studio film of his beloved Big Red One when John Wayne was going to have the lead. Fuller thought Wayne was too much of a hero type.

Most of Fuller's films were made during the '50s and were regarded at the time as "B-movies," that is, low budget projects studio-produced by yeomen on a tight schedule. He fell out of favor with the Hollywood studios, but became a celebrity in France, where he was lauded by the intellectual leaders of the French New Wave.

Fuller had a reputation in Hollywood for making violent films with raw emotions. His war films, *Steel Helmet* and *Fixed Bayonets*, both in 1951, were popular moneymakers. Fuller stated that the only way to make a realistic war movie was to shoot live ammunition at the audience, which he admitted would be tough on sales. He made several films also about war veterans: *China Gate, Crimson Kimono, House of Bamboo,* and *Verboten!* He tried for most of his career to get his cherished *The Big Red One* filmed, and finally succeeded in 1980, although completing it on a very tight budget. He commented that making the movie about his own unit caused him to have nightmares and intrusive images.

Fuller's comment about war emotions is worth noting. "War is not about emotions. It's about the absence of emotions. That void *is* the emotion of war" (p. 234). He observed that he worked out many of his disturbing feelings and images in his violent, hard-hitting films, and ironically but clinically true, toward the end of his life, one of his ongoing nightmares was of being a character in his own films (p. 557).

As a film director, Samuel Fuller had great respect for his actors, but also apparently something of a temper that he brushes over in his autobiography. Among his quirks was his habit of starting a scene by firing off a pistol. Because of his defiant independence, many of his film projects did not come to fruition. He once went into the Brazilian jungle to make a film, hoping that it would take his mind off his painful memories (p. 325). He writes,

> With eight pictures under my belt, now established as a writer-director in Hollywood, I should have been sleeping peacefully under those silk sheets in my big house in Beverly Hills. Nothing could have been further from the truth. I tossed and turned all night long, racked by horrific nightmares. Terrible visions from the war buried in my brain rose up as soon as I dozed off. Heaps of dead bodies. A gaunt hand stretching skyward for help. Bombs exploding. Soldiers ripped apart [p. 325].

One of his frequent comments addressed the casualties caused by "friendly fire." Like more than a few vets with PTSD, Fuller walked away from his first marriage after his wife was attracted to another man. He left her his house and his entire estate, moving into a little place he called "The Shack."

Fuller wrote something that must be very true about the end of any war.

> The ending of all hostilities was a quiet shock. It was hard to accept that the war was really over. I couldn't believe that I didn't have to sleep with my hand on my rifle anymore, that every noise wasn't the start of an enemy attack, that I could light a cigar at night without worrying about a sniper putting a bullet through my brain [p. 218].

About his return to the states, he writes:

> Though it was good beyond words to put my arms around her (his mother) again, it became quickly evident that my homecoming was burdensome for me and everyone around me. I spent a helluva lot of time in bed but couldn't sleep for long stretches. Horrible nightmares kept rattling my head. Every-day sounds made me jump and shake uncontrollably. My family couldn't understand my constant grumpiness. No one who hadn't lived through the front lines of the war could. I was a textbook case of "war hysteria" [p. 233].

Fullers' company that landed in Normandy lost 100 men out of the 183 who embarked.

Samuel Fuller's 2002 autobiography, *A Third Face: My Tale of Writing, Fighting, and Filmmaking,* is an enjoyable book to read for a number of reasons: his old fashioned, tough dialog; his perpetual optimism and zeal to write; the characters he's known, from Damon Runyon in the early days, to Hollywood personalities and army generals. He ridiculed the right wing newspaper columnists in the day when it was not fashionable. Warfare marked his career, and at times he is eloquent in describing its effects, as when he writes: "To this day, that first face of death is imprinted on my mind like a leaf in a fossil, never to fade away" (p. 114).

Ironically, I had the impression that the first psychological trauma came when the young Sammy Fuller, as a crime reporter, had to witness an execution by electric chair. He wrote about it in his first novel, *Burn, Baby, Burn*:

> The yarn kicks off with a pregnant woman condemned to die in the chair. I must have been so obsessed with the electric chair that I used it as a fictional hook, finding a release for some of my nightmarish memories of prisoners getting fried at Sing Sing [p. 77].

Fuller made one of his last pictures of his Hollywood period, *Shock Corridor,* about the hospital treatment of mental illness. His story has a reporter going undercover disguised as a hospital mental patient. The reporter eventually goes crazy.

To convey how appalling electric-shock treatment is for a patient, we put together a montage, superimposing it across Johnny's convulsive body, along with shrieking sounds. The scene still makes me shiver, dredging up memories of electric-chair executions at Sing Sing that I had to witness as a crime reporter" [p. 409].

Samuel Fuller seems to brag and boast in his book, but it is not narcissism so much as the events in the life of an extraordinary man. When he writes, "I tailored the script for her like a seamstress fitting a wedding dress to a bride" (p. 447), he seems to be savoring his craft.

His career was obviously influenced by his war experiences and he expressed gratitude for surviving.

> For those lucky enough to survive it, war turned your deepest convictions upside down and inside out. Life was supposed to be precious. Every human being was supposed to be valuable. Yet all around you were the corpses of people killed in a conflict they hardly understood, lives wasted in intolerable ways and unthinkable proportions. What could those young men have accomplished, if only they'd survived? It was enough to drive you crazy. Many soldiers did go nuts. If you retained any sanity, you never thought about time the same way again. You were grateful for every moment of existence you were granted, and you didn't want to waste another split second on bullshit [p. 189].

A Third Face credits Christa Lang Fuller, his second wife, and Jerome Henry Rudes as co-authors assisting Samuel Fuller, who was a noted raconteur and probably dictated much of his book after the first of his late-life strokes. The book thankfully retains a sense of casual immediacy. For example, when Fuller is describing his first encounter with death on the battlefield, he significantly shifts person, in a manner that suggests dissociation.

> During the North African campaign, I had to kill a man for the first time. The act begets the most basic revulsion. I couldn't believe it was me pulling the trigger. It left me feeling hollow inside. But a soldier must overcome that disgust if he is to survive. Afterward, when you kill, you're shooting the same man over and over again. Your will to survive surprises you, eventually kicking abstract thoughts like remorse or mercy out of your brain [p. 123].

From my perspective, Samuel Fuller is truly the war veteran in film.

Films Reviewed in Text, by Release Date

Heroes for Sale (1933, U.S.). World War I veteran tries to cope with wound-related opiate habit and frustrations of the Great Depression.

I Am a Fugitive from a Chain Gang (1933, U.S.). World War I veteran gets trapped by criminal justice system.

The Fallen Sparrow (1943, U.S.). Veteran of the Spanish Civil War pursues the killers of his friend, who helped him escape from a wartime prison.

Cornered (1945, U.S.). World War II veteran searches for Nazi murderer of wife.

The Blue Dahlia (1946, U.S.). World War II veteran returns from war to find wife murdered and searches for killer.

The Best Years of Our Lives (1946, U.S.). World War II veterans return to three different home situations.

Crossfire (1947, U.S.). World War II veterans involved in murder of fellow veteran.

Dead Reckoning (1947, U.S.). World War II veteran seeks killer of war veteran buddy.

Fort Apache (1948, U.S.). Civil War veterans occupy a frontier outpost and continue fighting.

Machine to Kill Bad People (*La Macchina Ammazza Cattivi*) (1948, Italy). World War II Italian-American veterans return as businessmen to an area of Italy where they fought.

Key Largo (1948, U.S.). World War II veteran seeks parents of dead buddy, fights gangsters.

Red River (1948, U.S.). U.S. Civil War veterans drive cattle from Texas to market.

She Wore a Yellow Ribbon (1949, U.S.). Civil War veterans serve with U.S. Cavalry on the Western Frontier. Captain confronts retirement.

The Men (1950, U.S.). Paraplegic World War II veteran struggles with readjustment, spouse, and identity.

Macao (1952, U.S.). World War II veteran gets mistaken for a cop in the borderland city of Macao.

The Sun Shines Bright (1953, U.S.). U.S. Civil War veterans from both sides of the war live competitive lives side by side in a Kentucky town.

Ulysses (1954, Italy). Trojan War veteran has difficulty returning home, and, once home, reclaiming his entitlement.

Bad Day at Black Rock (1955, U.S.). World War II veteran fights resistance in desert town population while searching for the father of Japanese-American soldier.

The Man in the Gray Flannel Suit (1956, U.S.). World War II veteran balances business promotion with family obligations, while sorting wartime baggage.

The Seventh Seal (1957, Sweden). Crusades veteran returns to home shore to find plague and death threatening.

The Sun Also Rises (1957, U.S.). Wounded World War I veteran vacations in Spain, attends bullfight spectacle.

A Hatful of Rain (1957, U.S.). Korean War veteran copes with opiate habit from wounds.

China Gate (1957, U.S.). War veterans from Korean War and World War II continue to fight Communists for the French in Indochina.

Some Came Running (1958, U.S.). World War II veteran returns to hometown to cope with his brother and his own identity as a writer.

Anatomy of a Murder (1958, U.S.). World War II and Korean War veteran on trial for murder of man who raped veteran's wife.

Ocean's Eleven (1960, U.S.). Korean War veterans gather for reunion heist of gambling casino.

Sundays and Cybèle (1962, French). French-Indochina War veteran develops relationship with young abandoned girl.

Manchurian Candidate (1962, U.S.). Korean War veteran tries to stop buddy from carrying out assassination ordered under hypnosis while POW.

The Glory Boys, (1964, UK). World War II British veteran called into government service to fight terrorist.

Motor Psycho (1965, U.S.). Vietnam War veteran goes on rampage with friends in California desert.

The Born Losers (1968, U.S.). Vietnam War veteran fights outlaw biker gang.

The Ballad of Andy Crocker (1969, U.S.). Vietnam War veteran rides stolen motorcycle home and copes with changes, beats his business partner, and re-enlists.

Looking for Mr. Goodbar (1969, U.S.). Vietnam War veteran is psychopathic lover.

Satan's Sadists (1969, U.S.). Vietnam War veteran fights motorcycle outlaw club.

Rio Lobo (1970, U.S.). U.S. Civil War Union army veteran pursues traitors after the war.

Ryan's Daughter (1970, UK). Wounded World War I veteran on assignment in western Ireland has affair with local woman.

The American Soldier (1970, German). Vietnam War veteran hired as German underworld assassin.

Billy Jack (1971, U.S.). Vietnam War veteran battles town ruffians in Southwest.

Johnny Got His Gun (1971, U.S.). World War I veteran copes with loss of limbs and face.

Chrome and Hot Leather (1971, U.S.). Vietnam War veteran fights outlaw biker gang.

The Visitors (1972, U.S.). Two Vietnam War veterans visit the man from their squad who turned them in for atrocities. World War II veteran father has a revived sense of wartime camaraderie.

To Kill a Clown (1972, U.S.). Vietnam War veteran terrorizes vacationers staying in a summer cabin.

Deathdream (1972, U.S.). Vietnam War veteran KIA keeps living and terrorizes friends and family.

Private Duty Nurses (1972, U.S.). Student nurse tries to help a wounded Vietnam War veteran on a destructive course.

Blackenstein (*The Black Frankenstein*) (1972, U.S.). Wounded Vietnam War veteran's treatment goes awry.

Electra Glide in Blue (1973, U.S.). Lonely Vietnam War veteran motorcycle cop seeks promotion to detective.

Gordon's War (1973, U.S.). Vietnam War veteran rounds up his veteran buddies to fight drug dealers in Harlem.

Mr. Majestyk (1974, U.S.). Vietnam War veteran ex-con melon farmer fights for justice.

Dog Day Afternoon (1975, U.S.). Putative Vietnam War veteran robs bank in Brooklyn.

Taxi Driver (1976, U.S.). Vietnam War veteran drives a cab in New York City, decompensates into a psychosis and recovers.

Tracks (1976, U.S.). Vietnam War veteran travels by train to deliver the body of wartime buddy in a coffin.

Rolling Thunder (1977, U.S.). Vietnam War POW returns home, is betrayed by wife and tortured by villains, then pursues them with vengeance.

Black Sunday (1977, U.S.). Vietnam War veteran, recruited as POW by terrorists, tries to bomb Superbowl from a blimp.

Heroes (1977, U.S.). Zany Vietnam War veteran escapes from a veterans hospital and travels across country with female companion.

Coming Home (1978, U.S.). Paraplegic Vietnam War veteran finds love in hospital helper while helper's spouse, also a war veteran, returns with PTSD and walks into the sea.

The Deer Hunter (1978, U.S.). Vietnam War veterans struggle with post-traumatic sequela.

Up in Smoke (1978, U.S.). Vietnam War veteran motorcyclist has flashback while companion grimaces in the sidecar.

Who'll Stop the Rain? (1978, U.S.). Vietnam War veteran conspires to smuggle heroin, battles rogue cops.

Saint Jack (1979, U.S.). Korean War veteran living in Singapore develops tourist trade catering to needs of GIs on R&R from Vietnam.

The Stunt Man (1980, U.S.). Vietnam War veteran on run from law becomes stunt man for war movie production.

Ruckus (1980, U.S.). Vietnam War veteran of Army Special Forces lays waste to the country boys who harass him.

Cutter's Way (1981, U.S.). Severely wounded Vietnam War veteran seeks murderer of girl with non-veteran friend.

Ashes and Embers (1982, U.S.). African-American Vietnam War veteran returns home in rural South and experiences alienation.

Some Kind of Hero (1982, U.S.). Vietnam War veteran POW returns home to find out that his wife has adapted to his death, becomes involved in a bank robbery.

Firefox (1982, U.S.). Vietnam War veteran pilot recruited for dangerous government mission.

First Blood (1982, U.S.). Vietnam War veteran persecuted by cops fights back with guerrilla tactics.

The Big Chill (1983, U.S.). Vietnam War veteran is in reunion of friends after a funeral.

Birdy (1984, U.S.). Vietnam War veteran friends meet in hospital and recall neighborhood life.

Choose Me (1984, U.S.). Vietnam War air force veteran in romantic, highly stylized love triangle.

Fleshburn (1984, U.S.). Native American Vietnam War veteran kidnaps four psychiatrists who sent him involuntarily to a mental hospital.

Alamo Bay (1985, U.S.). Vietnam War veteran Texas shrimper caught up in ethnic tensions.

The Park Is Mine (1985, U.S.). Vietnam War veteran takes over Central Park with an abundance of pyrotechnics, but limited philosophy.

Desert Bloom (1986, U.S.). Alcoholic World War II veteran struggles to cope with family and news during Korean War.

O. C. & Stiggs (1987, U.S.). Vietnam War veterans are comic survivalists in satire of teen exploitation movie.

Gardens of Stone (1987, U.S.). Army old guard bury the Vietnam War dead and experience the guilt of not training recruits for combat.

Extreme Prejudice (1987, U.S.). Vietnam War veterans are duped to fight on as rogues in secret group.

Distant Thunder (1988, U.S.). Vietnam War veteran, a former POW, seeks revenge against outlaws.

The Presidio (1988, U.S.). Vietnam War veterans, still in the army and recently retired, in a murder mystery and dispute over jurisdictions.

Born on the Forth of July (1989, U.S.). Vietnam War veteran returns home to cope with paralysis, his identity, and his family.

Jacknife (1989, U.S.). Vietnam War veterans meet years after loss of friend in war, struggle with memories.

In Country (1989, U.S.). Vietnam War veteran raises niece and copes with PTSD.

The Desperate Hours (1990, U.S.). Vietnam War veteran fights for family against outlaws.

Wild at Heart (1990, U.S.). Vietnam War veteran persuades fellow-traveler to rob feed store.

Jacob's Ladder (1990, U.S.). Vietnam War veterans haunted by government experiment with psychedelic motivator.

Men at Work (1990, U.S.). Vietnam War veteran tries to shepherd zany garbage men.

Akira Kurosawa's Dreams. "The Tunnel" (1990, Japan). World War II veteran POW returns home to face ghosts.

A Dangerous Man: Lawrence After Arabia (1990, UK). The World War I veteran is disillusioned and frustrated by the colonial powers betrayal of his cause.

Dances with Wolves (1990, U.S.). U.S. Civil War veteran nearly loses his leg, becomes suicidal, and is transferred to the Western frontier, where he meets and becomes one of the Sioux.

The Indian Runner (1991, U.S.). Vietnam War veteran returns to hometown and takes up outlaw life.

Lethal Weapon (1991, U.S.). Vietnam War veteran cops fight crime and PTSD.

Nothing but Trouble (1991, U.S.). World War I veteran is bizarre justice of the peace in a dump town.

Lawrence of Arabia (1962). World War I veteran resigns from British army after betrayal of his Arab cause, drives his motorcycle at high speed and is killed.

Article 99 (1992, U.S.). war veterans are affronted by services at VA hospital.

Le Retour de Martin Guerre (1992, French). Veteran of Franco-Spanish War of 1557 returns as fraud.

Sommersby (1993, U.S.-French). U.S. Civil War Confederate veteran returns to family farm posing as another.

Red Rock West (1993, U.S.). wounded Vietnam War veteran, unable to work, is mistakenly recruited by a husband to murder man's wife.

Troubles (1993, UK). World War I veteran travels to Ireland to encounter prejudice among the British colonialists, along with Irish antipathy.

Forrest Gump (1994, U.S.). Vietnam War veteran copes with success and amputee friend's PTSD.

The War (1994, U.S.). Vietnam War veteran tries to raise family in poverty conditions in rural south.

Dead Presidents (1995, U.S.). African-American Vietnam War veterans conspire to rob an armored car.

Last Stand at Saber River (1996, U.S.). U.S. Civil War veteran keeps fighting after war is over.

The Devil in a Blue Dress (1996, U.S.). World War II veteran becomes detective to search for missing woman.

Conspiracy Theory (1997, U.S.). Vietnam War veteran becomes paranoid after government mind tricks.

Ulee's Gold (1997, U.S.). Vietnam War veteran must face off with outlaws while coping with family, and work as a beekeeper.

Absolute Power (1997, U.S.). Korean War veteran burglar more righteous than U.S. president.

The Spitfire Grill (1997, U.S.). A traumatized girl becomes infatuated with a Vietnam War Veteran, who lives as a

hermit in woods near the grill where she works.

Photographing Fairies (1997, UK). A World War I veteran photographer becomes fascinated investigating fairies, realizes his own grief.

Fairytale: A True Story (1997, UK). World War I veterans populate scenery of girls' sensational story.

Ivanhoe (1998, UK). Crusades veteran returns home in disguise to reclaim his reputation.

Mrs. Dalloway (1998, UK). World War I veteran becomes suicidal over post-war grief, crosses the path of a society woman planning a party.

The Big Lebowski (1998, U.S.). Vietnam War veteran bowling partner satirizes lowbrow sentiments.

Rushmore (1999, U.S.). Vietnam War veteran businessman befriends oddball high school student.

The Straight Story (1999, U.S.). Aging World War II veteran travels across state in a riding lawn mower to visit dying brother.

The Patriot (2000, U.S.). veteran of French and Indian War resists participation in Revolutionary War, but joins the ranks after his son is killed by Redcoats.

Meet the Parents (2000, U.S.). Vietnam War veteran and overprotective father quizzes daughter's lover.

Snow Falling on Cedars (2000, U.S.). World War II veterans in murder trial involving Japanese-American veteran in Pacific Northwest.

Lawn Dogs (2000, U.S.). Korean War veteran scorned by son for his chronic illness.

The Legend of Bagger Vance (2000, U.S.). World War I veteran returns after 10 years to play golf with the assistance of his soulful caddy.

Gosford Park (2001, UK). World War I veteran part of a houseparty with his war service extolled and compared to the slackards and conscientious objectors.

The Man Who Wasn't There (2001, U.S.). Navy veteran lies about his participation in combat, gets stabbed to death.

War Veteran Films, Alphabetically

These films have been identified as being about war veterans. Titles in bold type are mentioned in the text. I have not included popular TV series involving Vietnam veterans as characters, notably *The A Team*; *Riptide*; *Simon & Simon*; *Magnum PI*; and *Miami Vice*. Lists are drawn from various sources, including Selby, 1984; Dittmar and Michaud, 1990; Walker, 1991; Lanning, 1994; Devine, 1995; Turner, 1996; McBride, 2001. Owens (2001, p. 83) discusses the influence of the TV series *Magnum PI* and the many shows depicting interactions between war veterans, both cooperative and hostile.

Above the Law (1988, U.S.)
Absolute Power (1997, U.S.) Korean War
Act of Violence (1949, U.S.)
Akira Kurosawa's Dreams (1990, Japan) World War II
Alamo Bay (1985, U.S.) Vietnam War
American Commandos (1986, U.S.)
American Eagle (1991, U.S.)
American Ninja (1986, U.S.)
The American Soldier (1970, Germany) Vietnam War
Americana (1981, U.S.)
Anatomy of a Murder (1958, U.S.) World War II and Korean War
Angels from Hell (1968, U.S.)
The Angry Breed (1968, U.S.)
The Annihilators (1985, U.S.)
Armed Response (1987, U.S.)
Article 99 (1992, U.S.) Vietnam War
Ashes and Embers (1982, U.S.) Vietnam War
Back to School (1986, U.S.)

Backfire (1950, 1987, U.S.)
Bad Day at Black Rock (1955, U.S.) World War II
The Ballad of Andy Crocker (1969, U.S.) Vietnam War
Band of the Hand (1986, U.S.)
The Bears and I (1974, U.S.)
Bell Diamond (1987, U.S.)
The Best Years of Our Lives (1946, U.S.) World War II
Betrayed (1988, U.S.)
The Big Bounce (1969, U.S.)
The Big Chill (1983, U.S.) Vietnam War
The Big Lebowski (1998, U.S.) Vietnam War
Billy Jack (1971, U.S.) Vietnam War
Billy Jack Goes to Washington (1974, U.S.)
Birdy (1984, U.S.) Vietnam War
Black Gunn (1972, U.S.)
The Black Six (1974, U.S.)
Black Sunday (1977, U.S.) Vietnam War

Blackenstein (*The Black Franken-
stein*) (1972, U.S.) Vietnam War
Blind Fury (1990, U.S.)
Blood of Ghastly Horror (1965, U.S.)
The Blue Dahlia (1946, U.S.) World
  War II
Blue Thunder (1983, U.S.)
Borderline (1980, U.S.)
The Born Losers (1968, U.S.) Viet-
  nam War
Born on the Fourth of July (1989,
  U.S.) Vietnam War
Le Boucher (1969, France)
Braddock: Missing in Action III (1988,
  U.S.)
Break Loose (see *Parades*)
The Brotherhood (1969, U.S.)
The Burbs (1988, U.S.)
The Bus Is Coming (1971, U.S.)
Bus Riley's Back in Town (1965, U.S.)
Cage (1989, U.S.)
Captain Milkshake (1970, U.S.)
Captive (see *Two*)
Carolina Skeletons (1991, U.S.)
Cartel (1991, U.S.)
Casualties of War (*1989, U.S.)*
Cease Fire (1984, U.S.)
Charley Varrick (1973, U.S.)
China Gate (1957, U.S.) Korean War,
  World War II
The Choirboys (1977, U.S.)
Choose Me (1984, U.S.) Vietnam War
Chrome and Hot Leather (1971, U.S.)
  Vietnam War
Clay Pigeon (1971, U.S.)
Code Name: Zebra (1987, U.S.)
Colors (1988, U.S.)
Combat Shock (1986, U.S.)
Coming Home (1978, U.S.) Vietnam
  War
Conspiracy Theory (1997, U.S.) Viet-
  nam War
Cool Breeze (1972, U.S.)
Cornered (1945, U.S.) World War II
Le Crabe-Tambour (1977, France)
The Crazies (1973, U.S.)
The Crazy World of Julius Vrooder
  (1974, U.S.)
The Crimson Kimono (1959, U.S.)

The Crooked Way (1949, U.S.)
Crossfire (1947, U.S.) World War II
Cutter's Way (1981, U.S.) Vietnam War
Dances with Wolves (1990, U.S.) U.S.
  Civil War
A Dangerous Man (1990, UK) World
  War I
Dangerously Close (1986, U.S.)
Dark Blue World (2001, Czech)
DC Cab (1983, U.S.)
Dead Presidents (1995, U.S.) Vietnam
  War
Dead Reckoning (1947, U.S.) World
  War II
Deadly Encounter (1982, U.S.)
Deathdream (1972, U.S.) Vietnam War
The Deer Hunter (1978, U.S.) Viet-
  nam War
Desert Bloom (1986, U.S.) World War
  II
The Desperate Hours (1990, U.S.)
  Vietnam War
The Desperate Miles (1975, U.S.)
The Devil in a Blue Dress (1996,
  U.S.) World War II
The Destroyers (1992, U.S.)
Distant Thunder (1988, U.S.) Viet-
  nam War
The Doberman Gang (1972, U.S.)
Dog Day Afternoon (1975, U.S.)
  Vietnam War
Don't Answer the Phone (1980, U.S.)
Electra Glide in Blue (1973, U.S.)
  Vietnam War
The Enforcer (1976, U.S.)
Exterminator (1980, U.S.)
Exterminator II (1984, U.S.)
Extreme Prejudice (1987, U.S.) Viet-
  nam War
Eye of the Tiger (1986, U.S.)
Eyewitness (1981, U.S.)
Fairytale: A True Story (1997, UK)
  World War I
The Fallen Sparrow (1943, U.S.)
False Identity (1990, U.S.)
Fear (1987, U.S.)
Fighting Back (1980, U.S.)
Fighting Mad (1977, U.S., Philippines)
Final Mission (1984, U.S.)

Firefox (1982, U.S.) Vietnam War
First Blood (1982, U.S.) Vietnam War
Five Days Home (see *Welcome Home, Soldier Boys*)
Flashpoint (1984, U.S.)
Fleshburn (1984, U.S.)
A Force of One (1979, U.S.)
Forced Vengeance (1982, U.S.)
The Forgotten Man (1971, U.S.)
Forrest Gump (1994, U.S.) Vietnam War
Fort Apache (1948, U.S.) U.S. Civil War
The Fourth War (1990, U.S.)
Gardens of Stone (1987, U.S.) Vietnam War
Georgia, Georgia (1972, U.S.)
Getting Straight (1970, U.S.)
The GI Executioner (1987, U.S.)
The Girl Who Came Between Them (1990, U.S.)
The Glory Boys (1964, UK) World War II
Godfather, Part I (1972, U.S.)
Godfather, Part 2 (1974, U.S.)
Godfather, Part 3 (1990, U.S.)
Good Guys Wear Black (1977, U.S.)
Gordon's War (1973, U.S.)
Gosford Park (2001, UK) World War I
Graveyard Shift (1990, U.S.)
Green Eyes (1976, U.S.)
The Green Glove (1952, U.S.)
Hail Hero (1969, U.S.)
The Hard Ride (1971, U.S.)
Hardcase and Fist (1987, U.S.)
A Hatful of Rain (1957, U.S.) Korean War
Heartbreak Ridge (1986, U.S.)
Heroes (1977, U.S.) Vietnam War
Heroes for Sale (1933, U.S.) World War I
High Crimes (2002, U.S.)
The High Wall (1947, U.S.)
Highway Dragnet (1954, U.S.)
Hi-Low Country (1998, UC)
Hitman (1986, U.S.)
Hoodlum Empire (1952, U.S.)
House (1986, U.S.)
House of Bamboo (1955, U.S.)

I Am a Fugitive from a Chain Gang (1932, U.S.) World War I
I Feel It Coming aka *The Soldier's Wife* (1969, U.S.)
In Country (1989, U.S.) Vietnam War
In the Bedroom (2001, U.S.)
The Indian Runner (1991, U.S.) Vietnam War
Ivanhoe (1998, UK) Crusades
Jacknife (1989, U.S.) Vietnam War
Jacob's Ladder (1990, U.S.) Vietnam War
Johnny Got His Gun (1971, U.S.) World War I
Journey Through Rosebud (1972, U.S.)
Jud (1971, U.S.)
Just a Little Inconvenience (1977, U.S.)
Key Largo (1948, U.S.) World War II
Kill Zone (1986, U.S.)
Kiss the Blood off My Hands (1948, U.S.)
Last Orders (2002, U.S.)
Last Stand at Saber River (1996, U.S.) U.S. Civil War
The Late Liz (1971, U.S.)
Lawn Dogs (2000, U.S.) Korean War
Lawrence of Arabia (1992, UK) World War I
The Legend of Bagger Vance (2000, U.S.) World War I
Lethal Weapon (1991, U.S.) Vietnam War
Let's Get Harry (1987, U.S.)
L.I.E. (2000, U.S.) Vietnam War
Limosine (1984, U.S.)
The Line (see *Parades*)
Little Lips (1999, Spain) World War I
The Lively Set (1964, U.S.)
Looking for Mr. Goodbar (1969, U.S.) Vietnam War
The Losers (1970, U.S.)
Macao (1952, U.S.)
Machine to Kill Bad People (*La Macchina Ammazza Cattivi*) (1948, Italy) World War II
Magnum Force (1973, U.S.)
The Majestic (2001, U.S.) World War II
Malone (1987, U.S.)
The Man in the Gray Flannel Suit (1956, U.S.) World War II

The Man Who Wasn't There (2001, U.S.)

The Man Who Would be King (1975, U.S.)

Manchurian Candidate (1962, U.S.) Korean War

Mean Johnny Barrows (1976, U.S.)

Meet the Parents (2000, U.S.) Vietnam War

Memorial Day (1983, U.S.)

The Men (1950, U.S.) World War II

Men at Work (1990, U.S.) Vietnam War

Missing in Action (1984, U.S.)

Moon in Scorpio (1987, U.S.)

Motor Psycho (1965, U.S.) Vietnam War

Mr. Majestyk (1974, U.S.) Vietnam War

Mrs. Dalloway (1998, UK) World War I

My Father, My Son (1988, U.S.)

Nam Angels (1986, U.S.)

Night Flowers (1979, U.S.)

Night Wars (1987, U.S.)

Nightforce (1987, U.S.)

1969 (1988, U.S.)

The Ninth Configuration (1980, U.S.)

No Dead Heroes (1986, U.S.)

The No Mercy Man (see *Trained to Kill*)

Nobody Lives Forever (1946, U.S.)

Norwood (1970, U.S.)

Nothing But Trouble (1991, U.S.) World War I

O. C. & Stiggs (1987, U.S.) Vietnam War

Ocean's Eleven (1960, U.S.) Korean War

Omega Syndrome (1987, U.S.)

Operation Warzone (1987, U.S.)

Opposing Force (1987, U.S.)

The Others (2001, UK)

Outlaw Force (1987, U.S.)

Outside In (1972, U.S.)

The Package (1987, U.S.)

Parades aka *Break Loose* aka *The Line* (1972, U.S.)

The Park Is Mine (1985, U.S.) Vietnam War

The Patriot (2000, U.S.) French and Indian War

Photographing Fairies (1997, UK) World War I

Poor White Trash (see *Scum of the Earth*)

The POW (1973, U.S.)

The Presidio (1988, U.S.) Vietnam War

Private Duty Nurses (1972, U.S.) Vietnam War

Rambo, First Blood Part II (1985, U.S.) Vietnam War

Rambo III (1988, U.S.) Vietnam War

The Ravager (1970, U.S.)

Rescue Me (1993, U.S.)

Red River (1948, U.S.) U.S. Civil War

Red Rock West (1993, U.S.) Vietnam War

Le Retour de Martin Guerre (1992, France) Franco-Spanish War of 1557

Returning Home (1975, U.S.)

Riders of the Storm (1986, U.S.)

Rio Lobo (1970, U.S.) U.S. Civil War

The Road Back (1931, U.S.) World War I

Rogue's Regiment (1948, U.S.)

Rolling Thunder (1977, U.S.) Vietnam War

Ruckus (1980 U.S.) Vietnam War

A Rumor of War (1980, U.S.)

Rushmore (1999, U.S.) Vietnam War

Ryan's Daughter (1970, UK) World War I

Saigon (1948, U.S.)

Saint Jack (1979, U.S.) Korean War

The Saint of Fort Washington (1993, U.S.)

Satan's Sadists (1969, U.S.) Vietnam War

Savage Dawn (1985, U.S.)

Scent of a Woman (1992, U.S.)

Scum of the Earth aka *Poor White Trash II* (1976, U.S.)

Search and Destroy (1981, U.S.)

The Seventh Seal (1957, Sweden) Crusades

She Wore a Yellow Ribbon (1949, U.S.) U.S. Civil War

Skyjacked (1972, U.S.)

Slaughter (1972, U.S.)

Snow Falling on Cedars (2000, U.S.) World War II

So Cool (1991, U.S.)
Soldier's Revenge (1987, U.S.)
The Soldier's Wife (see *I Feel It Coming*)
Some Came Running (1958, U.S.) World War II
Some Kind of Hero (1982, U.S.) Vietnam War
Somewhere In the Night (1946, U.S.)
Sommersby (1993, U.S.-French) U.S. Civil War
Special Delivery (1976, U.S.)
The Spitfire Grill (1997, U.S.) Vietnam War
Stanley (1972, U.S.)
Star Witness (1931, U.S.)
The Straight Story (1999, U.S.) World War II
Steele Justice (1987, U.S.)
Stigma (1972, U.S.)
The Stone Killer (1973, U.S.)
A Street to Die (1985, Australia)
Street Trash (1987, U.S.)
The Stunt Man (1980, U.S.) Vietnam War
The Sun Also Rises (1957, U.S.) World War II
The Sun Shines Bright (1953, U.S.) U.S. Civil War
Sundays and Cybèle (1962, France) French-Indochina War
Suspect (1987, U.S.)
Tagget (1991, U.S.)
Targets (1968, U.S.)
Taxi Driver (1976, U.S.) Vietnam War
The Texas Chainsaw Massacre Part 2 (1986, U.S.)
Thieves Highway (1949, U.S.)
Thou Shalt Not Kill ... Except (1987, U.S.)
Three Steps North (1946, U.S.)
To Heal a Nation (1988, U.S.)
To Kill a Clown (1972, U.S.) Vietnam War
Tough Guys Don't Dance (1987, U.S.)
Tracks (1976, U.S.) Vietnam War

Trained to Kill aka *The No Mercy Man* (1973, U.S.)
The Trial of Billy Jack (1977, U.S.)
Troubles (1993, UK) World War I
Try and Get Me (1950, U.S.)
Twilight Zone — The Movie (1983, U.S.)
Twilight's Last Gleaming (1977, U.S.)
Two aka *Captive* (1975, U.S.)
Two People (1973, U.S.)
Ulee's Gold (1997, U.S.) Vietnam War
Ulysses (1954, Italian) Trojan War
Uncommon Valor (1983, U.S.)
Under Siege (1992, U.S.)
Undertow (1949, U.S.)
Unnatural Causes (1986, U.S.)
Up in Smoke (1978, U.S.) Vietnam War
Vanishing Point *(1971)*
Verboten! (1958, U.S.)
Vietnam, Texas (1990, U.S.)
Vigilante Force (1975, U.S.)
The Visitors (1972, U.S.) Vietnam War
The War (1994, U.S.) Vietnam War
Welcome Home (1988, U.S.)
Welcome Home Johnny Bristol (1972, U.S.)
Welcome Home, Soldier Boys aka *Five Days Home* (1972, U.S.)
Whatever It Takes (1986, U.S.)
When Love Kills: The Seduction of John Hearn (1992, U.S.)
When You Comin' Back Red Rider? (1979, U.S.)
White Ghost (1985, U.S.)
White Line Fever (1975, U.S.)
White Nights (1985, U.S.)
Who'll Stop the Rain? (1978, U.S.) Vietnam War
Wild at Heart (1990, U.S.) Vietnam War
The Wild Life (1984, U.S.)
Wolf Lake (1987, U.S.)
The Woman Inside (1981, U.S.)
The Woman on the Beach (1947, France)
Year of the Dragon (1986, U.S.)

War Veteran Films Reviewed, by War

U.S. Civil War

Dances with Wolves (1990, U.S.)
Fort Apache (1948, U.S.)
Last Stand at Saber River (1996, U.S.)
Red River (1948, U.S.)
Rio Lobo (1970, U.S.)
The Searchers (1956, U.S.)
She Wore a Yellow Ribbon (1949, U.S.)
Sommersby (1993, U.S.-French)
The Sun Shines Bright (1953, U.S.)

World War I

A Dangerous Man (1990, UK)
Fairytale: A True Story (1997, UK)
Gosford Park (2002, UK)
Heroes for Sale (1933, U.S.)
I Am a Fugitive from a Chain Gang (1932, U.S.)
Johnny Got His Gun (1971, U.S.)
Lawrence of Arabia (1962, UK)
The Legend of Bagger Vance (2000, U.S.)
Mrs. Dalloway (1998, UK)
Nothing but Trouble (1991, U.S.)
Photographing Fairies (1997, UK)
Ryan's Daughter (1970, UK)
The Road Back (1931, U.S.)
The Straight Story (1999, U.S.)
The Sun Also Rises (1957, U.S.)
Troubles (1993, UK)

World War II

Akira Kurosawa's Dreams (1990, Japan)
Bad Day at Black Rock (1955, U.S.)
Best Years of Our Lives (1946, U.S.)
The Blue Dahlia (1946, U.S.)
Cornered (1945, U.S.)
Crossfire (1947, U.S.)
Dead Reckoning (1947, U.S.)
Desert Bloom (1986, U.S.)
The Glory Boys (1964, UK)
Key Largo (1948, U.S.)
Macao (1952, U.S.)
Machine to Kill Bad People (La Macchina Ammazza Cattivi) (1948, Italy)
The Man in the Gray Flannel Suit (1956, U.S.)
The Man Who Wasn't There (2001, U.S.)
The Men (1950, U.S.)
Snow Falling On Cedars (2000, U.S.)
Some Came Running (1958, U.S.)

Korean War

Absolute Power (1997, U.S.)
Anatomy of a Murder (1958, U.S.)
China Gate (1957, U.S.)
A Hatful of Rain (1957, U.S.)
Lawn Dogs (2000, U.S.)
Manchurian Candidate (1962, U.S.)
Ocean's Eleven (1960, U.S.)
Saint Jack (1979, U.S.)

Vietnam War

Alamo Bay (1985, U.S.)
The American Soldier (1970, Germany)
Article 99 (1992, U.S.)
Ashes and Embers (1982, U.S.)
The Ballad of Andy Crocker (1969, U.S.)
The Big Chill (1983, U.S.)
The Big Lebowski (1998, U.S.)
Billy Jack (1971, U.S.)
Birdy (1984, U.S.)
Black Sunday (1977, U.S.)
Blackenstein (*The Black Frankenstein*)
    (1972, U.S.)
The Born Losers (1968, U.S.)
Born on the Fourth of July (1989, U.S.)
Choose Me (1984, U.S.)
Chrome and Hot Leather (1971, U.S.)
Coming Home (1978, U.S.)
Conspiracy Theory (1997, U.S.)
Cutter's Way (1981, U.S.)
Dead Presidents (1995, U.S.)
Deathdream (1972, U.S.)
The Deer Hunter (1978, U.S.)
The Desperate Hours (1990, U.S.)
Distant Thunder (1988, U.S.)
Dog Day Afternoon (U.S., 1975)
Electra Glide in Blue (1973, U.S.)
Extreme Prejudice (1987, U.S.)
Fleshburn (1984, U.S.)
Firefox (1982, U.S.)
First Blood (1982, U.S.)
Forrest Gump (1994, U.S.)
Gardens of Stone (1987, U.S.)
Gordon's War (1973, U.S.)
Heroes (1977, U.S.)
In Country (1989, U.S.)
The Indian Runner (1991, U.S.)
Jacknife (1989, U.S.)
Jacob's Ladder (1990, U.S.)
Lethal Weapon (1991, U.S.)
Looking for Mr. Goodbar (1969, U.S.)
Meet the Parents (2000, U.S.)

Men at Work (1990, U.S.)
Motor Psycho (1965, U.S.)
Mr. Majestyk (1974, U.S.)
O. C. & Stiggs (1987, U.S.)
The Park Is Mine (1985, U.S.)
The Presidio (1988, U.S.)
Private Duty Nurses (1972, U.S.)
Rambo III (1988, U.S.)
Rambo, First Blood Part II (1985, U.S.)
Red Rock West (1993, U.S.)
Rolling Thunder (1977, U.S.)
Ruckus (1980 U.S.)
Rushmore (1999, U.S.)
Satan's Sadists (1969, U.S.)
Some Kind of Hero (1982, U.S.)
The Spitfire Grill (1997, U.S.)
The Stunt Man (1980, U.S.)
Taxi Driver (1976, U.S.)
To Kill a Clown (1972, U.S.)
Tracks (1976, U.S.)
Ulee's Gold (1997, U.S.)
Up in Smoke (1978, U.S.)
The Visitors (1972, U.S.)
The War (1994, U.S.)
Wild at Heart (1990, U.S.)
Who'll Stop the Rain? (1978, U.S.)

Other Wars

The Fallen Sparrow (1943, U.S.) The
    Spanish Civil War
Ivanhoe (1998, UK) Crusades
Le Retour de Martin Guerre (1992,
    France) Franco-Spanish War of 1557
The Patriot (2000, U.S.) French and
    Indian War
The Seventh Seal (1957, Sweden) Cru-
    sades
Sundays and Cybele (1962, France)
    French-Indochina War
Ulysses (1954, Italian) Trojan War

Bibliography

American Psychiatric Association (2000). *Diagnostic Criteria from DSM-IV-TR*. Washington, D.C.

Anderson, Maxwell (1939). *Key Largo: A Play in a Prologue and Two Acts*. Washington, D.C.: Anderson House.

Bergman, Ingmar (1960). *The Seventh Seal*. In *Four Screenplays*. New York: Simon & Schuster.

Bram, Christopher (1995). *Father of Frankenstein*. New York: Dutton.

Brodeur, Paul (1970). *Stunt Man*. New York: Atheneum.

Cohen, Deborah (2001). *The War Come Home: Disabled Veterans in Britain and Germany, 1914–1939*. Berkeley: University of California Press.

Curtis, James (1998). *James Whale: A World of Gods and Monsters*. London: Faber and Faber.

Damasio, Antonio (2000). *The Feeling of What Happens*. New York: Harcourt-Brace.

Dalieli, Yael (1997). *International Handbook of Multigenerational Legacies of Trauma*. Reviewed in *PTSD Research Quarterly* 8 (1).

Davis, Natalie Zemon (1983). *The Return of Martin Guerre*. Cambridge: Harvard University Press.

Dean, Eric T., Jr. (1997). *Shook Over Hell: Post-traumatic Stress, Vietnam, and the Civil War*. Cambridge: Harvard University Press.

Devine, Jeremy M. (1995). *Vietnam at 24 Frames a Second*. Austin: University of Texas Press.

Dittmar, Linda, and Gene Michaud (eds.) (1990). *From Hanoi to Hollywood: Hollywood, American Culture, and World War II*. New Brunswick, N.J.: Rutgers University Press.

Doherty, Thomas. (1993) *Pre-code Hollywood: Sex, Immorality, and Insurrection in American Cinema, 1930–1934*. New York: Columbia University Press.

Doherty, Thomas (1993b). *Projections of War: Hollywood, American Culture, and World War II*. New York: Columbia University Press.

Fuller, Samuel (2002). *A Third Face: My Tale of Writing, Fighting and Filmmaking*. New York: Alfred A. Knopf.

Gillingham, John (1999). *Richard I*. New Haven: Yale University Press.

Grimm, Jacob, and Wilhelm Grimm (1840, 1972). "Bearskin." In *The Complete Grimms' Fairy Tales*. Margaret Hunt, trans. New York: Pantheon.

Gutterson, David (1999). *Snow Falling on Cedars*. New York: Vintage Books.

Halberstam, David (2000). "Platoon." In *Oliver Stone's U.S.A.*, R. Brent Toplin, ed. Lawrence: University Press of Kansas.

Harmetz, Aljean (2000). "The 15th Man Who Was Asked to Direct *M*A*S*H* (and Did) Makes a Peculiar Western." In David Sterritt (ed.), *Robert Altman Interviews* (3–18). Jackson: University Press of Mississippi.

Hemingway, Ernest (1926). *The Sun Also Rises*. New York: Simon and Schuster.

Herman, Judith Lewis (1997). *Trauma and Recovery*. New York: Basic Books.

Hirsh, Foster (1981). *Film Noir: The Dark Side of the Screen*. London: Da Capo Press.

Homer (B.C.). *The Odyssey*. Robert Fagles, trans. New York: Viking, 1996.

Houston, John (1980). *An Open Book*. New York: Ballantine Books.

Hoy, Pat (2002). From a speech, "Reverberations," at the dedication of the Class of '61 Reconciliation Plaza at their 40th Reunion. In *Assembly*, Jan/Feb, 38–39.

Jones, James (1957). *Some Came Running*. New York: Charles Scribner.

Jung, C. G. (1927, 1978). "Mind and Earth." In *Civilization in Transition*, v. 10, *The Collected Works of C.G. Jung*. Princeton, N.J.: Princeton University Press.

_____ (1934, 1971). *Archetypes of the Collective Unconscious*, v. 9a, *The Collected Works of C.G. Jung*. Princeton, N.J.: Princeton University Press.

_____ (1957, 1978). *Civilization in Transition*, v. 10, *The Collected Works of C.G. Jung*, Princeton, N.J.: Princeton University Press.

_____ (1958, 1972). *Schizophrenia*, v. 3, *The Collected Works of C.G. Jung*. Princeton, N.J.: Princeton University Press.

Kael, Pauline (1954, 1965). *I Lost It at the Movies*. Boston: Little, Brown.

_____ (1991). *Movie Love: Complete Reviews 1988–1991*. New York: Penguin Books.

Kovic, Ron (1976). *Born on the Fourth of July*. New York: McGraw-Hill.

Krystal, Henry (1967). *Massive Psychic Trauma*. New York: International Universities Press.

Lanning, Michael Lee (1994). *Vietnam at the Movies*. New York: Fawcett Columbine.

Lavigne, Yves (1993). *Hell's Angels: Three Can Keep a Secret If Two Are Dead*. New York: Carol Publishing Group.

Lembcke, Jerry (1998). *The Spitting Image: Myth, Memory, and the Legacy of Vietnam*. New York: New York University Press.

Leonard, Elmore (1959). *Last Stand at Saber River*. Maine: Thorndike Press.

Malle, Louis (1993). *Malle on Malle*, P. French, ed. London: Faber & Faber.

Marshall, Randall D., et al. (2001). "Comorbidity, Impairment, and Suicidality in Subthreshold PTSD." In *American Journal of Psychiatry*, 158 (9), 1467–1473.

Mason, Bobby Ann (1985). *In Country*. New York: Harper Perennial.

Maugham, W. Somerset (1944). *The Razor's Edge*. London: Penguin.

McBride, Joseph (2001). *Searching for John Ford: A Life*. New York: St. Martin's Press.

Mellor, Anne K. (1989). *Mary Shelley: Her Life, Her Fiction, Her Monsters*. New York: Routledge.

Miller, Henry (1960). "The Alcoholic Veteran with the Washboard Cranium." In *Wisdom of the Heart*. New York: New Directions.

Morgan, C. A., III (1997). "From *Let There Be Light* to *Shades of Gray*: The Construction of Authoritative Knowledge about Combat Fatigue (1945–1948)." Paper presented to the annual meeting of the International Society for Traumatic Stress Studies, Montreal, Quebec, November 8, 1997.

Muller, Eddie (1998). *Dark City: The Lost World of Film Noir.* New York: St. Martin's Griffin.

Nagy, Gregory (1996). *Homeric Questions.* Austin: University of Texas Press.

Naremore, James (1998). *More Than Night: Film Noir in Its Contexts.* Berkeley: University of California Press.

Niederland, W. G. (1984). "Compulsive Gambling and the 'Survivor Syndrome.'" Letter, *American Journal of Psychiatry,* 141 (8): 1008–1013.

Otto, Walter F. (1954). *The Homeric Gods: The Spiritual Significance of Greek Religion,* Moses Hadas, trans. New York: Pantheon.

Owens, Richard H. (2001). "Perspectives on the Vietnam War Experience in the TV Series 'Magnum P.I.'" *Viet Nam War Generation Journal,* 1 (1), 81–87.

Page, Tim (2002). "Harold Russell: Oscar winner, veterans activist." *Seattle Times-Post-Intelligencer,* February 3, 2002, p. 11.

Philpott, Tom (2001). "The Prisoner: The bitter heroism of America's longest held P.O.W." *New Yorker,* April 2, 2001, pp. 52–65.

Pitman, Roger (2000). "Stress Hormones and the Amygdala in PTSD: Possible Implications for Secondary Prevention." Address to the 16th annual meeting of the International Society for Traumatic Stress Studies, San Antonio, Texas, November 19, 2000.

Port, Cynthia Lindman, Brian Engdhal and Patricia Frazier (2001). "A Longitudinal and Retrospective Study of PTSD Among Older Prisoners of War." *American Journal of Psychiatry,* 158 (9), 1474–1479.

Pucci, Pietro (1987). *Odysseus Polutropos: Intertextual Readings in The Odyssey, and The Iliad.* Ithaca, N.Y.: Cornell University Press.

Reid, Alatair (1995). "Remembering Robert Graves." *New Yorker,* September 4, 1995, pp. 70–81.

Remarque, Eric Maria (1920, 1998). *The Road Back.* New York: Ballantine.

Richie, Donald (1996). *The Films of Akira Kurosawa.* Berkeley: University of California Press.

Schein, Seth L. (1996). *Reading the Odyssey.* Princeton, N.J.: Princeton University Press.

Scorsese, Martin (1989). *Scorsese on Scorsese,* D. Thompson and I. Christie, eds. London: Faber and Faber.

Scott, Sir Walter (1820, 1996). *Ivanhoe.* London: Oxford University Press.

Seals, David (1979). *The Powwow Highway.* New York: Penguin Books.

Selby, Spencer (1984). *Dark City: The Film Noir.* Jefferson, N.C.: McFarland & Company.

Shay, Jonathan (1994). *Achilles in Vietnam: Combat Trauma and the Undoing of Character.* New York: Atheneum.

Sinclair, Andrew (1984). *John Ford: A Biography.* London: Lorrimer.

Stanford, W. B. (1963). *The Ulysses Theme: A Study of the Adaptability of a Traditional Hero.* Dallas: Spring Publications.

Stone, Robert (1973). *Dog Soldiers.* Boston: Houghton Mifflin.

Theroux, Paul (1973). *Saint Jack.* New York: Penguin.

Thompson, Frank T. (1983). *William A. Wellman.* Metuchen, N.J.: Scarecrow Press.

Thornberg, Newton (1976). *Cutter and Bone.* London: Serpent's Tail.

Toplin, R. Brent, ed. (2000). *Oliver Stone's U.S.A.* Lawrence: University Press of Kansas.

Traver, Robert (1958). *Anatomy of a Murder.* New York: St. Martin's Press.

Trumbo, Dalton (1939, 1980). *Johnny Got His Gun*. New York: Bantam.

Turner, Fred (1996). *Echoes of Combat: The Vietnam War in American Memory*. New York: Anchor Books.

Van der Kolk, Bessel (1994). "The Body Keeps the Score: Memory and the Evolving Psychobiology of Posttraumatic Stress." *Harvard Review of Psychiatry*, 1 (1), 253–265.

Walker, Mark (1991). *Vietnam Veteran Films*. Metuchen, N.J.: Scarecrow Press.

Wharton, William (1978). *Birdy*. New York: Vintage Contemporaries.

Willeford, William (1969). *The Fool and His Scepter*. Chicago: Northwestern University Press.

Wilson, Sloan (1956). *The Man in the Gray Flannel Suit*. New York: Amereon House.

Wolf, Daniel (1991). *The Rebels: A Brotherhood of Outlaw Bikers*. Toronto: University of Toronto Press.

Wolfe, Virginia (1925). *Mrs Dalloway*. New York: Harcourt.

Index

273